ETHNIC MINORITIES AND EDUCATION

ETHNIC MINORITIES AND EDUCATION

ROBERT JEFFCOATE

Harper & Row, Publishers
London

Cambridge
Hagerstown
Philadelphia
New York

San Francisco
Mexico City
Sao Paulo
Sydney

First published 1984

Harper & Row Ltd
28 Tavistock Street
London WC2E 7PN

British Library Cataloguing in Publication Data

Jeffcoate, Robert
Ethnic minorities and education.
1. Children of minorities—Education—
Great Britain
I. Title
371.97'00941 LC3736.G6

ISBN 0–06–318284–X

Typeset by Inforum Ltd, Portsmouth
Printed and bound by Butler & Tanner Ltd, Frome and London

THE AUTHOR

Robert Jeffcoate was born in Liverpool in 1940 and attended schools in the city. He read English at Cambridge University and received educational qualifications from Bristol and Lancaster Universities. For 11 years he taught English in secondary schools, most recently between 1976 and 1978 as Head of Department. Between 1973 and 1976 he was Development Officer on the Schools Council project 'Education for a Multiracial Society', and between 1978 and 1983 Lecturer in Education at the Open University. He is the author of *Positive Image* (Writers and Readers, 1979), co-author of *Education for a Multiracial Society* (Schools Council, 1981), and co-editor of *The School in the Multicultural Society* (Harper & Row, 1982).

In memory of Annette

CONTENTS

	Preface	xi
Chapter 1	**Ethnic Minorities in Britain**	1
Chapter 2	**The Educational Context**	29
Chapter 3	**Equality of Opportunity**	52
Chapter 4	**Positive Discrimination**	75
Chapter 5	**Integration or Segregation?**	96
Chapter 6	**The Limits to Pluralism**	116
Chapter 7	**Combating Racism**	139
Chapter 8	**Conclusion: liberty, equality, fraternity**	164
Bibliography		174
Index		179

The Remove

The Sikh from Ambala in East Punjab,
India, formerly the British Empire,
the Muslim from Sialkot in West Punjab,
Pakistan, formerly British India,
the Sikh boy and the Muslim boy are two
of twenty such Sikhs and Muslims
from East Punjab and West Punjab, which
formerly were the Punjab,
standing together in assembly, fearfully
miming the words of a Christian hymn.

Later, their firework voices explode
in Punjabi until Mr Iqbal –
which can be a Sikh name or a Muslim name,
Mohammed Iqbal or Iqbal *Singh* –
who comes from Jullundur in East Punjab
but near enough to the border to be almost
West Punjab, who is a specialist in
the archaic intonations of the *Raj*,
until the three-piece-suited Mr Iqbal
gives a stiff-collared voice to his
Punjabi command to shut their thick wet
lips on the scattering sparks of their
white Secondary Modern teeth.

Mr Iqbal has come to London to teach
English to Punjabi Sikhs and Muslims
and has pinned up in his class pictures
of Gandhi and Jinnah, Nehru and Ayub
in case the parents come to ask in Punjabi
how the kids are doing in English.

And so; twenty years after
the Union Jack came down on Delhi
and the Punjab became East Punjab and
West Punjab and the Sikhs did not like it
and the Muslims did not like the Sikhs
not liking it and they killed each other
not by the hundred nor by the thousand
but by the hundred thousand, here then

is Mr Iqbal with his remove class of
twenty Punjabis, some Sikh and some Muslim,
in a Secondary Modern School in London,
all of them trying to learn English.

Back home the fastidious guardians of freedom,
the Sikh army and the Muslim army, convinced
that East is East and West is West etcetera,
periodically accuse each other of aggression.

Zulfikar Ghose

From *Jets of Orange* (Macmillan, 1967)

Preface

In 1978 I wrote a book *Positive Image* in which I explored a number of topics in multicultural education from the point of view of a classroom teacher. The book also included excerpts from my research experience on the Schools Council project 'Education for a Multiracial Society' between 1973 and 1976. The project team's report had been rejected by the Schools Council's programme committee early in 1978 on the grounds (never actually made public) that it made too much of racism and was unnecessarily critical of schools and teachers for their inaction. The Schools Council subsequently published its own version of the report, minus the names of the authors, in the summer of 1981. This version consisted essentially of a discussion of the theory and practice of developing a multicultural curriculum prepared by Mary Worrall and myself. Entirely omitted was a section on racism in British society and its impact on schoolchildren prepared by Rosalind Street Porter, though this had in fact already been published in amended form in 1977 by the Open University as part of the correspondence material for its course E361 'Education and the Urban Environment'.

This book is intended to complement *Positive Image* and my work for the Schools Council project in the sense that its focus is on analysis and policy rather than curriculum development or classroom activity. I have set myself two tasks: first, I want to try to describe and explain the situation of pupils from the ethnic minorities within the British school system. This will involve considering such questions as whether they enjoy equality of opportunity or are in some way disadvantaged or discriminated against, either directly or indirectly (see Chapter 3). Second, and partly in the light of the answers given to the above questions, I shall examine what I believe to be the four most important policy issues raised by their presence: positive discrimination (Chapter 4); integration or segregation (Chapter 5); putting pluralism into practice (Chapter 6); and combating racism (Chapter 7). In the course of tackling these tasks I shall also attempt to develop a coherent argument – an individual viewpoint – which is not fully stated until the last chapter (Chapter 8) but which can, for the moment, be identified as liberal, egalitarian and integrationist. Intermittently, as part of that developing argument, I shall test out, sometimes explicitly and sometimes implicitly, the hypothesis that recently settled ethnic minorities have highlighted weaknesses in the educational system which existed prior to their arrival. I shall further suggest that their presence has had the effect of inviting us to renew our commitment to state education and to make clear what purposes we want it to serve. Before broaching either task, or embarking on my argument, a certain amount of ground clearing has to be done in order to set all three in a proper context; this is done in Chapters 1 and 2.

This book also represents an extension and elaboration of material originally prepared for Open University course E354 'Ethnic Minorities and Community Relations' (the replacement for E361), which was presented to students for the first time in 1982 and published the following year. I should like to express my thanks to the University and the course team for giving me permission to make use of the course in this way, and to acknowledge a particular indebtedness to my former colleagues Peter Braham, Barbara Mayor and Bill Prescott, who together with myself constituted the 'core' team, for all that I learned from our four years of discussion and collaboration.

I have a number of other debts to acknowledge as well, none more so than to Alan James who has been such a conscientious and constructive critic over the years. He read through the whole book when it was in draft form and commented in detail; he will find many of his suggestions on matters of content and expression incorporated into the final text. Linda Chanan also generously gave up time to read through all eight draft chapters critically, while Janet Evans, Barbara Mayor and Christopher McCrudden read and commented on individual ones. Finally, I should like to thank Marianne Lagrange of Harper & Row for her support and Carolyn Hawkins who typed the manuscript. I alone, of course, am responsible for the opinions expressed and for any errors or infelicities there may be.

Since the book is intended for a general as well as a specialist audience, I have kept references in the text to a minimum. Much of the statistical data comes from Open University course E354; what does not could have been picked up by anyone following the press and the relevant journals since 1982. Somewhat reluctantly I have followed the current practice in race relations literature of using 'blacks' and 'black people' to include South Asians as well as those of African or Afro-Caribbean origin.

CHAPTER 1

ETHNIC MINORITIES IN BRITAIN

These are the heroes who despise the Dutch,
And rail at new-come foreigners so much;
Forgetting that themselves are all deriv'd
From the most scoundrel race that ever liv'd,
A horrid crowd of rambling thieves and drones,
Who ransack'd kingdoms, and dispeopled towns:
The Pict and painted Britain, treach'rous Scot,
By hunger, theft, and rapine, hither brought;
Norwegian pirates, buccaneering Danes,
Whose red-hair'd offspring ev'ry where remains;
Who join'd with Norman-French compound the breed
From whence your true-born Englishmen proceed.
(Daniel Defoe, 1701, *The True-born Englishman*)

Who are Britain's ethnic minorities? The term was borrowed from the United States in the 1970s to take account of the fact that the immigrant workers and their families who arrived in the 1950s and 1960s from southern Europe, the Caribbean and the Indian subcontinent had become settled communities with British-born children and grandchildren; and in common parlance it is frequently still reserved for those communities. Sometimes it is further restricted, excluding southern Europeans, to communities of New Commonwealth origin and occasionally even to black people, forgetting perhaps that the New Commonwealth includes Hong Kong, Cyprus and Malta. Yet, if one asks what the term 'ethnic minorities' actually means, limiting its application in these ways seems odd, even perverse. If pressed for a definition most people would, I think, say something like: 'an ethnic minority is a comparatively small community with a way of life which differs in salient respects from that of the majority and probably as a result of fairly recent foreign extraction'. Some might want to add that there is a second sense to 'minority' – minority status – which is of greater relevance; for them an ethnic minority is distinguished more by its comparative powerlessness than by its comparative smallness. The definition of 'ethnic minority' is, then, to some extent a subject for disagreement; and I shall return to it later in the chapter. For the time being I want to make use of the phrase in the broader sense (not limiting it to blacks or New Commonwealth communities or post-1945 immigrants, and incorporating both meanings of 'minority') in order to make a start on answering my opening question.

The Irish

By the broader definition Britain's biggest ethnic minority is the Irish. It is also one of the longest established. (Was there ever a time when there were no Irish in Britain?) Its size is primarily due to the mass migration of the Irish rural poor to Britain's industrial cities in the nineteenth century. In 1841, the first national census to enquire about country of birth recorded 400,000 Irish people living in Great Britain. Twenty years later, as a consequence of the severe Irish famines of the 1840s, this figure had doubled. In 1861 the Irish-born accounted for three percent of the total population of England and Wales and no less than one-quarter of the population of Liverpool. Their migration has often been compared to the migration of European and New Commonwealth workers in the 1950s and 1960s, since they came to occupy positions at the bottom end of the labour market which indigenous workers would not or could not fill. They were as essential to the Industrial Revolution as were European and New Commonwealth workers to the economic boom which followed the Second World War. In addition, they were obliged to inhabit some of the least salubrious areas of industrial Britain and to contend with the prejudices and opprobrium of the native populace. The historian E.J. Hobsbawm has sketched a graphic portrait of their plight:

> They became the dockers and coal-heavers, the navvies and construction gangs, the iron and steelworkers, the miners, and when the English and Scots did not want the jobs, or could no longer live on the wage, those who did the unwanted work – the handloom weavers or unskilled labourers. They became, more than any other people, the soldiers of the Queen . . . while their sisters became the servants, nurses and prostitutes of the big cities. Their wages were lower than anyone else's, they lived in the worst slums, and the English and

> Scots despised them as semi-barbarians, distrusted them as Catholics and hated them as undercutters of their wages.
>
> (Hobsbawm, 1969, p.310)

They remained ethnically as well as residentially distinct. As Hobsbawm adds, the culture they brought with them was already that of an oppressed people:

> They came as members of a pauperized, degraded peasantry whose own native society had been crushed by some centuries of English oppression into fragments of old custom, mutual aid and kinship solidarity, held together by a generically Irish 'way of life' (wakes, songs, and so on), by a hatred of England and by a Catholic priesthood of peasants' sons and brothers.
>
> (Hobsbawm, op.cit.)

Bearing in mind that the high noon of Victorian imperialism was also a period in which quasi-scientific theorizing about race flourished, it is hardly surprising that the Irish in Britain should have become the targets for some of the crudest and most insulting of racist stereotypes. Karl Marx, in a letter of 1870, even went so far as to claim that the working class in England was divided into two hostile camps, 'English proletarians and Irish proletarians' (with the former regarding the latter in much the same way as 'poor whites' regarded 'niggers' in 'the former slave states of the USA'), and that this was the secret of its impotence (quoted in Castles and Kosack, 1973, p.243). Twentieth-century historians have not always agreed – E. P. Thompson, for example:

> It would have been difficult to have made a people who spoke the same language and were British citizens under the Act of Union (1800) into a subject minority. There was a great deal of inter-marriage. And it is not the friction but the relative ease with which the Irish were absorbed into working-class communities which is remarkable.
>
> (Thompson, 1968, p.480)

In support of his case Thompson points to 'a clear consecutive alliance between Irish nationalism and English Radicalism between 1790 and 1850'. Just as English reformers, he argues, generally supported the cause of Catholic emancipation (eventually granted in 1829), so Irish immigrants were influential and prominent in English Jacobinism, Ludditism, Chartism and the trades union movement (Thompson, op.cit., pp. 481–485).

During the final decades of the nineteenth century and the early decades of the twentieth, the size of the Irish community in Britain diminished.

However, after the Second World War the combination of economic depression in Ireland and expansion in Britian produced a further mass migration of the rural Irish poor. This second exodus was of a piece with the migration of workers from southern Europe and the New Commonwealth; and both were part of the settlement of approximately 15 million workers and their dependents from less developed countries in industrialized North-west Europe between 1945 and 1975. In 1961 there were close to one million people of Irish birth in Britain, equivalent to one-quarter of the population of all Ireland and one-third of the population of the Republic. Had those of recent Irish descent, as opposed to Irish birth, been added, the total figure for the Irish community as a whole would have been at least double. E. J. Hobsbawm maintains that the size of the Irish minority is most accurately measured by the size of the Roman Catholic population. If he is right, this puts it in the region of five million people or one-tenth of the population of Great Britain.

Since 1961, with the economic recession in Britain and improved economic prospects in Ireland, there has undoubtedly been an increase in return migration, but nowhere near enough to disturb the Irish claim to being our biggest ethnic minority. Whether they are also an integrated one is still as much a matter for dispute as it was in regard to their nineteenth-century forebears; and so, of course, is the meaning of integration and whether it is a good or bad thing. There has been considerable inter-marriage, for example, and it would be interesting to know how many Britons can boast at least one Irish grandparent or great-grandparent. There is also an Irish middle class; in the 1960s 12 percent of all doctors were of Irish origin. Yet a degree of residential segregation persists, and the employment profile remains skewed towards unskilled manual labour with particular concentrations of Irish workers on building sites or in motorway construction and repair. In addition, Irish pubs, clubs, associations and institutions continue to thrive.

As for relations with the British, Hobsbawn reminds us that a largely Catholic constituency in Liverpool returned an Irish nationalist MP for many years in the latter part of the nineteenth century and that it was not until 1964 that the Protestant working class in the city forgave the Labour Party for being pro-Catholic and pro-Irish and stopped voting Conservative. Perhaps it would not be an exaggeration to say that the Irish will not become integrated in the social sense so long as the struggle in Northern Ireland remains unresolved.

Italians

Two other long-established British ethnic minorities which underwent expansion in the nineteenth century were the Italians and the Jews. Britain's Italian community can trace its genealogy back to traders in fourteenth-century Southampton, bankers in fifteenth-century London and Renaissance scholars, musicians and artists at the court of Elizabeth I. In the nineteenth century Italy became, like Ireland, a country of mass emigration. Since 1861 over 25 million emigrants have left Italy; their descendants around the world now number some 40 million. It was Republican exiles like Mazzini who laid the basis for the major expansion of Britain's Italian population. Between the 1881 and 1901 Censuses it actually tripled from 6500 to 20,300 as Italians, mainly from the north of Italy, ensconced themselves in catering and the service sectors.

In the twentieth century the stability of the Italian community was rudely interrupted by the Second World War, when adult Italians were interned as hostile aliens, their property was confiscated and they were subjected to xenophobic abuse. After the war, agreements between British and Italian governments produced a further wave of mass immigration. Unemployed labour in the *mezzogiorno* was recruited to fill positions in British heavy industry which indigenous labour had vacated or shunned. As many as 180,000 Italians have migrated to Britain since 1945, 15,000 of them to work in the brick industry. It has been estimated that one-tenth of the population of Bedford, Britain's brick-making capital, is of Italian origin. Some, of course, returned home when their work contracts expired and others have followed them on reaching retirement. But the size of the Italian community remains substantial – over 200,000 – and it should not be forgotten, our prime concern here being educational, that the majority of them are southerners from impoverished and barely educated peasant backgrounds. In the early 1950s, when so many of them migrated, 25 percent of the population of southern Italy was officially classified as illiterate and a further 25 percent had had less than five years of elementary education.

The Italian community is in a sense marginal to British society, not just because those who are Italian-born and have retained Italian nationality are effectively disenfranchised aliens (though enjoying rights as EEC nationals), but because of the maintenance of Italian identity for economic as well as cultural reasons.

> Culturally they are proud of their ethnicity which is preserved by a large number of organisations, many of them church-based, which bind the second and even third generations into the 'Italian fold'; whilst economically they have been able to trade on their ethnicity and their special links to the food and catering industries by building up a relatively uncontested sector of the British service economy.
>
> (King, 1979, p.6)

The conventional image of Britain's Italians is of a model minority – industrious, law-abiding and family-centred. Though still predominantly working class, there has been considerable upward mobility both professionally and residentially. Significant numbers are skilled manual or white-collar workers; almost 10 percent are self-employed; and a very high proportion, over 90 percent in Bedford, are owner-occupiers. Moreover, there are clear signs of social integration among the British-born. Ethnic concentration in housing is decreasing and nearly one-third of the marriages at Bedford's Italian church between 1977 and 1980 were to non-Italian partners, with almost as many women as men marrying 'out'.

Jews

The origins of British Jewry go back to the Norman Conquest; but it is a fractured history too, with a hiatus of three and a half centuries. Following increased persecution and mob violence directed against them, the Jews were expelled from England in 1290, and their property was confiscated and their religion proscribed. They were not officially readmitted until 1656 when Cromwell's government granted a petition from Dutch Sephardic Jews to be allowed to settle and practise Judaism. Their absence in the intervening period did not, however, betoken the disappearance of anti-Semitism, as is only too evident from Chaucer's *Pardoner's Tale*, Marlowe's *Jew of Malta* and Shakespeare's *Merchant of Venice*.

The resettlement paved the way for what was to become 200 years later, at the time of political emancipation in 1858, a prosperous community of around 65,000 people. But in the last two decades of the nineteenth century the equilibrium of Anglo-Jewry was seriously disturbed by the recrudescence of virulent anti-Semitism in response to the mass immigration of 150,000 Ashkenazi Jewish refugees from the pogroms of Tsarist Russia and Eastern Europe. In the 1902 debate on the Queen's speech, Major William Evans Gordon, Conservative MP for Stepney (where many of the refugees had settled), argued:

> Not a day passes but English families are ruthlessly turned out to make room for foreign invaders. Out they go to make room for Rumanians, Russians and Poles. Rents are raised 50 to 100 per cent and a house which formerly contained a couple of families living in comparative decency is made to contain four or five families living under conditions which baffle description . . . It is only a matter of time before the population becomes entirely foreign . . . The rates are burdened with the education of thousands of children of foreign parents. . . .
>
> (Quoted in Foot, 1965, p.88)

The strength of sentiments such as these led eventually to this country's first serious statutory exercise in immigration control, the 1905 Aliens Act, which was specifically designed to halt the Jewish 'invasion'. Thirty years later the hospitable reception of 50,000 Jewish refugees from Nazi Germany was vitiated by the resilience of British anti-Semitism, most notoriously manifested in the violent street campaign conducted by the British Union of Fascists' 'blackshirts'.

Nowadays British Jewry has regained some of the prosperity and stability of the mid-nineteenth century; anti-Semitism is almost, but not quite, a nightmare of the past. At around 350,000 it is one of the half-dozen or so surviving sizeable Jewish communities outside Israel. For many it is our most successful, and our most successfully integrated, ethnic minority. Over the last century it has diversified occupationally, dispersed residentially and adopted English as its first language. It is prominent in business, the arts and sciences, and in public life with a record 46 Members of Parliament in 1974 (and five Ministers in the Conservative Government in 1983). At the same time it pursues its own vigorous community life through its Board of Deputies, its synagogues, its schools, its newspapers, its commercial networks and its family and friendship ties. On the other hand, to the religiously orthodox British Jewry is, notwithstanding prosperity and social acceptance, a community in decline. The birthrate is falling; emigration to Israel and elsewhere is increasing; and one in four Jews marries 'out'. Whether declining or successful, the most important fact for our purposes is that there are some 60,000 Jewish children in our schools, the vast majority of them in the non-denominational state sector.

Gypsies

The other long-standing British ethnic minority is the Gypsies or travellers. Their genesis is shrouded in mystery and the subject of dispute among anthropologists, several of whom have queried the popular notion of exotic origins in Egypt or India. Their first recorded appearance in Europe was in the fifteenth century and in the British Isles in the early sixteenth century. Whatever the truth of their origins, there is no dispute over the nature of the treatment they have consistently received at the hands of the people they call '*gorgios*': 'from the first appearance of persons called or calling themselves Gypsies in Britain in the sixteenth century, the state has attempted to control, disperse, deport, convert or destroy them' (Okely, 1983, p.231).

Yet it is an unresolved legal nicety whether Gypsies are protected by the 1976 Race Relations Act or not. Physically they do not look any different from other white Britons, but they are incontrovertibly an ethnic minority possessing a clear image of their own identity ('a birthright reinforced by upbringing within a distinct community'), based on 'the principle of descent, the practice of self-employment, a commitment to certain values, an ideology of travelling and pollution taboos' (Okely, op.cit., pp.34,67). In their resistance to settled residence and wage labour they stand further apart from mainstream British society than any other ethnic group, though they have secured a niche of a kind within the informal economy through scrap clearing, tarmac laying, hawking, seasonal agricultural work, fairground entertainment and fortune telling. They have also been generally antipathetic towards formal education since the inception of the state system in 1870. Theirs is a non-literate culture, and they perceive *gorgio* education as fundamentally alien since one of its objects is preparation for wage labour: 'they fear that the sedentary majority may use [formal education] as an instrument to enforce settlement and conformity. They provide within their community their own system of child rearing and training in the skills of economic and social subsistence' (Reiss, 1975). Though they may now see the point of literacy, their children are still 'the bane of attendance officers and educational administrators' (Reiss, op.cit.). The size of the Gypsy population is almost as hotly disputed as their origins, perhaps because of the confusion created by the myth of the 'true' Gypsy. In 1977 it was generally accepted that there were between 8000 and 9000 families in England and Wales. On this basis the size of the total population is probably somewhere between 30,000 and 50,000.

The meaning of 'ethnic minority'

These vignettes of four long-established communities provide a way of putting to the test the rough and ready definition of 'ethnic minority' with which I began. I identified three main elements – relative smallness, relative powerlessness and cultural difference probably arising from foreign extraction. Now we can see that while all four communities meet these criteria they do so in various ways and to differing extents. For example, if the estimates I have given are correct, there are something like 100 times as many Irish as Gypsies in Britain (some people, of course, are both). Similarly, although Irish, Italians, Jews and Gypsies have all encountered prejudice and discrimination from the majority at some point in their history, there seems to be a sharp contrast between the current position of the Jews, so well represented in Parliament and public life, and that of the Gypsies, still locked in conflict with *gorgio* society and still the victims of constant harassment. Neither the Irish, Italians nor Jews appear to be so very different from the majority culturally, any more than they are physically, compared with minorities such as the Pakistanis or Chinese, if one thinks of 'culture' first and foremost in terms of religion, language, dress, diet and marriage customs. However, orthodox Jews and devout Irish and Italian Catholics all maintain important distinctive customs. The Gypsies are perhaps more distinctive, if 'culture' is defined in terms of social and economic values; no other ethnic minority challenges some of the majority's most cherished assumptions about the good life quite so blatantly as they do.

The association between foreign extraction and ethnic minority status now looks mistaken. Some anthropologists believe that the Gypsies are as indigenous as anyone else, taking to the road when they did because of the collapse of feudalism; and, historically speaking, the Irish immigration of the nineteenth century was more an internal movement of labour than an incursion of foreigners. It represented a shift from the periphery to the centre of the colonial economy as well as part of the large-scale migration from countryside to city generated by the Industrial Revolution. With regard to those communities which are of recent overseas origin, the case of the Jews (the size of whose community is due to the mass influx of refugees between 1880 and 1905 and again in the 1930s) should remind us that some of them have their roots in flight from political or religious persecution rather than in labour migration. The Jews were neither the first nor the last of the refugee minorities. They were preceded in the seventeenth century by Protestant Huguenots from France and followed after World War II by Polish ex-servicemen under the Polish Resettlement Act of 1947, European Voluntary Workers from camps for 'displaced persons' in continental Europe between 1946 and 1950, Hungarians after the suppression of the 1956 rising and, in the 1970s, by Ugandan Asians expelled by Idi Amin,

Chileans after the overthrow of Allende, Greek Cypriots after the Turkish invasion and Vietnamese 'boat people'.

There is another problem with the term 'ethnic minority'. Its use perhaps implies that the communities so designated constitute discrete, homogeneous and unchanging entities. I hope my own portraits of Irish, Italians, Jews and Gypsies have not implied this, for nothing could be further from the truth. They are as diverse as the 'ethnic majority', stratified not only by class and sex but as often as not by language, religion and regional origin as well. Moreover, if they are of foreign extraction, they are bound to have undergone or be undergoing some degree of cultural adaptation or accommodation to settlement in Britain. Equally, despite restrictive immigration control and the 1981 British Nationality Act, and no matter how 'integrated' they may or may not be said to be, ethnic minorities are not detachable appendages but integral constituents of British society. They have both secured cultural concessions from the institutions of the state (as in the case of the exemption for Sikhs over crash helmets) and inspired cultural change within the majority (most notably in diet and musical taste). Furthermore, individuals whom members of the ethnic majority may simply see as members of a single ethnic minority, may identify their own cultural affiliations in a host of different ways.

I noted earlier some of the more obvious changes that have affected British Jewry in the past 100 years. Nowadays a British Jew may be Sephardic or Ashkenazi; religiously orthodox or reformist (or indeed agnostic); Zionist or anti-Zionist; may have married 'in' or 'out'; may send his or her children to Jewish independent or voluntary schools or to non-denominational state or independent schools; may observe Jewish customs and festivals or ignore them completely; and may live in a mainly Jewish residential area and have mainly Jewish friends or in a mixed area and have friends from a range of ethnic backgrounds. An adult student of mine of German Jewish parentage once wrote in an essay that she never thought of herself as Jewish, let alone as a member of an ethnic minority, since culturally she was neither. She did not believe in Judaism, was anti-Zionist, had married a Gentile and brought up her children to think of themselves as simply British, observed no Jewish customs and had no contact with Jewish institutional life. Her experience raises that age-old question: what makes a Jew a Jew? To which one answer has always been: anti-Semitism.

Her experience also raises the wider question of whether ethnicity is chosen, ascribed or objectively determined. Obviously an individual's choices, the perceptions of others and objective facts about ancestry and culture all come into play, interacting with one another complexly, but I think it would be generally accepted that ethnic affiliation is essentially something chosen. My student was certainly Jewish by descent, and some people would have said that she 'looked Jewish' too. Therefore, although her non-Jewish way of life might have reduced her chances of exposure to anti-Semitism, it could never have eliminated them completely. However, the way of life she had chosen meant that she had lost much of the sense of Jewishness into which she had been initiated as a child. Her marriage 'out', together with her decision to bring up her children outside the Jewish fold, probably also meant that any sense or knowledge, of Jewishness would eventually disappear entirely from among her descendants. That is why an anthropological approach to the study of ethnic minorities stresses so firmly the subjective dimension to ethnicity. For an anthropologist an ethnic group is distinguished, first and foremost, by its awareness of a common ancestry and a shared identity and by its determination to preserve both through endogamy and the initiation of the young into valued beliefs, practices and rituals. A degree of exogamy can be accommodated and may even be normal, but a point must come when the integrity and survival of the group are seriously threatened. All of which leaves us, I hope, with a working definition of 'ethnic minority' to serve the purposes of this book: namely, that it is a comparatively small and powerless community, whose culture differs in significant respects from that of the majority, and which is possessed of a sense of shared ancestry and identity and committed to self-preservation through endogamy and the initiation of its young.

The question of race

The other function of my vignettes of four long-established ethnic minorities is that they can be drawn on to ask precisely why so little research attention has been paid to their children's progress through school (none at all in the case of Italians and Jews). Also, precisely why has the debate about ethnic minorities and education so very largely ignored them in favour of more recently established communities, particularly those of New Commonwealth origin? Obviously recent arrival is in itself one explanation. But it is far from a complete one for, although significant numbers of Irish and Italian immigrants also arrived in the 1950s and 1960s, it was West Indians and South Asians who captured public attention. The most recently arrived group, Vietnamese refugees, has still to make a serious impression in the field of multicultural education. Another explanation points to degree of cultural difference. But, if this is the key factor, why have West Indians and South Asians been more of an object for enquiry and concern than the Chinese and Vietnamese? Perhaps because there are more of them or because the latter are, with a few exceptions, widely dispersed. A third explanation stresses the colonial connection, the theory being that the 'mother country' and her former colonies remain bound by a special nexus of affection and antipathy, pride and guilt, cultural commonality and cultural dissonance. Were this the dominant factor, however, one would have expected Cypriots, Hong Kong Chinese and (above all) the Irish to have attracted the same amount of attention as West Indians and South Asians. Manifestly they have not.

Undoubtedly the most popular sorts of explanation are those emphasizing the significance of race or, to be precise, of skin colour or, to be even more precise, of dark skin colour. The relationship between race and ethnicity is an intriguing one. Strictly speaking there is no necessary connection between them at all, for ethnicity refers to cultural differences and race refers to physical differences. British Gypsies are culturally but not physically distinct, while many British blacks (those of mixed race, for example, or those who have been adopted or fostered into white families) can hardly be said to belong to a distinct ethnic group. However, during the nineteenth century, from which the modern usage of 'race' derives, there was believed to be a very precise and close relationship between race and ethnicity. From the mid-century onwards biologists and anthropologists propounded the theory that humanity could be divided into genetically discrete races with separate geographical origins which could be further distinguished from one another culturally, temperamentally and intellectually. They also believed that races could be ranked on a kind of evolutionary scale of human development. Today this theory has been largely discredited; indeed it is what we now call 'racism'. Remnants survive, in the view entertained by some twentieth-century psychologists that the differences in the mean scores registered by various racial groups on IQ tests are primarily attributable to differences in inherited intelligence. In addition there is, of course, a long-standing popular tradition of speculation (frequently inaccurate and stereotyped) about physical differences, which antedated nineteenth-century theorizing about race and continues to surface in everyday prejudices and myths. But altogether it no longer seems wholly satisfactory to speak of racial, as opposed to ethnic, groups, because whereas ethnic identity is essentially something one chooses, racial identity is essentially something imposed by others, more often than not on the basis of ignorance and misconception. Not surprisingly considerable confusion now surrounds the application of the epithet 'racial', notably as a result of the widespread limitation of 'race' to skin colour, or rather to a small number of differences in physical features, of which skin colour is held to be the most significant.

When people say that racial difference is the main reason for the disproportionate amount of attention paid to South Asians and West Indians in the debate about ethnic minorities and education, they are referring not so much to race in its nineteenth-century sense – the Irish, Italians, Jews and Gypsies have all been treated or regarded as racially (that is to say, biologically) different – as to skin colour, or even to dark skin colour (for attitudes towards the Chinese and Vietnamese remain ambiguous or at least unclear). The assumption is that because of the relative conspicuousness of dark skins and the ancient, deep-seated and overwhelmingly negative connotations of blackness in European and Judaeo-Christian culture, the sharpest racial hostility has been reserved for black immigrants.

Whether this is true or not is hard to determine. Were Irish and Jewish immigrants in the nineteenth century less abused and maligned than black immigrants have been in the twentieth? Are the Italians in Switzerland, the Turks in West Germany and the Portuguese in France better treated than blacks in Britain? Has indeed the same degree of discrimination and prejudice been levelled at West Indians as at South Asians? And has any black group been so persistently harassed by the majority as the Gypsies? We may well have opinions on these questions, strongly held ones too, but there really is no way of quantifying or evaluating such evidence as there is, to answer them with confidence. My main point, however, is not that there are right answers to them, but rather that there does not seem to be a *good* reason why some ethnic minorities should have merited more attention than others. It must remain an open issue for the moment whether some are more at risk in the education system than others, and therefore in need of preferential treatment.

'Coloured' minorities

None of this is intended to play down the significance of the presence in our schools of large numbers of children who are both physically and culturally different, nor of the remarkable transformation which the complexion of British society underwent in the 1950s and 1960s. It is sometimes argued that Britain's 'coloured' minorities should also be seen as long-established communities. There is some substance to this claim but it only really applies to seaports such as London, Liverpool, Bristol and Cardiff. Although there was certainly a sizeable community of black slaves in London during the reign of Elizabeth I (hence her oft-quoted edict of 1601 complaining about 'the great number of Negroes and blackamoors which . . . are carried into this realm') and an even larger one of slaves and sailors in the eighteenth century, by the middle of the nineteenth there was virtually no distinct population of African or Afro-Caribbean descent left. Despite further settlement in the seaports in the late nineteenth and early twentieth centuries and in several parts of the country during the two world wars, this population had still reached only 10,000 people in the whole of Britain by 1945.

Indians and Chinese were even fewer in number than those of African origin prior to the mass immigration that followed the Second World War. The small Indian pedlar communities to be found in many British cities between the two world wars cannot have amounted to more than a few thousand in total. Although there were seamen's Chinatowns in London and Liverpool by the turn of the century, the 1901 Census recorded only 545 people of Chinese birth, which compares strikingly with the 80,000 Hong Kong Chinese estimated to have migrated to Britain by the end of the 1970s to service the huge expansion in the Chinese restaurant and take-away trade.

Blacks continue to represent only a small fraction of the overall British population: 4.1 percent, according to the Office of Population Census and Surveys in 1983, or 2.2 million, of whom the three largest constituents are Indians, West Indians and Pakistanis, followed by East African Asians and Bangladeshis. This proportion is unlikely to change much in the foreseeable future, unless there is an extraordinary about-turn in government policy on immigration control, as the black profile in terms of sex balance, age structure and family size gradually comes to resemble that of the white population. However, the most important demographic fact about the black population is not its size but its uneven distribution. Black communities can be found in towns and cities from Newcastle in the north to Southampton in the south and from Bristol in the west to Ipswich in the east, but the black population as a whole is heavily concentrated in Greater London, the Midlands, West Yorkshire and south Lancashire. The 1971 Census found that as many as 70 percent of all South Asians and West Indians were living in London and the South-east or in the West Midlands. However, this bald figure masked variations between the different black groups, with two-thirds of West Indians living in London and the South-east as against less than half of Indians and only one in seven of Pakistanis. The uneven distribution of the black population is a natural outcome of the patterns of labour demand which obtained between the mid-1950s and the mid-1960s; areas of traditionally high unemployment like Northern Ireland, Merseyside and Tyneside were avoided by the immigrants of that period.

The economic context to black immigration

I have already said something briefly about the current social and economic positions of the other ethnic minorities. What of the current position of black people? There is a common, and often unexamined, notion abroad that theirs is the most disadvantaged position of all, a notion succinctly captured in the title of a *Time* magazine article on Britain's blacks in August 1979 – 'Underclass in the making'. How much truth is there in this common view? Before we can answer that, it is important to take stock of some of the major changes which have affected British society since the period of mass immigration from the New Commonwealth. At that time, between say 1953 and 1963, Britain was experiencing an almost unprecedented economic boom. Without that economic expansion there would, of course, have been no mass immigration; nor would there have been much economic expansion without that level of immigration.

In the popular memory, those years conjure up Harold Macmillan's famous catchphrase about never having 'had it so good' (in material terms 'an unquestionable fact', according to E.J. Hobsbawm). Suddenly Britain had become an 'affluent' society of 'conspicuous consumption' in which more of its population than ever before could afford to participate, in strong contrast to the depression of the 1930s and the rationing of the 1940s. In the 1970s the British economy ceased to expand and moved into ever deepening recession. To some extent this has been a worldwide phenomenon, popularly associated with the crisis over oil prices in 1973 and the subsequent inflation. In Britain, however, it has assumed a particularly acute form in the erosion of the base of manufacturing industry, with some of our longest established industrial activities – textiles, steelmaking, shipbuilding – bearing the brunt of a decline which really began in the Great Depression of 100 years ago, when we ceased to be the 'workshop of the world'.

One obvious result of this economic decline has been a staggering increase in the level of unemployment. Unemployment virtually disappeared during the Second World War and averaged under two percent during the 1950s. In 1983 the official level of unemployment in Britain was

12 percent (well over three million people); for those under 25 it was 28 percent and for those under 18 almost 50 percent. The actual numbers of those out of work, however, were widely believed to be much higher because of the way statistics were arrived at and the failure of many to register. In addition, it should be remembered that the figures for under-25 and under-18 unemployment include neither those in full-time education nor those on job training schemes. The worst hit areas in the United Kingdom, according to the 1981 Census, were the traditional blackspots of Northern Ireland, Wales and the North-east of England; the worst hit single place was the steel town of Corby in Northamptonshire with an unemployment rate of 23 percent. But unemployment rates of around 20 percent are by no means unusual in other industrial towns and cities including those, for example in the West Midlands, previously having reputations for relatively low levels of unemployment. In some inner-city areas and on some housing estates the unemployment rate may be at least twice as high as this.

The most vulnerable groups in the population, apart from the young and setting ethnic minorities for the moment on one side, are the over-55s, the disabled, women, the unskilled and (naturally enough) workers in manufacturing industry. Yet paradoxically Britain remains an affluent society of conspicuous consumption. What the recession has done is to open up deep rifts between north and south, inner cities and suburbia, and between the majority of the working population who are paid more than they need (in many cases very much more) to feed, clothe and house themselves and their families, and the minority of the low paid and the unemployed who, while not exactly destitute, could hardly be said to have equal access to what most people regard as the good things of life. In April 1983, according to a government earnings survey, the average weekly pay of doctors was three times as high as that of agricultural workers and five times as high as that of waitresses and hairdressers; the average pay for women generally was 50 percent below that for men. In February of the same year a record 7.2 million people were estimated to be dependent on supplementary benefits.

The gathering recession over the past decade has been accompanied by other changes in the employment profile of Britain. There has been an increase (paradoxically enough) in the proportion of women in the work-force, a movement from blue-collar to white-collar employment (according to the 1981 Census non-manual workers are now in the majority) and from the secondary to the tertiary sector, and a population shift to the south of England. There has also been some kind of convergence between middle-

and working-class value systems. Skilled manual workers have undergone 'embourgeoisement' (actually a sociological coinage of the 1950s) – increasing their home ownership and deserting the Labour Party at elections. For their part, white-collar unions have shown themselves as prepared to resort to militant action when it suits them as their blue-collar counterparts. But perhaps the two most important developments have been the improved ability of international corporations to transfer employment from one country to another in pursuit of higher profit margins, and the emergence of automation and micro-electronic technology as forces to be reckoned with in the workplace. These two developments almost certainly mean that high levels of unemployment, and higher levels of long-term unemployment, will characterize the British economy for the remainder of the twentieth century, even if recession is replaced by boom.

One final effect of the recession has been an acceleration in the decline of the great Victorian cities created by the Industrial Revolution; they have experienced considerable job and population losses in the past 10 years. A radical change in government policy, from slum clearance and the encouragement of new towns in the years after 1945, to the regenerative inner-city programmes of the later 1960s and the 1970s, has failed to stem this process. The inner cities of Britain have become crucibles of multiple deprivation associated not only with high levels of unemployment but also with large proportions of overcrowded and single-parent households, of households without the exclusive use of basic amenities and of pensioners living alone, and with high rates of mortality and population turnover.

Blacks as an 'underclass'?

How does the black population fit into this picture? The evidence on employment supplied by national censuses, Political and Economic Planning (PEP) research, the National Dwelling and Household Survey and a number of local studies paints a portrait of overall disadvantage: black men are disproportionately represented in poorly paid, low-status, insecure jobs in manufacturing industry which often involve unsocial hours and disagreeable physical conditions. At the same time the evidence warns us off generalizations of this kind, for the differences in job level between the various black groups are as striking as the differences between blacks as a whole and whites. For example, the employment profiles of East African and Indian men are closer to the profile of whites than they are to those of West Indians, Pakistanis or Bangladeshis; and, although very few West Indians are in white-collar jobs (in fact less than 10 percent), the majority are in skilled, not semi-skilled or unskilled manual work. The only conspicuously disadvantaged groups of black men are Pakistanis and Bangladeshis. In the case of black women (on whom much less information is available), the 1971 Census found that 67 percent of West Indian women were economically active (above the national average) compared with 39 percent of Indians and 16 percent of Pakistanis. It also found that black women as a whole earned more than white women. However, this was because more of them worked full-time and, of course, they only fared comparatively well as women, earning far less than men. As for unemployment rates, it certainly does seem that blacks are a vulnerable category, especially during a period of recession and particularly in those conurbations where they are heavily and densely concentrated (but not in towns and cities where they are fewer in number and more broadly dispersed). Between 1971 and 1981 the rate of unemployment went up 300 percent generally and 500 percent for blacks. In 1981 17.2 percent of blacks were registered as unemployed compared with 9.9 percent of the workforce as a whole.

The data on housing yield a similar portrait, combining overall disadvantage with distinct variations between the different black groups. Blacks are not only unevenly dispersed around the country but concentrated in certain downtown and inner-city areas (the 1971 Census found 78 percent of them resident in 10 percent of enumeration districts), characterized by high levels of multiple deprivation. Predictably, therefore, they tend to inhabit inferior housing stock both as owner-occupiers and as tenants, whether renting from local councils or private landlords. However, whereas a significant proportion of West Indians are council tenants and comparatively few are owner-occupiers, the great majority of Asians own their own homes. This does not mean that the latter are necessarily in a more privileged position. Noting that home ownership among Asians increases the lower down the socioeconomic scale one goes, David Smith has commented: 'For a substantial proportion of Asians, buying their own home is not a way of getting superior housing at a premium price, but a way of getting poor housing cheaply' (Smith, 1977–1978, p.19).

Where data are deficient (and this is partly because national censuses have up to now confined their questions on ethnicity to country of birth) is in relation to the position of the British-born and any changes that may or may not have occurred in the situation of black minorities over the past 20 years. The conventional media image of black British youth is of a group which is particularly underprivileged in economic terms. How far is this the truth and how far is it an unsubstantiated stereotype? The Department of

Employment's 1981 Labour Force Survey found no significant difference in the rate of unemployment between white and South Asian 16–24-year-olds, but a marked difference in the case of West Indians; 28 percent of West Indian males and 16 percent of West Indian females were registered as unemployed, compared with 15 percent of white males and 11 percent of white females. In June 1982 the Opinion Research Centre conducted over 1000 interviews with 16–20-year-olds in the inner cities on behalf of the Commission for Racial Equality. Of 376 whites 26 percent were in further education, 42 percent were employed and 30 percent were unemployed; of 348 Asians 45 percent were in further education, 31 percent were employed and 21 percent were unemployed; and of 331 West Indians 36 percent were in further education, 24 percent were employed and 36 percent were unemployed.

There is also some evidence to support the view that South Asians not only started off with a more privileged profile compared with West Indians, but have actually improved their position, notwithstanding the recession. The National Child Development Study is a longitudinal investigation carried out by the National Children's Bureau of all children born in one week in March 1958. From looking at ethnic minority children when they were 16 in 1974, the study concluded that there had been very little change in the backgrounds of West Indians – in terms of employment, housing and financial position – between first and second generations. The position of South Asians, however, had improved to such a degree that there was very little to distinguish the second generation from the rest of the population. This is how one sociologist summarized the position of South Asians in 1978 after reviewing the available evidence:

> A majority [of South Asians] are manual workers, frequently concentrated in ethnic work groups in particular sectors of industry in Lancashire and Yorkshire, the Midlands and London, many of them with little command of English, and living quite often as extended families in dense ethnic clusters in houses they have bought in depressed areas. A substantial minority, however, are professionals and businessmen living in white suburbia with household composition, employment profile and housing circumstances which mirror those of their white neighbours.
>
> (Ward, 1978, p.474)

Everything considered, the notion of blacks as some kind of socio-economic 'underclass' does not really stand up to examination. Westergaard and Resler (1975) dismissed the idea 10 years ago, drawing on data from the mid-term Census of 1966, when the overwhelming majority of black workers were immigrants and hence more likely to be disadvantaged:

> Coloured people are not uniformly concentrated at the bottom of the economic order. They are certainly handicapped in the labour market, as they are in a wide range of other respects, but in no way so as make them, *en bloc*, an 'under-class'. . . . The plain point is that professional, white-collar and skilled manual blacks tend to be left aside in the stereotypes of public debate and research alike. The visibility of colour diminishes the higher the socio-economic position of the coloured, in the eyes of liberal reformers no less than the prejudiced.
>
> (Westergaard and Resler, 1975, pp.356–357)

Moreover, the disparities, already evident in 1966, between the positions of the various black groups, and within a broad category like South Asians (to say nothing of the variations and fluctuations in the economic health of different multi-ethnic localities), are now so great that it has to be seriously questioned whether it makes much sense to continue talking about their situation in a simple undifferentiating way. 'Britain's non-whites', an American observer has written, 'sometimes seem less a meaningful group or class than a categorical artifact, rather like redheads' (Kirp, 1979, p.118). In addition, it is hard to escape the conclusion that the economic inequalities experienced by blacks are relatively minor when set against the grosser inequalities of region, social class and gender. This is not to say, however, that specific groups in specific localities, such as the Bangladeshis in London's East End, might not be in a particularly disadvantaged position.

Racial discrimination

Group disadvantages affecting the ethnic minorities undoubtedly exist. As important as ascertaining accurately their gravity and extent is trying to establish their causes. One obvious explanation is racial discrimination. A range of evidence has amply demonstrated that, although there has been a decrease in the incidence of the cruder forms of discrimination in recent years, it remains a significant barrier to advancement in both labour and housing markets. But it is not the only factor involved, nor is it necessarily the most significant. For example, the ethnic minority with the worst unemployment rate, over 80 percent, is the Vietnamese. It would clearly be naive to suggest that this was because they had met more discrimination than other groups. A likelier explanation is that they arrived during a period of recession with little or no knowledge of English or Britain, having in many instances undergone traumatic experiences in their flight from Vietnam. In addition, after a period of orientation and instruction in

English in camps run by volunteers, they were dispersed to isolated family pockets on council estates around the country without regard to employment prospects.

Circumstances of migration can also be used to explain disadvantages among black minorities. Their present position, it could be argued, is essentially a consequence of the fact that they were originally recruited and employed in the 1950s and 1960s as replacement labour to perform jobs that native labour was unavailable or unwilling to do; in other words, the disadvantage antedated their arrival. Their lack of advancement since then, together with their comparatively high unemployment rates, can be accounted for by a variety of factors: the shrinkage in opportunities due to the recession; their concentration in vulnerable manual jobs and in vulnerable manufacturing industries; and the conservative practices and ethos of workplaces and trades unions, particularly in the case of small employers, where the 'nepotism' favouring 'mates' of existing workers, and 'lads of dads', can be such an important factor in recruiting new workers. In housing, blacks were almost predestined to be at a disadvantage as late arrivals in an already competitive market where supply could not match demand (not even in the boom period) and where the poor, the single, and large families had traditionally always fared badly. This is not intended to undervalue the importance of racial discrimination as a factor in explaining disadvantage; it is simply to suggest that we should not automatically turn to it as the most plausible before considering the other possibilities. David Smith concluded from the 1974 PEP survey of a sample of ethnic minorities: 'Minorities do not identify racial discrimination as their major difficulty in making a life in Britain . . . they do not see themselves first and foremost as members of an oppressed minority . . . but as relative newcomers in a country where prices are rising and jobs are hard to get' (Smith, 1976, p.186). It is only fair to add, however, that the PEP data primarily concerned immigrants rather than British-born, and that minorities have consistently been shown to underestimate the degree of racial discrimination directed against them.

Racism and racialism

This brings us finally to the knotty issue of racism, which many would take to be a key ingredient of the ethnic minority experience in Britain and about which I have so far said little. I have reserved Chapter 7 exclusively for a discussion of racism and education but some preliminary points need to be made here. The main trouble with the concept of racism is semantic: what does it mean and how is it to be applied? It is of course a derivative of 'race' and therein lies the root of the problem, for it is now generally accepted that dividing up humanity into races, however real the visible differences between them, makes little sense scientifically. Though this does not of itself invalidate the concept of racism, it has led to considerable confusion, because if there are no such things as distinct races what can racism mean and who can be its victims or objects? Classically, 'racism' refers to the nineteenth-century doctrine identified earlier in the section on race – the doctrine, in Michael Banton's words, 'that a man's behaviour is determined by stable inherited characters derived from separate racial stocks having distinctive attributes and usually considered to stand to one another in relations of superiority and inferiority' (Banton, 1970, p.18). Despite being generally discredited, this doctrine continues to attract a good deal of attention in discussions of racism, particularly from writers and speakers of a Marxist persuasion.

According to Marxists, racism (in the classical sense) is specific to, and an ideological product of, the development of European capitalism. For them the original doctrine functioned, first and foremost, to justify the exploitation of subordinate racial groups by a ruling racial group under Victorian imperialism. It had been foreshadowed in the doctrine of black inferiority propagated by apologists for the transatlantic slave trade and plantation slavery in the previous century. Though both these institutions had been abolished in the British Empire by the time the doctrine of racism was first fully stated in the 1850s, their contribution to the financing of industrial capitalism remained an irrefutable fact. Racial exploitation is, of course, not the only (or even the main) form of exploitation during the Victorian period to have engaged Marxists' attention. Nor was the quasi-biological theorizing of that era, sometimes known as Social Darwinism, confined to race. E.J. Hobsbawm, a Marxist historian, has pointed out that social classes were also widely held to possess immutable characteristics and to be hence equally amenable to hierarchical classification. 'The bourgeois', according to Hobsbawm, 'was, if not a different species, then at least the member of a superior race, a higher stage in human evolution, distinct from the lower orders who remained in the historical or cultural equivalent of childhood or at most adolescence.' His explanation for this phenomenon runs as follows:

> Racism pervades the thought of our period [1848–1875] to an extent hard to appreciate today, and not always easy to understand . . . Apart from its

> convenience as a legitimation of the rule of white over coloured, rich over poor, it is perhaps best explained as a mechanism by means of which a fundamentally inegalitarian society based upon a fundamentally egalitarian ideology [i.e. liberalism] rationalised its inequalities, and attempted to justify and defend those privileges which the democracy implicit in its institutions must inevitably challenge.
>
> (Hobsbawm, 1977, pp.290, 313)

To the extent that Marxists speak or write of racism in the modern world, it is primarily with reference to forms of racial exploitation (of black countries' resources, for example, or black immigrant labour) which are in a sense the legacy of the imperialist ideology of a century ago.

Whatever its merits as historical interpretation, the Marxist view has a major drawback so far as discussions of racism today are concerned. It does not coincide with most people's understanding of 'racism'. For, in restricting it to an ideological product of European capitalism (i.e. to the need to justify slavery, imperialist expansion and neocolonialist exploitation), Marxists have also effectively restricted it to something done to blacks by whites, and thereby confirmed the not uncommon confusion of race with skin colour. What, then, is to be made of forms of racial antagonism and exploitation in other periods and other parts of the world, and in which the oppressors are not white or the oppressed are not black? Is the Hindu caste system not profoundly racist, and how else are we to interpret the East African slave trade, whose perpetrators were Arabs, or the discrimination and hostility experienced by Jews in the Soviet Union, African students in China, Turks in West Germany and Irish and Gypsies in Britain? The Marxists' answer seems to be that these are not forms of racism but forms of ethnocentricism. This can readily be exposed as semantic juggling to suit an ideological case, for there is little if anything to separate the content of the racism that evolved as an adjunct of the transatlantic slave trade and European colonialism from the content of pre-capitalist modes of racial antagonism or of the racial antagonism to be found in modern socialist societies.

Marxist usage is also an example of the philosophical fallacy of 'essentialism', whereby a word is defined not according to its actual use but to some supposed 'true' meaning 'out there'. Actual use suggests that, for most people, racism refers to the demeaning and prejudiced attitudes or discriminatory and antagonistic behaviour that members of one racial group direct against those of another. This is sometimes called popular or 'folk' racism, to distinguish it from racism in the original sense of quasi-scientific, nineteenth-century doctrine, and it is the sense I shall principally have in mind in this book. At the same time I shall observe the convention common in race relations literature of reserving racism for ideas, views and attitudes and referring to antagonistic and discriminatory behaviour as racialism. I shall also follow the spirit of the 1976 Race Relations Act in assuming that the victims of racism and racialism can include those who are ethnically or nationally rather than racially (i.e. physically) distinct.

It is important to keep the two main senses of racism, 'scientific' and 'folk', separate from one another, although this is not to say that they might not be historically related. Some manifestations of folk racism could fairly be described as part of the legacy of nineteenth-century doctrine, while the derogatory popular stereotypes, deep-rooted in European culture, of (say) the Jew, the black African and the Gypsy, may well have facilitated the emergence of Social Darwinism a century ago. Perhaps the most intractable problem of popular racism is assessing its extent and significance. There is a collection of hard evidence on racial discrimination in labour and housing markets, as there is on the disquietingly high incidence of racially motivated attacks on ethnic minorities and their property. But beyond that, facts give way, almost inevitably, to personal impressions, experiences and opinions. Some sociologists have tried to quantify the extent of racist views among the population by the crude device of administering attitude scales. Interpreting the results, however, has been a matter for dispute. What can a response in the artificial context of an attitude test possibly tell us of an individual's likely behaviour towards ethnic minorities? Stereotypes and prejudices entertained by sections of the majority population about blacks, Jews, Gypsies, the Irish, foreigners as a whole, undoubtedly abound in everyday conversation and jokes, in media images and cartoons. How widely or deeply held they are, or what effects they have on those at whom they are directed, is virtually impossible to say.

Another perplexing area is the debate over immigration control, where popular racism has interacted with right-wing politics. Hostility to immigrants is a universal phenomenon, and Britain has been no exception to the rule. Successive waves of immigrants since the Middle Ages have met with rejection and resentment. However, it is a moot historical point whether this hostility is to be construed as racism or something else – say, xenophobic insularity or fear for employment or other material prospects. Even if it is the case that racially and ethnically distinctive immigrants have encountered more hostility than others, this could simply have been due to their relative conspicuousness or because natives have not wanted to see the character of their neighbourhoods, or the ethnic identity of the nation, radically transformed. British immigration control is often said to be racist. It is certainly stringent, and in operation has been harsh, inhuman and uncivilized. It also openly discriminates against women, in the rules applying to foreign husbands and fiancés. But whether it is racist or not is more contentious. Critics of the introduction of control on Commonwealth immigration, from Hugh Gaitskell (who opposed the first Commonwealth Immigrants Bill so vigorously) onwards, have had no doubt that it was racist in conception and has proved racialist in effect. This is not to say that the politicians responsible for the legislation and regulations are themselves accused of being racists; rather, that the principal motivation is alleged to have been the appeasement of a largely racist electorate who believed that the fewer black, brown and yellow people there were in Britain the better. The charge of racism was considerably strengthened by the introduction of the patriality principle in the 1968 Commonwealth Immigrants Act, and its retention in the 1971 Immigration Act and the 1981 British Nationality Act. Although there is not a perfect fit between whiteness and patriality and non-whiteness and non-patriality, it is hard to conceive of a closer approximation for politicians anxious to reduce the level of non-white immigration without saying so in so many words.

Apologists for such legislation might well retort that immigration control is inevitably harsh because it is designed to keep out of the country people who want to enter it. In their opinion, this is a reasonable aim for an overcrowded island in a period of economic difficulty. It is non-white immigrants who are being kept out because it is they who, for historical reasons, want to enter; the legislation applies whatever the colour of the prospective immigrant, and was necessary in order to remove an anachronistic anomaly (the 'open door' being a remnant of the ideology of Empire) and subject Commonwealth immigrants to the kind of strict controls that already applied to aliens. As for the patriality principle, is it not quite natural for any country to favour immigrants with an ancestral link, and is not British policy in this respect as justifiable as, for instance, Israeli immigration policy which guarantees all Jews the right of return to their ancestral homeland? Apologists have also maintained that strict immigration control is a prerequisite of good race relations, since it reduces the pressure on resources in inner-city areas, defuses white antagonism, and hence renders unlikely any repetition of the anti-black riots in Notting Hill and Nottingham in 1958. Whatever the merits of the apologists' argument, I do not find it very helpful to regard them as racists per se, for there is not necessarily any link between support for immigration control and either 'scientific' or 'folk' racism. Even Peter Griffiths, who was widely believed to have won Smethwick from Labour in the 1964 General Election because of his unscrupulous manipulation of local hostility to Commonwealth immigrants, could write two years after his success: 'Any doctrine which preaches the superiority of one race over another is specious, evil nonsense' (quoted in Banton, op.cit., p.29). However, such a connection indisputably exists in the policies of small neo-Fascist parties like the National Front. Yet their ideologies are anti-Semitic rather than anti-black (although they have certainly exploited and expressed anti-black sentiments to swell their ranks). Marxists at least like to preserve a conceptual distinction between anti-Semitism (about which they have been notoriously ambivalent) and racism, on account of the different functions they are said to have fulfilled under capitalism.

Recent discussions of racism have been further hampered by the introduction of the concept of 'institutional' racism. This was an American coinage of the 1960s referring to institutional rules and practices which operated unintentionally to the disadvantage of racial minorities, particularly blacks. Its appearance was one reflection of an important development in American civil rights and anti-discrimination legislation – the shift from concern for equality of opportunity to concern for equality of outcome. Laudable as the aim of equality of outcome is, the usefulness of institutional racism as a conceptual tool to facilitate its realization remains suspect. Its weakness has been neatly encapsulated by one American critic, Natham Glazer:

> The rise of the popularity of the term 'institutional racism' points to one happy development, namely, that racism pure and simple is less often found or expressed. But the rise of this term has less happy consequences in that it tends to assume that all cases of differential representation in an institution demonstrate 'institutional racism'.
>
> (Glazer, 1975, p.343)

However flawed the concept may be, one can at least understand why institutional racism should have emerged in the United States as a way of trying to explain how racial inequality reproduces itself over generations and proves resistant to remedial action. The USA is a society in which blacks, for example, have been systematically oppressed for several centuries. What is less comprehensible is how such a concept can possibly be translated to Britain, where nine-tenths of all black adults in the early 1970s (when the concept was imported) were immigrants who had arrived during the previous 20 years, half of them within the previous 12 years. The other concept imported along with it, indirect discrimination, which was later to be enshrined in the 1976 Race Relations Act, does, on the other hand, possess a certain usefulness. One can see the sense in calling the nepotism in small firms' recruiting methods (see p.21) indirect, or indeed institutional, discrimination, when it has the unintended effect of disproportionately excluding ethnic minorities from employment. But to call it institutional racism is manifestly absurd, for it has nothing whatsoever to do with either 'scientific' or 'folk' racism.

Lord Scarman, a shrewd and perspicacious observer, was evidently puzzled by the concept of institutional racism in the evidence submitted to him on the causes of the Brixton disorders in 1981. In rejecting the allegation that Britain is 'an institutionally racist society' he was not dismissing the evidence on disadvantage. Rather, he was challenging the notion of Britain as a society which, in his own words, 'knowingly, as a matter of policy, discriminates against' ethnic minorities (Home Office, 1981a, p.11). He had, of course, a commonsense definition of racism in mind, and it is hard not to feel sympathy for his point of view. From the vantage point of common sense the only institutionally racist society in the world is probably South Africa; and it does seem odd to apply the same appellation both to a society like South Africa, which has legalized racial discrimination in the shape of apartheid, and to one like Britain, which has introduced increasingly stringent legislation to combat it.

This is not to say that forms of institutional racism, in Lord Scarman's sense, cannot be found in Britain. They can; in employment, for example, or, many would say, in immigration and nationality legislation, whose combined effect is to restrict the number of British citizens who are not white. But it does seem strange to characterize a whole society as racist on the basis of such examples of institutional racism as there undoubtedly are; still more so when this concept is so stretched as to accommodate all forms of disadvantage irrespective of causation.

Let us take a concrete case like the allocation of council housing. During the 1950s Bedford town corporation refused to place Italian immigrants on the council house list, for the reason, admitted to the House of Commons Select Committee on Immigration and Race Relations in 1971, that 'public opinion would not have tolerated' it. This was in spite of the fact, pointed out by critics, that the Italians were the ones making the bricks for the people who were on the list. More often, however, the under-representation of ethnic minorities in council housing has not been due to deliberate discrimination but to residential requirements which they, as comparative newcomers, have been unable to meet. I would call Bedford's former policy both direct discrimination and institutional racism, but residential requirements are neither (though they are certainly indirect discrimination and now unlawful). To call residential requirements institutional racism seems to me totally unwarranted since it has never been the intention of the housing authorities concerned to use these requirements to discriminate against ethnic minorities. They have simply been availing themselves of the well-established principle of 'first come first served' as one criterion in allocating public housing when demand greatly exceeds supply. The habit of referring to patterns of inequality or under-representation affecting ethnic minorities as institutional racism, regardless of causes or reasons, seems to me confusing and unhelpful. It has had the effect of undermining the meaning of racism and has considerably detracted from its emotive potency.

CHAPTER 2

THE EDUCATIONAL CONTEXT

The truth of the matter is that the immigrants have thrown into sharp relief the fact that a sizeable proportion of the indigenous population has not been well served by our educational system.

(Alfred Davey, 1973)

The hereditary curse upon English education is its organisation along lines of social class.

(R. H. Tawney, 1931)

Chapter 1 stressed the importance of approaching the topic of education and ethnic minorities from a historical perspective and setting it in a social and economic context. In this chapter I want to warn against the danger of detaching it from the development and confines of the educational system. A number of commentators have, like Alfred Davey, argued that the mass immigration of European and New Commonwealth families in the 1950s and 1960s highlighted cracks and defects in the system which had been present long before their arrival – the so-called 'litmus paper' or 'barium meal' hypothesis. But the impression has sometimes been given that this was the first major encounter between the system and children from the ethnic minorities. Although information is lacking for most of the minorities established before the Second World War, we do know that the educational authorities were locked in conflict with the Gypsies more or less from the outset. From the report of the Royal Commission on Alien Immigration (1902–1903), which paved the way for the Aliens Act of 1905, we also know a good deal about what happened to Jewish children in London schools in the final decades of the last century. Yet, despite the fact that the period of mass Jewish immigration coincided almost exactly with the inauguration of the state system of education between 1870 and 1902, only one writer on immigration and social policy, Catherine Jones (1977), has noted the significance of this historical encounter for today's discussions. Before examining that episode in some detail we should perhaps remind ourselves of the system's origins.

The origins of state education in Britain

Looking back with the benefit of hindsight it is possible to isolate three sorts of pressure impelling the movement that culminated in the first Education Act of 1870 – philanthropic, democratic and economic. In the first place, there was increasing evidence that the existing system of (predominantly Anglican) voluntary provision, which had enjoyed government subsidies since 1833, was simply not reaching the majority of urban working-class children. Clearly the Liberal Party, which came to power in 1868 with a record of commitment to public health and factory legislation, was not going to tolerate such an affront to its social reformist conscience. Second, the long-standing recognition that an extension of the franchise demanded an educated electorate acquired renewed urgency after the passing of the second Reform Act in 1867. And, third, the visible evidence furnished by the Paris Exhibition in the same year, of the economic threat posed by the United States and European competitors, brought home to politicians and industrialists the need for an adequately trained workforce. Historians have on the whole attached greatest weight to economic factors:

> Education, in addition to the miscellaneous functions previously assigned to it such as the promotion of social harmony, moral regeneration and the protection of the young, was now assigned the economic function of promoting national prosperity through the creation of an efficient, disciplined and literate labour force.
>
> (Jones, D.K., 1977, p.4)

However, if the inauguration of state education really was a response to industrialization, it was both a belated and an inefficient one. Britain had been the leading capitalist economy, and 'the workshop of the world', since the Napoleonic Wars. Yet it did not possess a national system of elementary education until 1870, nor a secondary system until 1902. E.J. Hobsbawm has claimed that the effect of state education was not so much to improve industrial performance as to maintain the social status quo – to the detriment of the former:

> Knowledge, especially scientific knowledge, . . . took second place in the new British educational system, to the maintenance of a rigid division between the

classes. In 1897 less than 7 percent of grammar school pupils came from the working class. The British therefore entered the twentieth century and the age of modern science and technology as a spectacularly ill-educated people.

(Hobsbawm, 1969, p.169)

The 1870 Act came as a bitter disappointment to the liberals and radicals who, partly inspired by 'hostility to squire and parson and the Anglican–Tory alliance' (Centre for Contemporary Cultural Studies, 1981, p.39), had campaigned so assiduously for an effective national system of education which could stand comparison with those of the United States and other European countries. The elementary provision it introduced was neither universal nor free nor compulsory nor secular. Indeed, though the Act could claim with some justice to have laid the basis for such a system, it was not until 1918 that fees in elementary schools were abolished and only in 1944 was the socialist dream of 'secondary education for all' achieved. But it was the Liberal government's abject failure to stand up to the Anglican Church that attracted the sharpest rancour of the Act's critics. The system instituted was a 'dual' one whereby responsibility for the education of the nation's young was divided between the non-denominational elementary schools run by the new democratically elected school boards, and the existing religious voluntary schools which sacrificed an element of control in exchange for direct government grants. John Stuart Mill spoke for many when he wrote:

A more effectual plan could have scarcely been devised by the strongest champion of ecclesiastical ascendancy for enabling the clergy of the Church of England to indoctrinate the children of the greater part of England and Wales in their religion at the expense of the public.

(Quoted in Jones, D.K., op.cit., p.69)

Introducing the 1870 Bill to Parliament, the Quaker W.E. Forster candidly admitted that it was intended 'to complete the present voluntary system, to fill up gaps, sparing the public money where it can be done'. As a consequence of this historic compromise between church and state, in the years following the Act the children attending voluntary schools greatly outnumbered those attending board schools; even in 1900 they accounted for 46 percent of the total elementary school population.

Jewish children in London board schools at the end of the nineteenth century

One aspect of the historic compromise which was in fact to its credit was the

1870 Act's famous Cowper-Temple clause. According to this clause, board schools and voluntary schools receiving government grant were obliged to provide 'conscience-free' education; they were debarred from including in the curriculum any 'religious catechism or religious formulary which is distinctive of any particular denomination'. The presence of this clause explains why the Jewish authorities did not follow the Roman Catholic Church, for whom the 1870 Act represented a real breakthrough, in building new voluntary schools to take advantage of the Act's generous terms. In 1870 there were a number of successful Jewish voluntary schools in existence which combined specifically Jewish instruction with a general elementary education. One of them, the Jews' Free School in Spitalfields in the East End of London, was to become the largest elementary school in the country by the end of the century with over 4000 children on roll. Outside London there were other Jewish schools in Birmingham, Liverpool and Manchester. After 1870, however, the growth in the size of the Jewish population, coupled with the reluctance of the Jewish authorities to found new voluntary schools, meant more and more Jewish children went to the religiously neutral board schools. Of 7000 Jewish pupils in London in 1882 only one-third attended them. Twelve years later the total had more than doubled and the proportion in board schools exceeded half; by the turn of the century 13,000 of the Jewish pupil population of 21,000 were in the non-denominational state sector.

There was another factor too that helped to account for this increase, and for the willingness of Jewish parents to send their children to non-Jewish schools: the attitude of the London School Board, which like the other boards enjoyed considerable freedom under the 1870 Act, and its statutory successors. The experience of Old Castle Street School, the first board school to be opened in the East End, was typical. Before 1880 it enrolled very few of the Jewish children who made up the majority of potential pupils in its catchment area. When the school managers voted to hire a Jewish headmaster and to introduce Hebrew studies for Jewish children, the situation altered dramatically. In 1882, and in spite of the proximity of the Jews' Free School, 95 percent of its 1200-strong pupil population were Jewish. At the turn of the century the number of Jewish school-age children was such that they even began attending Church of England voluntary schools as well. One Anglican elementary school in Spitalfields had over 60 percent Jewish children. Initial parental fears of the threat of Christian indoctrination proved groundless; the liberal attitudes of the London School Board prevailed in the voluntary sector as well. 'Thus developed the interesting arrangement that Jewish religious teaching was given under the roof of an English church' (Gartner, 1960, p.229).

The London School Board and its statutory successors were prepared to go to remarkable lengths to satisfy the needs of the Jewish community. In 1902 16 elementary schools, with an aggregate of 15,000 pupils on their rolls, were effectively run by the Jewish community on behalf of the local authority. The supervisor of East End schools told the Royal Commission on Alien Immigration that such schools

> are practically Jewish – that is to say, we observe the Jewish holidays, and they are carried out to suit the wishes of the Jews, for very few children in those schools are of the Christian persuasion, so that the schools are practically run as Jewish schools. Jewish ladies and gentlemen are on the management . . . the Board's plan has been, when the larger number of children has become Jewish to add the school to the list of Jewish schools.
>
> (Quoted in Gartner, op.cit., p. 227 and Jones, C., 1977, p.106)

Running a school 'on Jewish lines' meant early closing on Friday afternoons in winter, up to five hours per week of Jewish religious instruction and a substantial proportion of Jewish teachers. Occasionally adjustments to school curriculum and organization seemed almost calculated to antagonize the non-Jewish section of the local community:

> The English attending Rutland Street School were deprived of their own Easter holidays, which were postponed for eight or ten days, so as to make them synchronise, or fit in with the Jewish passover . . . It is making them [i.e. English parents] conform to the aliens instead of the aliens conforming to them.
>
> (*Report of Royal Commission on Alien Immigration* 1902–1903, quoted in Jones, C., op.cit., p. 108)

On the whole, however, the propriety of having supposedly non-denominational state elementary schools openly reserved for Jewish children was not queried. 'The existence of a special Jewish sub-system within the State school system was regarded with some justice as a sound solution to the problem of schooling immigrant children' (Gartner, op.cit., p.229). This solution, which stands in such sharp contrast to the response of central and local government to the arrival of European and New Commonwealth immigrant children over half a century later, was essentially a pragmatic one. It also reflected the influence of the native Anglo-Jewish establishment and perhaps betrayed some confusion about the purpose of a national system of education. 'In its "Jewish schools" policy and in its direction of surplus Jewish pupils into Anglican establishments, the

[London] Board was acting completely within its rights and within the terms of the [1870] Act, so far as these went. Whether so drastic an adjustment was within the spirit of the Act, however, was a matter of opinion' (Jones, C., op.cit., p.114).

Such flexibility on the part of the state, or at least on the part of the London School Board and its successors, did not, however, signal the demise of British Jewry's own schools. Jewish voluntary and independent schools survived, and so for a while did the *hederim* – adaptations of the single-room schoolhouses of Eastern Europe – which offered out-of-school religious instruction by rote in Yiddish. The latter were anathema to the native Anglo-Jewish establishment who despised the quality of education they provided and believed that they impeded the 'Anglicization' of immigrant children. Immigrant Jews saw matters quite differently. They 'did not greatly care who made Englishmen of their children, but they jealously guarded their right to make Jews of their children in their own way' (Gartner, op.cit., p.231).

The faith entrusted by both native and immigrant Jews in the new state schools seems, to judge by the results, to have been well placed. The verdict of headteachers and class teachers on Jewish pupils was highly favourable. Among the assessments quoted by the report of the Royal Commission on Alien Immigration were 'bright', 'superior intellectually', 'excellent workers in school', 'anxious to learn', 'superior . . . in facility, in industry, and in perseverence'. A contemporary author wrote: 'The foreign children at the East End Board schools are universally allowed to be sharper and more intelligent than the English, and they carry off a large proportion of prizes and scholarships'. On the other hand the report also quoted evidence of the fear of the clever Jew in teachers' comments on the children's 'smartness, especially in commercial things' (not to mention their 'perfect want of moral sense'). The success of immigrant Jewish pupils was as much the object of hostility as their numbers and the efforts made by the local authority to accommodate their cultural needs (Gartner, op.cit., p.230; Jones, C., op.cit., pp.108–109). The indigenous working class, many of whom resented and distrusted the state system of education imposed upon them, found it particularly galling that an alien population should be so determined to make use of it for self-advancement. It should not be forgotten that this was a period of intense anti-Semitism when 'the child of the Ghetto . . . had to suffer daily insults and often had to fight his way to school' (Krausz, 1964, p.22). Nor was the immigrant children's success particularly welcome to the established Anglo-Jewish community:

> Along with the rest of propertied opinion, native Jewry had seen popular education, whether provided by themselves or the state, very much as a means of . . . civilizing the masses – in this case the alien immigrants. These same immigrants, however, showed themselves to be if anything rather more ambitious on their own behalf. In the event, indeed, their children became rather more civilized, or Anglicized, as a result of statutory education than English (or even immigrant) Jewry had envisaged.
>
> (Jones, C., op.cit., p.109)

This raises two pertinent questions. First, was popular education instituted in the final quarter of the last century, as Marxists since have so often alleged, to 'gentle the masses' – to provide an 'appropriate' and limited education for those who were destined to be the 'hewers of wood and drawers of water'; or was it really designed, as Victorian liberals hoped and Jewish immigrants at least appeared to believe, to open up avenues for self-advancement and upward social mobility? Second, so far as policy is concerned, should the aim of state education be to 'anglicize' children from the ethnic minorities or to help them maintain their own culture, if necessary by making special and separate arrangements? Or should it be to effect some kind of compromise between the two – what has since become known as 'biculturalism'? I shall respond to the first question later in this chapter. The complex ramifications to the second one are explored in subsequent chapters.

Separatism in British education

For the moment I want to concentrate on whether the Jewish experience of a century ago did in fact throw 'into sharp relief' any weaknesses in the state provision of education. Those were, of course, early days but one weakness stands out immediately: the profound divisiveness of British education as embodied in the institutional split between voluntary and non-voluntary sectors. The 'dual system' introduced by the 1870 Education Act remains intact today. Indeed religious influence is more deeply embedded now, institutionally if not in practice, than it was then. For the 1944 Education Act not only extended the system to the secondary sector but also made religious worship and instruction compulsory in all county schools. At the same time the Act preserved the spirit of the Cowper-Temple clause by stipulating that this must be non-denominational in character and by permitting teachers and parents exemption on grounds of conscience. In addition the 1944 Act created three categories of voluntary school –

controlled, aided and special agreement. The final category need not detain us here, since very few schools belong to it. The important one is that of the voluntary-aided schools which, unlike those in the controlled category, enjoy a significant degree of independence from their local education authorities – in the appointment of governors, the admission of pupils and the teaching of religion. At the same time 85 percent of their capital and running costs are met out of public funds. In England only voluntary-controlled schools are entirely funded at the public's expense; in Scotland all voluntary schools have been funded in this way since 1918.

Although the proportion of voluntary schools in relation to county schools has declined since the beginning of the century, it is still far from negligible. Roughly one-third of all maintained schools in England are in the voluntary sector, the majority being in the aided rather than the controlled or special agreement category. The Church of England has 5500 schools, the Roman Catholic Church 2500, the Methodists have 47 and the Jews 21. Nearly all Roman Catholic schools are voluntary aided, as are all bar one of those run by the Jewish authorities; most Anglican and Methodist schools are voluntary controlled. It is sometimes implied that religious apartheid in education is a peculiarity of Northern Ireland. In fact it is also a characteristic of Liverpool, Glasgow and indeed all British towns and cities with a substantial Catholic population. Half of Liverpool's children are educated in the voluntary sector, the great majority of them in Roman Catholic voluntary–aided schools. As we shall see in Chapter 5, recently established religious minorities – Hindus, Muslims and Sikhs – have added an extra dimension to the debate about the rights and wrongs of such segregation.

Separatism has been one of the most persistently prominent features of British education. Although religious segregation has been the only form of segregation to be endorsed by legislation, three others – segregation for handicap and by sex and 'ability' – have enjoyed official approval for at least some period in the past. For example, from the time of the 1944 Education Act until the late 1970s it was accepted practice, if not exactly accepted wisdom, for children with physical or mental handicap or those designated as maladjusted to be educated separately from their peers. The justification for this segregation was that a concentration of specialist staff and resources made it more likely that such children's special needs could be met. During this time, while the proportion of children with sensory handicaps in special schools declined, the proportion of children designated as physically handicapped, educationally subnormal and maladjusted and being educated separately increased – quite spectacularly for the last two groups. In the case of maladjustment the 1970s also saw the establishment of special disruptive units, or 'sin bins', in some local authorities, as well as an increase in suspensions and explusions, in an effort to reduce disciplinary difficulties in the classroom. By the end of the decade the tradition of segregation for handicap had been challenged. Educationists, handicapped groups themselves (apart from the deaf) and the parents of the children involved were united in arguing that, if handicapped children were to achieve equality of opportunity and be freed from social isolation and stigmatization, they had to be educated in ordinary county schools along with unhandicapped children. The Warnock Report of 1978 firmly supported the principle of integration and the 1981 Education Act supplied the necessary statutory sanction. Under Section 2 of the Act local authorities are expected to educate children with special needs in ordinary schools provided this is compatible with the efficient use of resources and does not conflict with the wishes of their parents or the educational needs of other children.

This development must have come as a considerable relief to the West Indian community. Their experience had exposed the unsatisfactory nature of the procedures for ESN assessment as clearly as the Jewish experience had exposed the absurdity of the 'dual system' a century earlier. ESN special schools had been a focus for concern among West Indian parents since the mid-1960s when it was discovered that in many areas they contained not only disproportionate numbers of working-class children but disproportionate numbers of West Indian pupils as well. In 1973, when the last national figures on 'immigrant' pupils showed West Indians to be more than four times over-represented in ESN schools, concern reached such a pitch that the DES took the unusual step of sending a letter on the subject to all Chief Education Officers. Although reliable statistics are not available, it is widely believed that West Indian pupils remain over-represented in special schools for the ESN and the maladjusted, not to mention 'sin bins', suspensions and expulsions.

Segregation between the sexes in education has run a similar course. At one time, certainly when I was at secondary school in the 1950s, it was normal for boys and girls to be educated separately from the age of 11 until they left school. In the 1980s, as a result of comprehensivization, falling rolls and a change in attitudes towards personal relations between the sexes, a single-sex secondary school is unusual in most areas outside the independent and selective sectors. This is not to say that integrationists have notched up another ideological victory. A vigorous rearguard action is being fought to preserve a few enclaves of girls' education by an unlikely alliance of 'conservative' parents and teachers (including Asians steeped in the conventions of *purdah* and fearful of the effects of 'permissive' Western attitudes on their daughters) and some 'radical' feminists. Both groups are preoccupied with girls' academic performance, but the feminist argument has a flavour of its own. It maintains that girls are likely to do better in separate schools, or at any rate in separate classes, especially in subjects like maths and science where, because of prevailing sexist norms (in, for example, teacher and peer group attitudes), they lack self-confidence. Such single-sex enclaves might also, the argument continues, lead to an increase in girls specializing in scientific and technical subjects and hence embarking on careers outside the stereotype of what is appropriate for females. In addition girls might acquire an enhanced capacity to resist the forces of male chauvinism. The validity of these various hypotheses remains untested – and perhaps, without a policy change over the desirability of coeducation, untestable. A majority of the remaining all-girls schools are in the independent and selective sectors and are not therefore strictly comparable with the coeducational comprehensives attended by most girls.

The fourth type of formal segregation – segregation according to 'ability' – has, like sexual segregation, been limited on the whole to the secondary sector. As with religious segregation, its origins can be traced back to some of the earliest steps in state education; but it is most commonly identified with the tripartite system. Having received the support of the Norwood Report in 1943, this system became established in most local authorities after 1945. It was founded on the strange premise that there were three identifiable 'types' of children who should be educated separately from one another. They were identified by a combination of an 11+ examination and primary school assessments, and on this basis allocated to grammar schools, technical high schools or secondary modern schools. More often than not segregation according to 'ability' between schools was accompanied by segregation according to 'ability' within schools in the shape of streaming, setting or banding. This practice had been regarded as an improvement on the existing practice of 'promoting' the bright and 'keeping down' the dull, and had become widespread in the 1930s, in primary as well as secondary schools, following the recommendations of the Hadow Report of 1931 and the Spens Report of 1938. The adoption of the tripartite system by so many local authorities, and of streaming by so many schools, is partly a testimony to the remarkable success of the educational psychologist Cyril Burt in converting the educational establishment to his now discredited view that children possess fixed innate intellectual abilities which can be measured.

By the end of the 1970s a radical reform had taken effect throughout England and Wales. The principle of integration had triumphed to such an extent that the great majority of children in the state sector of education attended common schools from the beginning to the end of their statutory school lives. In 1965, when the Labour government published its circular on comprehensive secondary education, there were over 1000 grammar schools in England and 3500 secondary moderns. Sixteen years later there were only 200 of the former and 380 of the latter, although one-third of English local authorities still retained at least one grammar school and relatively intact selective systems survived in eight of them. The dismantling of the tripartite system in the 1960s and 1970s was complemented by the abandonment of streaming in many primary schools and by experiments with different styles of mixed-ability teaching in secondary schools. Much of the comprehensive reorganization was, admittedly, dictated by pragmatic exigencies rather than principle, or by concern for economic growth ('maximizing society's talents') rather then socialist ideals, and some of it was of a makeshift and nominal nature. Much of it also occurred after the Labour defeat at the 1970 General Election and in Conservative-controlled local authorities.

Yet the significance of the ideological and political campaign prosecuted by Labour governments and Labour-controlled authorities during this period should not be underestimated. 'Our belief in comprehensive reorganization', stated Tony Crosland, the Labour Minister responsible for the 1965 circular, 'was a product of fundamental value-judgments about equity and equal opportunity and social division as well as about education' (quoted in Centre for Contemporary Cultural Studies, 1981, p.72). Labour's campaign was essentially a continuation of the struggle launched by Victorian liberals and radicals for an effective system of popular education. It marked a concerted attempt to realize more fully the old socialist dream of 'secondary education for all', making available to the whole nation what had previously been reserved for an academic élite. The campaign was fired by the conviction that the tripartite system was both divisive and inegalitarian, since it labelled a majority of the country's children 'failures' at the age of 11, and a product of precisely the same kind of class thinking as had led the Taunton Commission of 1867 to propose three grades of secondary school corresponding 'roughly, but by no means exactly, to the gradations of society'. No one had been deceived by the official rhetoric about 'parity' between the three types of secondary school; to be allocated to a secondary modern school, as 75 percent of 11-year-olds were, was to have 'failed' the 11+ examination.

The deleterious effects of both the tripartite system and streaming are vividly conveyed in the following account of a classroom incident in the early 1970s:

> A lesson taking place in a city centre, deprived area, mixed secondary modern school, with a group of fourth-year leavers. It was a four-form entry school, streamed into A,B,C, and D classes. This class was the lowest stream in the fourth year. This was an introductory lesson at the start of the year, with the objective of showing the children that they had potentialities and abilities which had previously gone unrecognized. This suggestion was immediately queried by the class:
>
> 'You don't understand the system in our town, sir.'
>
> 'All right, then, you explain it to me.'
>
> 'Well, sir, when we were eleven, we took this test. All the bright kids went to the grammar school, and the dunces came here.'
>
> The whole class was highly amused by this, and many inaudible comments were made.
>
> 'Yes, sir,' said another boy, 'and when we got here, they divided us up into four groups. The clever dunces went into the "A" form, and the next best dunces went into the "B" form and . . .' The rest was drowned in laughter.
>
> 'And', said a third boy, 'We're the "D" form, – we're the dustbin!'
>
> At this, the whole classroom dissolved into laughter, and became very animated, with much shouting out, guffaws and catcalls.
>
> (Shipman and Raynor, 1972, pp.64–65)

Such effects, coupled with the fact that comprehensivization and mixed-ability grouping have been consistently shown (contrary to the predictions of conservative educationists) to disadvantage nobody academically, have rendered segregation by 'ability' both socially and educationally indefensible.

Three of the four separatist traditions in British education – segregation for handicap and by sex and 'ability' – are, then, despite the odd reactionary flourish, in retreat; the fourth – religious segregation – is on the defensive (see Chapter 5). There is, however, a fifth tradition which is neither in retreat nor on the defensive, and which has never been either official policy or sanctioned by national legislation. Indeed for much of the time it has not been *willed* at all. Yet it has proved far more potent and resilient than the four which have, and it has particular significance for the situation of ethnic minorities. I refer, of course, to the tradition of segregation by social class. This tradition has its origins in the simple Victorian belief that, as middle- and working-class children could be distinguished by differences in inherited ability, and were destined for different social and economic roles, they should receive different sorts of education. Although this belief would now be generally dismissed as eccentric, it is remarkable how influential it has been in the twentieth century. Indeed, both segregation for handicap and by ability are to some extent products of it; it is no accident that working-class children have always been over-represented in ESN schools, bottom streams and remedial classes or under-represented in selective schools and higher education. The elimination of these social class inequalities, and the destruction of the social class barriers accompanying them, was the principal object behind the campaign for comprehensivization.

However, despite the fact that most children who spend their compulsory school life in the state sector (and the survival of the small but influential independent sector should not be forgotten) now attend comprehensive primary and secondary schools, there is still a clear tendency for them to be divided by social class between the ages of 5 and 16. This is more apparent in urban areas than in rural ones. This division is, of course, a consequence of residential separation between the social classes and acceptance of the neighbourhood school principle. It might, therefore, be thought to have a certain inevitability about it, but it was not always thought inevitable. During the 1960s a number of local authorities embarking on secondary school reorganization schemes made some attempt to counteract the effect of residential segregation even at the expense of the neighbourhood school principle. Bristol, for example, a pioneer local authority in the comprehensivization campaign, built a ring of secondary schools round the city perimeter in the 1950s. Having ended the 11+ examination in the mid-1960s, the authority drove catchment area wedges into the inner city in order to guarantee socially balanced intakes and forestall the emergence of 'sink' schools which would have resulted from a more strictly neighbourhood policy of catchment areas. I was a teacher in a Bristol comprehensive school at the time, and as far as my school was concerned the policy was implemented successfully. Pupils came from local housing estates, from downtown and from owner-occupied suburbs; moreover, after 1965 they were not divided into streams or 'ability' groups except for maths and foreign languages. Yet socially enlightened policies of this kind were soon to come under attack from both 'conservatives' and 'radicals': from the political right for 'social engineering' and disregarding parental wishes, and from the political left for threatening the solidarity of working-class neighbourhoods and infringing the principle of the 'community' school. I shall return to this issue, and to the whole question of the desirability of integration in education, in Chapter 5.

Inequality in British education

We come now to the second prominent feature of British education – inequality – which is often closely bound in with the first. I have already referred to two forms of educational inequality – gender inequality and social class inequality. There is also a third – geographical inequality – which is partially, but by no means entirely, a reflection of the second. DES statistics have regularly painted a vivid picture of the 'geography of deprivation' in education. Statistics for 1981 showed a wide discrepancy in 16+ performance (proportions of students gaining five or more 0-Level passes or CSE grade ones; going on to full-time further education; and leaving without any graded exam results) between the five most successful English local education authorities – Buckinghamshire, Surrey, East and West Sussex, and Hertfordshire – and the five least successful – Wolverhampton, Manchester, Inner London, Sandwell, and Salford. No one would, I think, be very surprised by this finding given what is known about the socioeconomic profiles of these 10 LEAs. DES statisticians certainly underlined the broad correlation between results and indices of deprivation in that particular year. Socioeconomic explanations have also been adduced to account for poor performance in Wales. Between 1979 and 1980 the proportion of pupils leaving schools in Wales without a single qualification increased from 23.8 to 25.1 percent, while in England it fell from 12.9 to 12.2 percent.

However, economic deprivation cannot claim to be a complete explanation for disparities in outcome. The proportion of pupils in Wales gaining five or more O-Levels or one or more A-Level in 1980–1981 was only just below the proportion in England (24.4 percent as opposed to 26 percent) and by 1982 the proportion leaving without qualifications had dropped to 18 percent. Moreover, students in Northern Ireland, the most deprived region in the United Kingdom, have always excelled. The level of local authority expenditure has even less explanatory power, though the DES statisticians did note a 'weak' connection in 1981 between the amount an authority spent on education and its results, once socioeconomic factors had been taken into consideration. Kirklees, for example, did not spend nearly as much money on education as ILEA and Manchester and scored highly on deprivation factors, yet the proportion of students gaining five or more O-Level passes or CSE grade ones was just 1 percent below the national average of 22 percent. The figure in both ILEA and Manchester was only 14 percent. Leeds, the lowest spending of all English authorities, managed a pass rate of 23 percent, and Dudley, lambasted by HM Inspectorate for shabby buildings, shortages of textbooks and poor staffing ratios, did even better with a pass rate of 25 percent.

What relevance do these statistics have for pupils from the ethnic minorities? Perhaps the most obvious point to make is that the populations of the five least successful English LEAs are, to varying degrees, conspicuously multi-ethnic and the populations of the five most successful are not. Many children of European and New Commonwealth immigrant origin attend schools in urban working-class areas where academic standards are often well below the national average. For instance, there was a rumpus in the London Borough of Haringey when it was revealed that in 1982 in six schools with large black populations only 5 percent of the fifth year gained an O-Level or CSE grade one in maths and only 12 percent in English. The proportions of all leavers in English schools (including the independent sector) passing at this level in 1979–1980 were 26 percent for maths and 37 percent for English. It would be reasonable to conclude from this that ethnic minority performance was likely to be depressed by attendance at underachieving schools in deprived neighbourhoods. Strangely enough, even though social deprivation and educational underachievement were features of inner-city and downtown areas long before mass immigration from Europe and the New Commonwealth, officialdom appears to have concluded that the presence of the newly established ethnic minorities is in itself a manifestation, or even a cause, of both. DES officials use the size of the ethnic minority population in an LEA as an index of deprivation and so do their counterparts at the Home Office and the Department of the Environment. This is a good example of what social policy critics call 'blaming the victim'. It should also be noted that the three LEAs which have secured good pass rates at 16+, against the odds, are all multi-ethnic as well, and markedly so in the case of Kirklees.

Although there are certainly discrepancies in academic performance between LEAs, and indeed schools, with similar socioeconomic profiles, there can be little doubt about the very close connection between scholastic success and social class. Social class is, and always has been, the fundamental basis for educational inequality in Britain. I referred earlier to the various forms of under-representation experienced by working-class children. Research has also consistently demonstrated that they do significantly worse than their middle-class peers in standardized tests and external examinations. In addition there is what has been aptly labelled an 'attrition' in working-class performance during the period of statutory education.

This has been amply illustrated by two famous longitudinal studies: the study conducted by J.W.B. Douglas and colleagues of a sample of children born in March 1946 and the National Child Development Study (NCDS) (see Chapter 1) carried out by the National Children's Bureau of all children born in one week in March 1958. The NCDS researchers found that the social class gap in reading and arithmetic attainment, clearly discernible as early as the age of seven, widened inexorably as the children progressed through school. Douglas and colleagues discovered that working-class children lost ground by the age of 11, and even more by the age of 15, to middle-class children with whom they had been adjudged equal in attainment at the age of eight. Nor has there been much improvement over the past half-century, despite some success in opening up better educational opportunities for the working class. In spite of considerable expansion in higher education, the chances of working-class pupils getting to university in the 1960s were pretty well the same as their parents' had been in the 1930s. During the 1970s the proportion of working-class students admitted to university actually declined, from a peak of 29 percent in 1970 to 23 percent at the end of the decade, which was much the same as it had been 50 years earlier. One researcher, A.H. Halsey, has reached the 'depressing conclusion' that 'over the century so far, the unequal relative educational chances of boys from different class origins have been remarkably stable . . . the conventional picture of a steady trend towards equality has been an optimistic myth' (Halsey, 1978, p.123).

Why should this be? There are two difficulties in answering this question. First of all, no matter how potent a factor social class may be in predicting children's life chances, it is not an unambiguous or uncontested indicator of social identity like, say, gender. It is what the sociologists call 'a summarizing variable', a shorthand expression for a complex of factors correlated with occupation. Most educational researchers investigating the role of social class have adopted the Registrar General's fivefold classification of occupational statuses or some derivation from it, such as a simple dichotomy between manual and non-manual workers. It is important to keep this sense of social class separate from Marxist usage which, by and large, recognizes only two social classes – the bourgeoisie and the proletariat – defined respectively by their ownership and non-ownership of the means of production. Second, the differences between working-class and middle-class performance as demonstrated by research are, on the whole, the differences between the mean or average performances of the two groups. The differences *within* the groups are far greater; and some working-class children do better than some middle-class children. It might fairly be queried how one can possibly explain something which is founded on a statistical convention, the mean score, and a sociological abstraction, social class. Certainly it would be quite wrong to make use of any explanation for the close correlation between social class and scholastic achievement, in order to try and explain why individual working-class children do not perform so well as they should – which is what most parents and teachers are interested in. It would also be a mistake to assume that close correlation indicates causation; in other words, that there is something about being working class which tends to produce poor academic results. Yet this is precisely what many have assumed or at least tried to prove. Middle-class Victorians would no doubt have argued that working-class underachievement was a natural outcome of the lower genetic potential of working-class communities – an argument by no means unknown in the twentieth century, even in academic circles, once it had been shown that social class correlated with measured intelligence as well as academic attainment and, of course, that academic attainment correlated with measured intelligence.

Most researchers, however, have taken the view that the explanation for underachievement is to be found in specific traits of working-class culture, and have directed their attention to trying to identify the most significant of these. On the whole they have concluded that it is the quality of parental support that goes furthest to explaining the discrepancy between middle-class success and working-class failure. That is why the disagreement between the two types of explanation is sometimes referred to as the 'nature versus nurture' debate. J.W.B. Douglas subscribed to the 'nurture' school of thought, and he was also one of those who set greatest store by parental attitude as the critical factor. His assessment of working-class underachievement, written 20 years ago, pointed also to the contributions made by material deprivation and the quality of the schools attended:

> Parents who are unskilled workers . . . will often be of low educational attainment, take little interest in their children's school work, have large families, live in grossly overcrowded homes lacking amenities . . . and may well send their children to primary schools which are ill-equipped, with large classes and less than first rate teaching.
>
> (Douglas, 1967, p.65)

Douglas was also one of the first to argue that the (at that time) widespread practice of dividing pupils into classes by 'ability' considerably exacerbated working-class children's underachievement.

Since Douglas wrote his assessment the influence of explanations in terms of inherited potential has declined and the 'nature versus nurture' debate has been replaced by the 'deficit or difference' debate. Are working-class children handicapped by being brought up in a defective culture, as Douglas and his contemporaries were inclined to believe? Or are they handicapped by a discontinuity between the values of home – as regards, say, discipline or the usefulness of book learning – and the values of school? Some Marxists have turned the debate upside down by alleging that it is defective schools which are to blame, not so much because of poor equipment, large classes and so forth, but because they are middle-class institutions staffed by middle-class personnel. Because their chief function under capitalism is to preserve the bourgeois hegemony, they inevitably come to disparage everything that working-class children bring with them to the classroom – their language, their appearance, their interests – and allot their experience and culture scant, if any, coverage in the curriculum.

Whichever of these explanations eventually prevails, the relevance of social class inequality to the educational position of ethnic minorities should be plain. Most ethnic minority pupils, except for the Jews, are of working-class parentage, live in predominantly working-class neighbourhoods and go to predominantly working-class schools. As we shall see in the next chapter, the debate about the causes of ethnic underachievement, insofar as it exists, has been a replication in miniature of the debate about the causes of working-class underachievement. However, this is not to say that social class necessarily operates to the disadvantage of members of ethnic minorities who are working class to the same extent, or in the same ways, as it does for the working class as a whole.

The same might be said of the third form of inequality in education – gender inequality. The discussion about the education of girls has taken a different route from the discussion about the education of the working class, or at any rate it has struck different emphases, although there are areas of overlap. The main reason for this is that girls do not underachieve academically. If anything they do better than boys in the subjects they take, up to and including the final year of compulsory schooling, apart from in maths where the evidence is conflicting. They secure better pass rates at 16+ and fewer girls leave school without a single graded result. At A-Level 13 percent gained two or more passes in 1981 compared with 14 percent for boys. In addition, considerably more girls are now found in the upper reaches of formal education than was previously the case. More girls than boys go on to some form of full-time education (but not part-time where they continue to be discriminated against); more girls than boys take

A-Level courses in state schools and sixth-form colleges (a reversal of the situation of 10 years ago); and over 40 percent of undergraduates are female compared with only 25 percent in the late 1960s. The principal thrust of the feminist critique of schools, therefore, has not been about achievement as such but towards an analysis of why girls, given the choice, continue to opt for, say, French and biology as examination courses rather than physics and technical drawing. More generally, feminist criticism centres around the sexist pressures in both the overt and the hidden curriculum which still guide girls overwhelmingly into conventionally female careers and life-styles. For Marxist feminists schools serve not only a capitalist society but a patriarchal and chauvinist one as well: 'the outcome of the schooling process continues to be a sexually segregated work-force in which women are trained less, paid less and promoted less' (Hannon, 1979, p.110).

Yet, to revert to a question posed earlier in the chapter, the academic advances made by girls and women over the century so far suggest that the faith invested in popular education by Victorian liberals was not misplaced. The unremitting reproduction of social class inequality, on the other hand, seems to support the Marxist hypothesis that the function of formal education in a capitalist society is to preserve and legitimate the status quo. Whether the experience of more recently settled ethnic minorities also supports the Marxist hypothesis, or like the experience of nineteenth-century Jewish immigrants tends to confirm liberal optimism, is a matter I turn to in the next chapter. The main point I want to make here is that it makes little sense to consider that experience outside the context of the long-established patterns of educational inequality I have just described.

Decentralization in British education

In Chapters 4–7 I shall be exploring what I believe to be the most important policy issues raised by the presence of pupils from the ethnic minorities. It would make equally little sense to do that without taking some account of the context of educational decision-making in Britain. How is power distributed and responsibility allocated; and how is control exerted and influence applied?

Undoubtedly decentralization is the main feature of educational administration in Britain, and it remains a constant source of bafflement to immigrants who have been educated in countries with quite different arrangements. Under the British system it is local, not central government which is essentially responsible for educational provision. In addition, individual schools and teachers enjoy considerable autonomy over decisions affecting curriculum and organization. This is not to say that central government is relatively powerless. In fact its powers are substantial although they are, by and large, limited to legislation and financial support. Neither of these should be underestimated. I have already noted the significance of the 1944 Education Act in regard to religious education, and of the 1981 Act for the education of the handicapped. The 1944 Act has further relevance, so far as the purposes of this book are concerned, in enshrining the principles of equality of opportunity and of education in accordance with parental wishes, the second of which was confirmed and reinforced by the 1980 Education Act. Also of relevance are the clauses covering direct and indirect discrimination in the 1976 Race Relations Act and the accompanying powers entrusted to the Commission for Racial Equality for investigating local authority policy and practice. As for finance, central government provides local authorities with a block grant, the rate support grant, which accounts for roughly half their educational expenditure and can be supplemented by further central funding to cater for the needs of the socially disadvantaged. Over and above those formal powers central government has the capacity to create climates of opinion and set agendas for educational debate. Normally this is done in a piecemeal fashion through the activities of HM Inspectorate and the publication of circulars, surveys and White and Green Papers. Occasionally, however, central government may choose to bring influence to bear in a more direct and concerted fashion, as when James Callaghan, then Prime Minister, in a speech at Ruskin College, Oxford, in 1976, initiated the 'great debate' in an attempt to improve relations between education and industry.

Since the return of the Conservative Party to office in 1979, there seems to have been a firm move by central government to increase its control, not only over how much money local authorities spend on education, but also over the curriculum. This tendency has become more pronounced since Sir Keith Joseph took over as Secretary of State for Education and Science. His readiness to intercede in the curriculum debate, coupled with his support for criterion-referenced testing and the stipulation of objectives, suggest we may be embarking on an era of central coercion. The question of precisely where power lies in relation to what is taught in school and how it is taught has always been a legal nicety. (The exception here is religious instruction, responsibility for which rests firmly with the Secretary of State.) In practice, responsibility for the curriculum (including religious instruction) has traditionally devolved upon headteachers and their staffs. A former

Conservative Minister of Education, David Eccles, once described the curriculum as a 'secret garden'; the teaching profession, and the teachers' unions, have long jealously guarded it as their sacred preserve and as a guarantee of their professional status. Now we appear to be witnessing attempts by both central and local government to invade that preserve – central government through its control of the public examination system, Sir Keith's interventions and initiatives undertaken by the Manpower Services Commission (described in the next section); and local government through the issuing of policy documents and curriculum guidelines.

Far from being a static, immutable affair, Britain's decentralized educational system is, then, a dynamic one. What has been aptly termed a 'triangle of tension' unites the three main partners (central government, local authorities and schools) in ever shifting patterns of control and a continuous struggle for power. One result is ambiguity and some confusion. According to Young and Connelly, authors of a recent study of policy and practice in six multi-ethnic authorities, English education 'is characterised by an opaqueness of policy determination . . . many of the issues which arise in the field of multi-racial education do so at the margin where policy and influence are contested between the various parties'. Another consequence, they note, of the 'customary autonomy' enjoyed by individual headteachers and schools – of the fact that 'the ultimate power to resist change lies in the headteacher's study and the staffroom' – has been the comparative absence of explicit government and local authority policy on topics of importance such as multicultural education (Young and Connelly, 1981, pp.98, 100, 132).

Since their study was undertaken, a number of local authority statements on multicultural or anti-racist education have, in fact, been published. Although this is testimony to the shift in the balance of curriculum power referred to above, it has yet to be seen if schools take any real notice of the injunctions now thrust upon them. However puzzled immigrants, themselves educated under centralized educational systems, may be by the relative lack of fiats from central governments, and whatever the drawbacks to our decentralized system, the 'customary autonomy' of schools and teachers remains one of its great strengths. It is right that curriculum power should be concentrated precisely where the curriculum is enacted, and in the hands of those with most experience of the business of teaching and learning. No matter how enlightened the content of the anti-racist and multicultural education guidelines recently promulgated by several local authorities, they seem to me to represent a retrograde step. But I am anticipating the argument of later chapters. My point here is that decentralization is a strong not a weak feature of British education.

The 'customary autonomy' of teachers, and the fact that they have so often been blamed for any shortcomings in the education of ethnic minority pupils, should alert us to the significance of the kind of profession they are. The dominant image evoked by the available evidence is of political and social conservatism. A survey carried out on behalf of the *Times Educational Supplement* shortly before the 1983 General Election revealed that 44 percent of teachers intended to vote Conservative, 28 percent SDP/Liberal Alliance and 26 percent Labour. Most were also in favour of retaining corporal punishment and compulsory religious education and opposed to admitting handicapped pupils into normal classrooms. Yet at the same time a majority clearly favoured schools adopting declared policies on combating sexist and racist attitudes among children.

Education and youth unemployment

A new ingredient in the British educational context is, of course, mass unemployment. It never occurred to me when I started teaching 20 years ago that pupils of mine might have difficulty finding jobs after they had left school, let alone that the teaching profession itself might ever be affected by the blight of unemployment. Yet, as a result of falling rolls and public expenditure cuts, unemployment, redeployment, redundancy and early retirement are all now established hazards of professional life. The situation for young people is far more acute. Only a minority now move from school to meaningful paid work. To the extent that the function of preparing young people for the world of work still exists, it has been largely annexed by the Manpower Services Commission, a Government 'quango' established in 1974 and at present operating with a budget of almost £2 million a year and considerably enhanced status and influence. Its two main undertakings so far, the Youth Training Scheme (YTS) (providing one year's training, education and work experience for 16-year-olds) and the Technical and Vocational Education Initiative (TVEI) (for 14–18-year-olds), were only launched in the autumn of 1983, which makes it hard to assess their likely significance or effectiveness. But the experience of the Youth Opportunities Programme (YOP) (the forerunner of YTS) hardly augurs well. Only one-third of school leavers in 1980–1981 joined YOP, and only one-third of those found jobs on leaving.

It seems paradoxical (to say the least) that the Government should invest so much in job training when there are fewer and fewer jobs to be trained for. However that may be, there can be little doubt that the school–work link has effectively been severed for the foreseeable future. Neither government nor the teaching profession nor society at large appears to have quite absorbed the shock or even wholly recorded the message. Nor for that matter have educational theorists. Popular education was instituted 100 years ago essentially as a response, albeit a tardy and insufficient one, to industrialization. Clearly liberal educationists are going to have to think again about the aims of formal statutory education in a post-industrial society – as indeed are Marxist educationists in relation to its possible functions under post-industrial capitalism.

CHAPTER 3

EQUALITY OF OPPORTUNITY

> I conceive it to be our duty to make a ladder from the gutter to the university along which any child may climb.
>
> (T.H. Huxley, 1871)

> All children should have an equal opportunity of acquiring intelligence, and of developing their talents and abilities to the full.
>
> (Sir Edward Boyle, 1963)

The most important questions we can ask about the situation of pupils from the ethnic minorities concern equality. In education these have traditionally revolved around the hallowed concept of 'equality of opportunity'. What is the meaning of this concept? What is it that all children should have an equal opportunity to achieve? Quite simply, in Sir Edward Boyle's words, it is to develop 'their talents and abilities to the full'. Put another way, the aim is that every child's school performance should represent the sum of effort plus natural aptitude and in no way be tainted by the influence of irrelevances such as social class, gender or ethnicity. Between T.H. Huxley's remark when a member of the first London School Board in 1871 and Sir Edward Boyle's introduction to the Newsom Report in 1963, this ideal state found support from most points of the political compass. In a sense it is hard to imagine any politician or any teacher, parent or pupil for that matter, wanting to dissociate themselves from so unexceptionable a notion.

Limitations to the equal opportunity philosophy

But the equal opportunity philosophy has come under regular attack from radicals and socialists – not so much for what it means in theory as for what it has meant in practice. As an ideological product of Victorian liberalism, it has revealed itself to be a meritocratic creed rather than an egalitarian one. The dream of its devotees has been not of a society in which gross disparities in wealth, power and status are eliminated or even much reduced, but of one in which these disparities are distributed according to merit as opposed to the privileges conferred by the circumstances of birth. They have notably failed to divest themselves of the belief that an education system should produce few winners and many losers. The dominant assumption has been that only a minority will ever surmount all the rungs on T.H. Huxley's ladder. This is why that doyen of socialist educationists, R.H. Tawney, dismissed the equal opportunity philosophy 50 years ago, in a memorable metaphor, as a 'tadpole philosophy'; a majority were consigned to an early death so that an élite could turn into frogs. With a handful of honourable exceptions like Sir Edward Boyle (whose idea of *acquiring* intelligence was strikingly at variance with beliefs prevailing at the time), advocates of the equal opportunity philosophy have all too often further compromised themselves in an unholy alliance with psychometricians purporting to measure innate ability. Some of them have even claimed that a state of equal opportunity has been realized when, for example, the social class composition of those pupils admitted to grammar schools in a particular authority corresponds to what might have been anticipated on the basis of tests of measured intelligence, irrespective of whether this still results in the under-representation of working-class children.

The other major socialist criticism has been that equality of opportunity is an individualistic creed stressing the enhancement of individual life chances rather than the encouragement of socially enlightened behaviour. Personal ambition and selfish acquisitiveness have been indulged at the expense of the spirit of altruism and cooperation. Here socialists are joined by radicals of a different complexion whose complaint is directed not so much at the equal opportunity philosophy's acquiescence in the perpetuation of social division and injustice as at its assumptions about what constitutes educational success and the good life. Radicals of this sort object to the notion that the most fully achieved educational career is one which negotiates the academic hurdles of school and university to gain entrance to well-paid and socially prestigious professions. For, in effect, this not only limits the successful to a minority but reduces the development of 'talents and abilities' to scholastic success as measured by 16+ and 18+ examinations, and in some subjects rather than others. Whatever the rhetoric may say, little heed is paid to artistic talent or athletic ability or to a whole range of human aptitudes which can contribute to the making of fulfilled adults and useful citizens.

There cannot be much doubt that the conventional assumptions about educational success and the good life are as widely held among the ethnic minorities, apart perhaps from Gypsies, as they are among the majority. Educational and socioeconomic advancement, both for themselves and their descendants, is one of the commonest reasons given by immigrants of the 1950s and 1960s for leaving their countries of birth. So do children from the ethnic minorities enjoy equality of opportunity? And do they perform academically in accordance with their aptitudes? Because of the theoretical and empirical problems involved – what precisely is an opportunity or an aptitude and how does one measure either? – these two questions have rarely been addressed much less answered. Nevertheless there are clearly several ways in which ethnic minority pupils might be said not to enjoy equal opportunities in education or at any rate to start out at a disadvantage. In the first place, most ethnic minority pupils are of working-class parentage, live in predominantly working-class neighbourhoods and attend predominantly working-class schools. I have indicated in the previous chapter the likely implications of these simple facts for educational performance (pp.42–46). Second, many of them arrive in their infant reception class speaking little or no English. Given what is known about the relationship between competence in the language of instruction and educational attainment, this might also be fairly construed as a handicap. Third, it seems at least conceivable that the cultural discontinuity so often discerned between the values of working-class homes and middle-class schools will become a cultural rift or gulf when the homes concerned are both working class and ethnically distinct. Finally, it is possible, maybe probable, that pupils from the ethnic minorities will all encounter racism or racialism at some stage in their school careers, either in the form of hostility from their peers, limited or negative expectations on the part of their teachers or ethnocentricism in the curriculum or other aspects of school policy. If so, such encounters could well have a depressing effect on school performance. All four of these considerations are, of course, rather speculative, markedly so in the case of the third and fourth, underlining the problems of getting to theoretical and empirical grips with questions of equal opportunity.

The educational performance of pupils from the ethnic minorities

Educational research has therefore turned its focus to questions which are amenable to empirical investigation and reasonably straightforward answers. These are essentially questions of equality of outcome, not of equality of opportunity. Researchers have sought to establish how pupils from the ethnic minorities actually perform in standardized tests, public examinations, university entrance and so forth, regardless of opportunities. It is important to keep the two concepts apart, since it is logically possible for equality of opportunity and *in*equalities in outcome to coexist. In other words, it is conceivable that ethnic minority pupils might achieve equality of opportunity – might perform in accordance with their aptitudes – and still perform differently from one another and, as a group, less well than the rest of the population. Unfortunately, the available research evidence on equality of outcome in relation to pupils from the ethnic minorities does not match the quality or quantity of the literature on working-class achievement. For a start, in the case of the four long-established communities portrayed in Chapter 1, there is no evidence at all on how Jewish or Italian children do at school, and very little on Irish children, though the general impression (correct or otherwise) seems to be that none of these groups presents or experiences any great difficulty. Gypsy children are quite another matter. In a well-known judgement the Plowden Report of 1967 referred to them as 'probably the most severely deprived children in the country'; it noted mass absenteeism, widespread illiteracy and general underachievement. Their situation does not appear to have altered much in the years since the Report. In 1983, a report by HM Inspectorate found that only half of Gypsy children go to primary school, and fewer than 1 in 10 to secondary school, and that even those who do go attend irregularly.

As regards more recently settled communities of European and New Commonwealth origin, little if anything is known about the performance of Chinese, Spanish or Portuguese pupils, all of whom are substantially represented in London. There is some evidence, from the ILEA Literacy Survey 1968–1975, to suggest that Cypriots in London might be under-achieving. However, no one appears to have been much moved by this, despite the fact that there were over 7000 Greek- and Turkish-speaking children in ILEA schools in 1978. During the period of the Literacy Survey Greek Cypriots had a mean reading score consistently below that of both Indians and Pakistanis, and Turkish Cypriots did worse than any other ethnic minority. When we turn to the evidence on South Asians and West

Indians, we find it invariably offers less information than might be hoped, simply because these two broad groupings are nearly always treated as undifferentiated entities. Gender and social class are rarely controlled for; island origin is usually ignored in the case of West Indians; and Pakistanis and Bangladeshis are not often considered separately from Indians or East African Asians. Furthermore, much of what is known is obsolete or in other ways unreliable.

Still, it does tell a story that cannot be disregarded. A useful article by Sally Tomlinson (1980) has summarized all the research investigations undertaken or reported between 1960 and 1980. These are of three types: investigations of performance on standardized tests, performance in 16+ (including course persistence) and representation in selective schools, special schools and streaming or banding systems. Three general trends emerge from Tomlinson's review: immigrant children tend to do significantly worse than British children on all three measures; British-born ethnic minorities do better than immigrants of the same ancestry and only in the case of West Indians do they do worse than the rest of the population; and South Asians are increasingly successful, particularly at 16+ (Tomlinson, op.cit.).

As a result of the inadequacies in the available research, the Rampton (later Swann) Committee of Inquiry into the Education of Children from Ethnic Minority Groups, set up by the Labour Government in 1979, commissioned two investigations. It asked the National Foundation for Educational Research (NFER) to review the research on West Indian pupils' attainment, and the DES to include a question on ethnic origins and achievement in its 1978–1979 leavers' survey for six multi-ethnic LEAs. Though confirming that there were relatively few research studies of any size or importance, and that the picture revealed was 'complex', the NFER review nevertheless felt able to conclude:

> . . . research evidence shows a strong trend to under-achievement of pupils of West Indian origin on the main indicators of academic performance. [They] perform less well on measures of IQ, verbal and non-verbal reasoning, reading and mathematics, and are more likely to be found in the lower streams of ordinary schools, in much higher proportions in ESN schools and there appears to be evidence that they suffer stress in the school environment.
>
> (Taylor, 1981, pp.216–217)

Further evidence to substantiate this conclusion, and to endorse the impression of South Asian success, was provided by the findings of the DES investigation. It revealed that only three percent of West Indian school leavers in the six LEAs gained five or more O-Level passes or CSE grade ones in 1978–1979, compared with 18 percent of South Asians, 16 percent of other leavers in those LEAs and 21 percent of all leavers in the English state school population. At A-Level only two percent of West Indians secured one or more passes compared with 13 percent of Asians, 12 percent of other leavers in those LEAs and 13 percent of leavers in the whole English state school population.

These figures do indeed suggest that West Indians are seriously underachieving, whereas South Asians are faring, if anything, better than the majority of their schoolmates and, by A-Level, as well as the overall state school population in England. However, several critics of the DES statistics were quick to point out that the figures made no allowance for parental occupation or educational background – that is, ignored the critical variable of social class. They argued that the relative failure of West Indians and the relative success of South Asians could have been predicted from the employment and educational profiles of these two groups as furnished by the 1971 Census. The NFER review, on the other hand, concluded that the few studies which had attempted to control for social class did not support a social class explanation for West Indian failure. One of these, the ILEA Literacy Survey, had monitored the reading performance of a cohort of London pupils from the ages of 8 to 15 between 1968 and 1975. The principal finding in relation to West Indian pupils was that their standard of reading as a group was 'well below the indigenous group' – a difference which could not 'be entirely explained by differences in social factors or time at school in England' – and that it actually deteriorated during the course of their school career (Mabey, 1981, pp.89–90).

Another (roughly contemporary) longitudinal investigation – the National Child Development Study – also tried to take account of social class factors and reached broadly similar conclusions in relation to West Indian pupils; namely, that poor attainment among ethnic minorities was confined to them, when only British-born children were compared, and after financial and other material circumstances had been taken into consideration. This general picture of relative South Asian success and relative West Indian failure was locally corroborated by a study of results in one London borough in the late 1970s, which also attempted to control for social class. Maurice and Alma Craft surveyed the examination performances, and subsequent destinations, of the cohort of pupils in the fifth and upper sixth forms of the borough's schools in 1979. Their findings for the 16+, but not the 18+ (where the numbers involved were rather small), tallied closely with what might have been anticipated from other research. The percentage of the different groups in the 'high' scoring category (i.e. passing five or more GCEs or three–four GCEs plus five CSEs) were as follows: middle-class whites, 31 percent; working-class whites, 18 percent; middle-class South Asians, 32 percent; working-class South Asians, 16 percent; middle-class West Indians, 20 percent; working-class West Indians, 9 percent (Craft and Craft, 1983).

The Crafts' survey also confirmed what is known about the participation of ethnic minorities in further and higher education: namely, that whereas there is a pronounced tendency for both South Asians and West Indians to continue with full-time education after 16, West Indians are inclined to prefer colleges of further education to school sixth-forms; and that South Asians, but not West Indians, are well represented in higher education. Although questions have occasionally been raised about the quality or usefulness, in career terms, of some of that participation, there can be little doubt that as a group South Asians, at any rate, have made it to the top of T.H. Huxley's ladder. Figures from the DES survey of six multi-ethnic LEAs in 1978–1979 showed that the same proportion of South Asians, three percent, as of other leavers (excluding West Indians) in those authorities, left to go to university, compared with five percent of the overall state school population. For all degree courses (there being some preference among South Asians for polytechnics) the figures were: South Asians five percent, all other leavers (excluding West Indians) in the six LEAs four percent, and the state school population as a whole six percent.

Other research into the first year, British-resident (excluding British-born) South Asian student population in British universities in 1979, has shown that although the size of their numbers was partly attributable to the over-representation among them of the more privileged East African communities, as a group they were comparatively free of some of the social class and gender bias that characterized the rest of the student body. South Asian female students shared their male counterparts' preferences for science and medicine (though not engineering), and more South Asians, 24.6 percent, came from working-class backgrounds, and fewer from the managerial and professional classes, 33.9 percent, than was the case for the bulk of the student population (i.e. those born in the United Kingdom), for whom the figures were 19.4 percent and 49.2 percent respectively (Vellins, 1982). West Indians, on the other hand, remain conspicuously under-represented among university students. The DES survey showed only 1 percent leaving to go to university from the six LEAs in 1978–1979 (the same proportion as went on to all degree courses); and in 1980 the National Union of Students estimated that only 300 of Britain's 250,000 university students were of West Indian origin.

The concept of underachievement

In the light of the evidence, deficient as it may be, the Rampton Committee would appear to be justified in its conclusion that 'West Indian children *as a group* are underachieving in our educational system' (Committee of Inquiry into the Education of Children from Ethnic Minority Groups, 1981, p.10). However, one or two qualifications are called for. The most important concerns the use of the concept of 'underachievement'. In relation to working-class performance this can mean one of two things: either that the attainment of working-class children is below what would have been predicted from their scores on standardized aptitude tests or from their attainment at an earlier point in their school careers; or that the attainment of working-class children is below the attainment of middle-class children. In the case of the latter, the assumption is that the same distribution of ability obtains for both social classes. The statement that West Indian children underachieve is usually taken in this group comparison sense, since standardized tests are held to be culturally biased. In other words, as a group West Indian children do less well than other groups or than the pupil population as a whole. The DES investigation undertaken for the Rampton Committee illustrates 'underachievement' in this sense. It simply recorded the difference in results between ethnic groups at 16+. On the other hand the ILEA Literacy Survey could be said to combine both senses in that it not only compared mean scores but compared them *over time*. It showed both that Turkish Cypriots and West Indians were the two lowest achieving groups when tested in 1975 at the age of 15 and that their test scores then were below what they had been seven years before when they were eight. In other words, there was a deterioration in their performance comparable to the 'attrition' of working-class performance charted by J.W.B. Douglas and colleagues in the 1960s.

But evidence on this point is conflicting. For example, the data yielded by two studies of small samples of urban schools in the mid-1970s, which are more recent than both the ILEA and the NCDS findings, pointed in the opposite direction. Geoffrey Driver examined the 16+ results in five multi-ethnic schools for the period 1975–1978 and concluded: that West Indians for the most part did better than their English peers (but worse than South Asians); that West Indian girls did better on average than West Indian boys; and that in some cases West Indians actually overtook English pupils during the course of their secondary school careers (Driver, 1980). Driver's study excited considerable controversy and has been criticized on methodological and other grounds, notably by the NFER review of research carried out on behalf of the Rampton Committee (Taylor, op. cit., pp. 113–122).

More persuasive is the evidence supplied by the study by Michael Rutter and colleagues of 12 inner London secondary schools and unfortunately not included in their original report *Fifteen Thousand Hours* (Rutter et al., 1979). This revealed a marked improvement in the West Indian position as a result of sheer perseverance. At the age of 14 West Indian performance was well below that of whites on measured IQ and in reading – by nine and six points respectively. When the main group under investigation came to take public examinations for the first time in 1976, only one percent of West Indians gained five or more O-Level passes or CSE grade ones compared with seven percent of whites. But 47 percent of West Indians, as opposed to 24 percent of whites, stayed on into the sixth form, leading to a transformation in educational outcomes. Taking fifth- and sixth-form experiences together, 19 percent of West Indians left with five or more O-Level passes or CSE grade ones compared with 11 percent of whites; 18 percent left without any graded results compared with 34 percent of whites; 10 percent gained at least one A-Level compared with 6 percent of whites; and 17 percent went on to tertiary education compared with only 3 percent of whites. Moreover West Indian pupils, especially girls, had better attendance records and far fewer left at Easter in their fifth year without sitting public examinations. These results really are remarkable, and in stark contrast with the DES's findings for six multi-ethnic LEAs in 1978–1979. They are particularly remarkable when one bears in mind that the schools in Rutter et al.'s sample were not only in the inner city, and hence predisposed towards academic standards below the national average, but did not at the time of his study have fully comprehensive intakes. They had lost the 'cream' of their potential intakes to surviving grammar schools and had only 10 percent of pupils in the top ability band compared with 25 percent in London as a whole (*Times Education Supplement*, 8 October 1982).

The other main qualification to be made in regard to the statement that West Indian pupils underachieve concerns the notion of West Indians as some kind of undifferentiated entity. Driver and Rutter have not been the only researchers to comment on differences between West Indian boys and

West Indian girls. It seems possible that West Indian girls may both have more positive attitudes towards school and secure better results than West Indian boys. It is also possible, though again the evidence is slight, that educational attainment among pupils of Jamaican origin (approximately half of all West Indians in Britain) may be below that of pupils from other islands in the Caribbean. It has been hypothesized that this is a reflection of the differences between the educational backgrounds and socioeconomic profiles of Jamaican and other West Indian immigrants. So the underachieving group may not be West Indians as a whole but West Indian boys and not West Indian boys as a whole but boys of Jamaican descent. However that may be, the West Indian community is no more a homogeneous population than any other ethnic minority or the nation as a whole.

One obvious form of social heterogeneity is social class stratification. In Chapter 1 I noted that the employment profile of West Indian males was characterized by a high proportion of skilled manual workers and only a small minority in white-collar jobs. It would not be unreasonable to infer that this might have some bearing on patterns of educational attainment among West Indian children. Although the few studies attempting to take some account of social and economic background do not support an explanation of West Indian underachievement exclusively in terms of social class, this does not mean that it might not be a significant factor.

Simple social class explanations of a mechanistic kind are, of course, to be avoided. An unpredictable dimension remains when the attainment levels of schools, local authorities and regions are compared and socioeconomic factors taken into account. The same is true of ethnic minorities. Pakistanis have a more disadvantaged economic profile nationally than Indians but Pakistani children outscored Indian children in the ILEA Literacy Survey; and the West Indians in Rutter's sample of London schools eventually outstripped their white peers despite a high incidence of socially deprived home backgrounds. Nevertheless the significance of social class for educational attainment cannot be disputed. The NCDS findings, for example, showed an improvement in educational performance between the first and second generation of South Asian children comparable to the improvement in their economic position, while in the case of West Indians both performance and financial circumstances stayed unaltered. The unanswered, perhaps unanswerable, question concerns the *extent* to which relative South Asian success and relative West Indian failure can be explained in terms of social class. How much Asian 'overachievement' and West Indian 'underachievement' is left once social class has been controlled for?

Although it is understandable how the Rampton Committee arrived at its conclusion, a more measured assessment of the situation of West Indian pupils seems to be indicated. After all, our knowledge of it is limited, as is our knowledge of the situation of South Asians and other ethnic minorities (there has been no systematic nationally based research enquiry), and most of what we do know is out of date or inadequate. Both the NCDS and the ILEA Literacy Survey data are now 10 years old and the DES's 1979 investigation of 16+ and 18+ performance controlled for neither social class, sex, nor national or regional origin. Bald statements about group attainment can degenerate all too easily into stereotypes; and, just as in the case of working-class underachievement where the evidence at least is irrefutable, it should not be forgotten that the inequalities in outcome within social groups are far greater than those between social groups. One of the ILEA researchers has commented on the Literacy Survey results: 'it should be noted that the analysis deals mainly with average scores and differences. For both the indigenous and West Indian groups the range in achievement was wide and many of the latter scored more highly than some of the former' (Mabey, 1981, p.85). For these reasons the few half-hearted attempts to develop the Marxist thesis that ethnic minorities or blacks constitute some kind of educational underclass carry little conviction. One can see how the West Indian experience might be manipulated to suit such a thesis, but the experience of South Asians, like that of the Jews before them, points in the opposite direction, upholding the faith invested by Victorian liberals in public education as an avenue for social and economic advancement.

Explaining West Indian underachievement

Given the uncertainty over the nature and extent of West Indian underachievement, it is hardly surprising that explaining it should have created even more confusion and dissension than in regard to working-class underachievement whose nature and extent are clear. Rarely, for example, is it apparent whether a particular theory is supposed to explain poor West Indian performance as a whole or just that degree of underachievement which persists after social class factors have been eliminated. This is in spite of the fact that the course of the debate has closely followed that about working-class underachievement, namely, 'nature' versus 'nurture', 'deficit' versus 'difference' and 'defective' homes versus 'defective' schools. On the one hand there have been explanations, associated particularly with the psychologists Jensen and Eysenck, claiming that disparities between the IQ test scores of different ethnic groups can largely be assigned to disparities in inherited intelligence. On the other hand there have been explanations in terms of material disadvantage (low incomes, poor housing) or cultural deprivation (high incidence of child-minding, inadequate linguistic stimulation in early childhood, authoritarian disciplinary practices) or both.

Since the late 1960s 'deficit' explanations have been rather upstaged by the now widely entertained hypothesis that West Indian underachievement is a product of racism. This hypothesis has its origins, like genetic explanations, in American psychological testing, but interpreted to suit a sociological style of analysis. Following the replication in this country of American doll and picture tests of racial identification and preference on young black and white children over 10 years ago, the argument developed that West Indian children were prone to low self-esteem and insecure self-identity, and hence poor academic attainment, because they found it difficult to resist the pejorative images of black people relayed to them by the institutions of a white racist society (Milner, 1975). One of these institutions, so it was claimed, was the school system itself. Though the parallels were not always noted explicitly, this argument was a re-run of similar arguments about sexism and 'classism'; the language used to frame the criticism was often identical and so were the targets – reading schemes, children's literature, history teaching, teachers' attitudes. School was declared to be not only a bourgeois and male chauvinist institution but a racist one too, deeply imbued with assumptions about the superiority of white over black, indigenous over foreign, European over Asian and African. Such allegations constructed a stark picture of the West Indian child's experience of school, of profound inequality in treatment, in which overtly racialist acts by teachers and almost unconscious stereotyping both figured.

This hypothesis had a seductive force when first enunciated but it seems to have failed the test of time. Apart from the doubtful ethics of the tests themselves (asking very young children to choose between, and make evaluative judgements about, white and black dolls) and the problem of interpreting responses in such an artificial and forbidding context, the simple logic – negative teacher attitudes plus ethnocentric curricula equals low black self-esteem equals poor black adademic performance – has proved empirically vulnerable and over-reliant on anecdote, impression and opinion. More recent research has suggested that, regardless of white society's images of blacks or white teachers' attitudes towards them, West Indian pupils are increasingly self-confident and perfectly capable of looking after themselves, at least in secondary schools. In the words of one researcher Maureen Stone, who discovered neither disproportionately poor self-concept nor disproportionately low self-esteem among her sample of West Indians: 'The West Indian children's unfavourable view of their teachers' feelings towards them did not correlate with an unfavourable view of themselves' (Stone, 1981, p.214). This knocks a key element out of the equation. If West Indians are not, in fact, more susceptible to derogatory views of themselves than other groups of children, precisely how does racism in the education system and the wider society produce West Indian underachievement? Moreover, if racism really is the decisive factor, why do South Asians, also presumably its victims, perform so well? Finally, how can we explain the comparative success of West Indian girls, indicated by some research, or the fact that the differences in attainment among individual West Indians are far greater than the differences between them as a group and other groups?

Turning to the first elements in the equation, it is virtually impossible in a decentralized system of education to determine at any given moment to what extent school curricula are ethnocentric (not to mention the difficulty of deciding what is to be interpreted as 'ethnocentric'), although limited critical appraisals of, for example, examination syllabuses or currently available textbooks, are feasible and have been attempted. What about teachers' attitudes, so persistently arraigned and incriminated over the past 10 years? Under the influence of the mainly American research on the self-fulfilling effect of teacher expectations, a number of commentators have argued that it is the teaching profession's low expectations of West Indian performance that is principally responsible for their under-achievement.

In fact, the evidence on the basis of which the teaching profession has been pilloried is flimsy, to put it mildly. Not only is the research into the self-fulfilling effect of teacher expectations the subject of academic dispute but none of it, either in this country or the United States, concerns the relationship between white teachers and black pupils. Like many others I have heard teachers say ghastly things about ethnic minorities in staffrooms and meetings, of the sort encountered by Rex and Tomlinson in their interviews with headteachers in Handsworth, Birmingham, in the mid-1970s:

> [West Indians] are bound to be slower. It's their personalities. They lack concentration.

> I've got a small representative bunch [of West Indians]. They are a slow, docile, low-functioning lot.
>
> The temperament of the West Indian child is more volatile, disruptive, easily stirred.
>
> A racial characteristic is that West Indians are voluble. Their fights look like riots.
>
> (Rex and Tomlinson, 1979, pp.198–203)

But what teachers say in such settings is not necessarily a reliable guide to their classroom behaviour or even perhaps to their real beliefs. In 20 years as a teacher and researcher I can think of perhaps half a dozen examples of racialist conduct likely to have a detrimental effect on pupils from the ethnic minorities, and all of those involved teachers notorious for their general insensitivity to children.

There has been only one systematic attempt to sample the attitudes, or rather opinions, of teachers in relation to ethnic minorities. In 1972 Townsend and Brittan administered a questionnaire on different aspects of multicultural education to 510 teachers from 25 schools around the country. The teachers were invited to respond on a five-point scale to more then 40 statements relating to school life. Discussing the findings one of the researchers, Elaine Brittan, identified the most outstanding feature as the 'high degree of consensus' among teachers concerning the academic and social behaviour of West Indians; namely, that they were of 'low ability' and created disciplinary problems. The degree of consensus, coupled with the additional remarks made by respondents ('some of which can only be described as racist'), led her to conclude that large-scale stereotyping was involved – 'self-contradictory' stereotyping, since West Indian pupils were labelled as both 'lazy/passive/withdrawn' and 'boisterous/aggressive/disruptive'. Striking as these findings undoubtedly were, it has again to be queried whether what teachers say – especially when expressed in the form of responses on a five-point scale – has much bearing on how they actually behave in school towards pupils from the ethnic minorities. But the crucial question, as the researcher herself notes, is whether the 'objective problem' of West Indian pupils 'should be located in the children or the teachers, or in some interaction of the two' (Brittan, 1976, pp.189–190).

Support for an 'interactive' explanation is to be found in Geoffrey Driver's study of a West Midlands secondary school. This is the only detailed ethnographic investigation of relations between West Indian pupils and white teachers yet published, and was carried out at roughly the same time as the research by Townsend and Brittan. In an attempt to explain the severe underachievement and increasing alienation of a group of West Indian boys, Driver certainly isolated the school's treatment of them (or rather how they interpreted the school's treatment of them) as a major factor, but he did not simply castigate teachers for low expectations, stereotyped perceptions or overall racism. Instead he chronicled the way their limited 'cultural competence' in regard to West Indian pupils involved them in confusion and perplexity, which combined with external pressures – family breakdown and peer-group power – to deny those pupils educational success (Driver, 1979).

Another ethnographic study (Hammersley, 1981) conducted in an inner-city secondary modern school in the same period, while not specifically concerned with race relations, also reached a conclusion of an 'interactive' kind, albeit rather different from that of Driver. Though recording a high degree of staffroom racism in the form of derogatory remarks ('They're thick', 'The coloured boys know no restraint', 'They're the closest to savages in this country'), Hammersley noted no carry over into the classroom: 'the teachers did *not* explicitly discriminate on grounds of race in their dealings with pupils, nor did I detect any covert discrimination, though this of course is much more difficult to identify'. He explained the teachers' racism in part as a rationalization for their dissatisfaction and resentment at what they perceived as the sharp decline in their 'social and professional status as a result of the changing character of the pupil intake'. This was not advanced as a complete explanation since the teachers identified West Indian pupils as a particular problem, especially in the area of discipline. There was indeed an objective problem involving West Indian pupils, as the researcher confirmed, but 'it must be seen as a product of the relationship between the orientations of Downtown teachers and those of "West Indian" pupils, not as reflecting some deficiency on the part of the latter' (Hammersley, 1981).

What we have here is a variation on the cultural discontinuity explanation for working-class underachievement. For me the appeal of this type of explanation is partly its ring of truth. Both Driver's and Hammersley's accounts chime in closely with my own experience as a classroom teacher and a classroom researcher. Their added attraction is that they studiously shun both pathology and criminology. They do not deprecate the West Indian community for intellectual deficiency or cultural deprivation, nor do they accuse British society and schools of endemic racism; unlike so many other contributions to the debate, they are not gunning for a guilty party.

However, in his later study of attainment in five urban secondary schools Driver (1980) did try to explain comparative success and failure among ethnic minorities in terms of relative cultural strengths. Many teachers have long believed that South Asians do well because of the firm cultural base provided by their communities, while West Indians do badly because their original cultures were fragmented by the combination of slavery and generations of indoctrination through a colonial education system, leaving them dazed in a kind of cultural no man's land. Driver formulated the hypothesis that West Indian girls outshone West Indian boys because they had been brought up to believe that family prosperity and status depended on what the woman achieved, not the man. Needless to say, cultural explanations of this ilk are anathema to radicals, because they detract from the significance of racism or 'structural' factors or both.

The views of West Indian parents and pupils

The *Colour and Citizenship* report of 1969 observed that 'children of West Indian parents . . . have been a source of bafflement, embarrassment and despair in the education system' (Rose et al., 1969, p.281). Among schoolteachers 'despair' has taken the form of what Elaine Brittan called a 'high degree of consensus' about West Indians' indiscipline and 'low ability'. What of the views of the parents and children themselves? Research on ethnic minority parents' views of their children's education is scanty and to some extent contradictory. Rex and Tomlinson's (1979) survey of parental attitudes in Handsworth found that the majority of all three groups sampled – South Asians, West Indians and whites – were satisfied with their children's schools, and that the minority of South Asian and West Indian parents who were not satisfied criticized lax discipline and informal teaching methods.

A more pessimistic picture of views among West Indians emerged from Maureen Stone's research in London in the late 1970s: 'There is real bitterness in the West Indian community at the way the school system is seen as treating black children . . . the West Indian community generally regards the school system as reinforcing and sanctioning the racist views which exist in society at large and which regard people of African descent as basically inferior to people of European descent' (Stone, op. cit., p.174). Maureen Stone also developed what might be termed a distinctively parental explanation for West Indian underachievement; namely, that it is a direct outcome of so many teachers forsaking their socially sanctioned duty of imparting necessary knowledge and skills in a business-like no-nonsense fashion, in preference for building up harmonious relationships with their pupils and dabbling in psychotherapy to foster self-esteem. Further indicators of parental dissatisfaction among West Indians have been campaigns on issues such as 'bussing' and ESN schools, but the clearest evidence is provided by black supplementary education. Maureen Stone, who visited most of the West Indian supplementary schools in London, distinguished them from the evening and weekend religious and language schools run by South Asian and European communities, since the latter did not necessarily imply any comment on the quality of statutory education. For her they 'mirrored' the Socialist Sunday School Movement of a century ago, in the sense that they were dedicated to the aim of promoting social mobility and founded on the principles of 'hard work, disciplined study and the will to succeed'. All those she visited stressed the teaching and learning of basic skills, while a few also saw themselves as inculcating 'black consciousness' or, alternatively, religious values.

With a few exceptions, such as Maureen Stone, educational researchers have paid even less attention to the views of the pupils themselves. Stone found that her London sample of West Indian children were highly antagonistic towards teachers, although not necessarily towards school or education: 'they perceive teachers as hostile and authoritarian, using their power in an arbitrary way'. So much so, she concluded, that if it was true, as Elaine Brittan's research had suggested, that teachers regarded West Indian children in a 'negative, stereotyped' manner, then it was equally true that West Indian children regarded their teachers similarly (Stone, op.cit., p.217). Peter Ratcliffe, a co-worker of Rex and Tomlinson in Handsworth, also recorded a hostile response among a group of 25 West Indians aged between 16 and 21, none of whom had progressed beyond CSE. Not only did they voice resentment at teachers' exercise of authority, but 'there appeared to be a distinct mood of dissatisfaction with the interest which the teachers had shown them . . . Many said that their teachers had effectively prevented them from studying "O" level examinations which they thought they could have passed' (Ratcliffe, 1981, p.301). A rather different criticism was expressed by a group of West Indian university students who submitted evidence to the Rampton Committee. They argued that to succeed in the system blacks had to deny their identity – a claim reminiscent of the social psychologists' theory of a decade ago that what black children learned from British society and its institutions (including school) was that it was 'better' to be white than black (*The Guardian*, 20 November 1980).

The students' viewpoint has received some qualified support from the few subcultural studies of West Indian pupils, such as that of Geoffrey Driver. Unfortunately, like the demographic research on achievement, these studies have not always taken note of the long-established tradition of enquiry based on social class. This tradition prompts the general conclusion that because schools are essentially middle-class institutions, they confront working-class pupils with the unenviable dilemma of having to choose between discarding working-class values in the pursuit of success and joining anti-school working-class subcultures. Jean Floud and colleagues suggested as long ago as 1957 that the ethos of the grammar school was fundamentally alien to the working-class child, while five years later Jackson and Marsden (1962) added that working-class children who succeeded at school were somehow disposed towards middle-class values.

Two well-known studies of the 1960s (Hargreaves, 1967; Lacey, 1970) found that, although the influences of home and peer group might incline a working-class boy to acceptance or rejection of school values, the polarization that eventually occurred into pro- and anti-school subcultural groups was an almost direct consequence of the school's 'differentiation' mechanism – streaming. Acknowledging this tradition in his study of West Indian boys in a single-sex secondary modern school, Barry Troyna (1978) discovered that those in the bottom streams were powerfully immersed in black culture and had exclusively West Indian peer-group affiliations while those in the top streams were more likely to associate with other races and to 'de-emphasize' black identity.

A culture of resistance?

There was an attempt in the 1970s to conceptualize anti-school working-class subgroups, using Marxist conventions of analysis, as a 'culture of resistance'. This was seen as part of the long history of working-class rejection of compulsory formal education as a devious ploy by the state under capitalism to produce appropriately trained and disciplined labour. A seminal work was Paul Willis's study of a counter-school culture among white working-class boys in the Midlands. Incidental to the main object of his investigation ('how working-class kids get working-class jobs') he observed the development of a 'hyper "lads" (i.e. anti-school) culture' among West Indians in inner-city schools. 'We are facing for the first time in this society the possibility of the rejection of contemporary forms and structures of work by at least a significant minority of our second generation immigrant population' (Willis, 1977, p.85).

Also influential was Farrukh Dhondy's polemic 'The Black Explosion in

Schools'), published in 1974. Its analysis too belonged within the Marxist ambit. Dhondy observed an 'active rebellion' of working-class youth in schools which, in the case of black pupils, amounted to 'nothing less than a crisis of schooling'. He interpreted their indiscipline and rejection of school values not only as a reaction to school as such but as part of a coordinated resistance to white society's efforts to 'process' or 'deskill' them for the labour market: 'Their [i.e. black pupils'] models of ambition don't include the work ethic . . . they challenge discipline, study and routine . . . they are the breed most dangerous to capital as they refuse to enter the productive partnership under the terms that this society lays down' (Dhondy, 1974). Here, then, was yet another explanation for West Indian underachievement. It was deliberate. West Indians, the implication seemed to be, misbehaved and rejected school work in much the same spirit as they were said later to refuse menial jobs and social security benefits.

Paradoxically some empirical support for Dhondy's Marxist thesis was provided by Geoffrey Driver's ethnographic study of a Midlands secondary modern school. The alienation and antipathy towards the school expressed by a group of West Indian pupils, which Driver described, could certainly be interpreted as a culture of resistance. But it is also noticeable, a fact Driver was at pains to stress, that the resistance was primarily associated with boys and particularly boys of Jamaican descent. Though Dhondy referred simply to 'blacks', one had the unmistakable impression he was talking about West Indians not South Asians, and about boys not girls. In a study of West Indian girls in a London comprehensive Mary Fuller has commented on the paucity of attention paid to girls in subcultural and ethnographic research. Her study seems to substantiate Driver's argument about the significance of relative cultural strengths. Though scornful of the pettiness of school, the girls in her sample managed to combine a carefully controlled degree of indiscipline with determination to succeed within the system, both educationally and economically. Their accurate perception of themselves as doubly discriminated against – being both black and female – simply increased their determination and reinforced their pride in their femininity and their blackness. Rejecting the idea of a simple equation between academic success and conformity to school values, Mary Fuller noted (like Maureen Stone) that these girls' achievement 'was not related to whether teachers saw them as good or bad pupils' (Fuller, 1980).

In common with much Marxist analysis, the 'culture of resistance' hypothesis faces two problems: a problem of evidence and a problem of interpretation. The evidence contained in the studies by Driver, Fuller,

Stone and Troyna suggests that Dhondy's polemic was insufficiently discriminating; that, empirically speaking, there is little justification for speaking of an 'active rebellion' among black youth at school in a simple undifferentiating fashion. I have already noted that, although West Indian pupils may well be over-represented in bottom streams, ESN schools and disruptive units, and may be sharply critical of their teachers and their schools, they remain firmly committed to formal education, certainly in the sense of staying on longer and truanting less than their white contemporaries. Two social psychologists (quoted in Kettle and Hodges, 1982) interviewed 240 black and white Londoners, aged between 16 and 25, in the winter of 1979–1980. Among the black group they found evidence of material deprivation, 'trouble with the law' and some despair about their prospects, but little sign of a general alienation from society or the education system:

> These young blacks . . . viewed society positively and wished to succeed in it . . . held positive attitudes towards going to college, towards Jobcentres, careers offices and benefit offices, towards the school system and further education, towards the media and towards other British people . . . Their aspirations were very conventional and straightforward: material possessions, a pleasant job, marriage, a happy family life. The jobs they would most like to do were in the skilled manual category.
>
> (Summarized in Kettle and Hodges, 1982, pp.152–153)

The interpretation problem facing the 'culture of resistance' thesis is that, insofar as an 'active rebellion' can be detected among West Indian pupils, is it anything other than a very visible manifestation of working-class revolt or indeed of a more general adolescent tendency to rebel? Paul Willis, for example, not only concedes that the non-conformists at his school were in the minority (his study was of a group of 12 boys) but also that 'all schools of whatever class always create oppositional cultures' (Willis, op.cit., p.58), a fact well known to those educated in the independent sector or familiar with the history of the Victorian public schools. schools.

In this section and the previous one I have identified no less than eight different explanations to account for such West Indian underachievement as can accurately be said to exist: genetic endowment; material deprivation; inadequate upbringing; a fragmented cultural inheritance; cultural discontinuity between home and school; racism in school and society; informal teaching methods; and rejection of school values. Given the gaps and contradictions in the research evidence, choosing the right explanation, or combination of explanations, is bound to be a bit of a lottery. My own hunch is that the 'objective problem' of a significant minority of West Indian pupils, which presents itself to teachers as a combination of low attainment and indiscipline, will eventually be revealed as essentially a social class phenomenon (similar to the 'objective problem' of a significant minority of working-class pupils). This problem has been exacerbated by cultural discontinuity and mutually antagonistic stereotypes bequeathed by the history of slavery and colonialism, from whose shackles many blacks and whites find it hard to break free. Whichever theory triumphs, however, or proves to have the greatest explanatory power or empirical support, it would be quite wrong, as in the case of working-class underachievement, to make use of it to try and explain why *individual* West Indian children are not getting the results they should.

Equality of opportunity reconsidered

So far as equality of outcome is concerned, it is clear that the academic attainment of at least two British ethnic minorities – West Indians and Gypsies – gives serious cause for concern. In addition, a question mark hangs over that of at least two other ethnic minorities – London's Greek and Turkish Cypriot communities. However, before concern can be translated into action, we really need a much fuller picture than we have at present, in regard to the attainment both of these groups and of the rest of the country's ethnic minorities, including those, such as the Chinese, Italians and Jews, which have up until now been ignored. In some cases, notably that of South Asians, a fuller picture would have to involve taking into consideration the relative performance of subgroups, for it seems more than possible that there is a world of difference between the situation of Ugandan Asians in Leicester and Bangladeshis in London's East End. A fuller picture should also involve setting the information on the attainment of ethnic minorities within the broader context of the information we already have on those deep-rooted patterns of inequality – of social class, gender and region – described in Chapter 2. Only when we have a picture of this scope and detail, can we be in a position to decide with any confidence what might be the most appropriate forms of intervention on the part of central government, local authorities and schools.

At the same time we need to think again about the concept of equality of opportunity. Earlier in this chapter I commented on the way the seemingly unexceptionable notion of developing all children's 'talents and abilities to the full' has been perverted into a preoccupation with the academic destinies of an intellectual élite. It is time we tried to recapture something of the concept's pristine purity. The prevailing obsession, in discussions of educational equality, with results in 16+ and 18+ examinations seems increasingly unwarranted. Even on their own terms these examinations hardly justify the reverence with which they are often regarded. They are known to be poor predictors of academic performance in higher education; and there does not appear to be any empirical foundation for prospective employers interpreting success in them as indicative of probable efficiency or effectiveness at work. Quite apart from that, only a small minority of pupils enter for 18+ examinations, and a majority emerge from the 16+ examinations as failures of one kind or another. Although there is now a growing recognition of the need for reform of the examination and assessment system, and of the 13+ curriculum that has been very largely shaped by it, employers and institutions of higher education are likely to remain the predominant influences determining the nature of that reform. This is despite the fact that most secondary school pupils do not go on to higher education and that much of their adult lives will be spent in leisure and social activities rather than in paid employment. A far better basis for curriculum reform would be provided by a fresh, and genuine, commitment to the aim of developing *all* the 'talents and abilities' of *all* children 'to the full'. As David Hargreaves has remarked in his recent book on the comprehensive school: 'The only way in which we can prevent so many pupils leaving school with a sense of failure and inferiority is to make sure that there are many more opportunities in schools for pupils to experience success' (Hargreaves, 1982, p.137) – and, one might add, to have the successes they do experience recognized as such.

The perversion of the equal opportunity philosophy, in the apparent interests of academics and employers, goes some way to explaining why those areas of school and public life in which West Indians have been conspicuously successful – sport, music, drama and dance – have been either disregarded by research or subjected to exclusively negative interpretations. Several researchers have noted the tendency for teachers' pejorative stereotypes of West Indians in regard to behaviour and academic ability to be complemented by favourable stereotypes in regard to physical movement and artistic expression. They have been inclined, therefore, to argue that black athletic and artistic success is as much a product of teachers' expectations as black scholastic failure – even, indeed, that success and failure may be causally connected. Ernest Cashmore, for example, has referred to black sports stars as 'champions of failure', because 'their success springs, in part from the failure of black youth to make progress educationally, and from the failure of the school system to accommodate their needs and interests' (Cashmore, 1982, p.218). On the face of it, this seems an unnecessarily churlish interpretation – blacks do well at running, singing and dancing because white teachers believe those to be the extent of their talents – and more a reflection of the academic snobberies of researchers than anything else.

However, there are other reasons for the predominance of such negative interpretations among academics. First, none of the areas in which West Indians shine could be said to be characterized by a wealth of secure career prospects. Quite the reverse; to the extent that careers in any of them exist, they are notoriously precarious and short-lived – for the few who win through to fame and riches there are a multitude of losers and also-rans. Second, and perhaps more importantly, academics and researchers in the field of race relations are notoriously sensitive to anything that might be construed as racism. For them, teachers' airy generalizations about West Indians' 'natural' talents are uncomfortably reminiscent of nineteenth-century theorizing about racial difference ('scientific' racism). In addition the caricature of the West Indian child, incorporating both positive and negative traits, that sometimes crystallizes from teachers' everyday discourse, is uncomfortably reminiscent of the stereotype of the black African that was pretty well fully formed by the time the transatlantic slave trade got underway in the sixteenth century ('folk' racism). However any of this may be, it seems curiously ungenerous not to acknowledge and celebrate every success children manage to accomplish. I cannot see any intrinsic reason for sporting and artistic success being less meritorious than academic success. After all, they also require discipline and determination as much as innate ability.

CHAPTER 4

POSITIVE DISCRIMINATION

> A policy of direct coordinated attack on racial disadvantage inevitably means that the ethnic minorities will enjoy for a time a positive discrimination in their favour.
>
> (Lord Scarman, 1981)

Questions of equality of educational opportunity, whether broached with a view to ameliorating the position of the disadvantaged or maximizing society's talents or both, are of more than academic interest. They have direct relevance to central and local government policy, and above all to the interpretation and implementation of the principle of positive discrimination. Positive discrimination is one approach to the goal of equal opportunity. What distinguishes it from other approaches is that it goes beyond simply trying to prevent discriminatory acts from occurring in the future; it involves taking steps, in addition, to compensate for past discrimination and eliminate well-entrenched inequalities and disadvantages. Though particularly associated with the 1960s, it was in fact a child, albeit an illegitimate one, of the social reconstructionism of the 1940s. The 'people's war' of 1939–1945 had bequeathed to the nation a fresh sense of unity and purpose, which found institutional expression in the establishment of the welfare state. The 1944 Education Act, with its boast of providing 'secondary education for all', was an important element in the new social philosophy. It was during this period that the principle of equality of opportunity achieved its apotheosis as an article of faith. Catherine Jones sketches the popular mood as follows:

> The 1940s were austere times for Britain: times when equal shares for all out of scarce resources, after an all-out war effort, seemed no more than appropriate

> and just. They were optimistic times also: when to legislate for equal opportunity – or an equal chance to take one's chance – seemed to be the same thing as to legislate for a new social order . . . Individual achievement would, henceforth, be none other than the measure of individual potential.
>
> (Jones, C., 1977, pp.37–38)

The egalitarian optimism of the 1940s was soon to be disappointed. With the increased prosperity of the 1950s, and despite considerable educational expansion after 1955, social deprivation became more, not less visible. By the 1960s the principle of positive discrimination – in the sense of directing extra resources to deprived urban areas – had captured a wide range of political support, not just from within the Labour Party but from the 'liberal' brand of Conservatism that then prevailed too. It was partly inspired by the model of President Johnson's 'war on poverty' in the United States and to some extent prompted by the effects of mass immigration from Europe and the New Commonwealth. It was an 'illegitimate' offspring of 1940s' reconstructionism in that it renounced the simple egalitarianism of 'equal shares for all' in the hope that preferential treatment for the socially disadvantaged might help to attain the equality of opportunity – 'an equal chance to take one's chance' – which had up to then proved so elusive.

Positive discrimination in the 1960s

The educational testament of positive discrimination was the Plowden Report of 1967. It argued both for an increase in the 'total volume' of resources devoted to education and for 'some redistribution' to 'make schools in the deprived areas as good as the best in the country', thereby closing 'the gap between the educational opportunities of the most fortunate and least fortunate' children. It recommended the setting up of Educational Priority Areas which were to be identified by what has since become a familiar litany of indices of deprivation: the proportions of unskilled, semi-skilled and unemployed workers; of large and single-parent families; of overcrowded households and households in receipt of social security benefits and free school meals; of poor school attenders and of retarded, disturbed and handicapped children. Also included, and for the first time in a list of this kind, was the proportion of children unable to speak English. Three of the forms of positive discrimination advocated were eventually implemented: more financial resources, better staffing quotas and extra allowances for teachers (CACE, 1967).

These recommendations had been partially anticipated in regard to immigrant children by government initiatives of the previous year. The

Labour Government had informed local authorities in Circular 7/65 *The Education of Immigrants* and in the 1965 White Paper *Immigration from the Commonwealth* that, if they had substantial numbers of immigrant pupils on roll, they would be able to apply for increases in their teacher quotas from January 1966. In that same month the DES began collecting statistics on the numbers of immigrant children in schools. 'Dovetailing neatly' (in the DES's own phrase) with the provision for extra staff in multi-ethnic areas was Section 11 of the 1966 Local Government Act. According to this, LEAs with two percent or more of Commonwealth immigrant pupils in the total school population were entitled to a 50 percent grant (raised to 75 percent in 1969) towards expenditure on extra personnel. This included social workers, welfare officers, ancillaries and so on, as well as teachers. Two years later the Labour Government announced its Urban Aid Programme (inaugurated in 1969) to assist areas of special social need. One of the two initial criteria for selecting a local authority was whether it had at least six percent of immigrant children on the school roll. Unlike Section 11, Urban Aid could be used for capital expenditure, but not to supplement spending on the statutory education service. Also in 1968 the Burnham Committee on teachers' salaries agreed to a special allowance for teachers serving in schools recognized as being of exceptional difficulty; the proportion of immigrant children on roll was once again a criterion.

The initiatives undertaken by government between 1965 and 1969 with reference to immigrant children, whether exclusively as in the case of Section 11 or partially as in the case of Urban Aid, were one ingredient in the bipartisan race relations philosophy developed in a curious ad hoc way by Labour and Conservative Parties in the 1960s. This was first fully stated in the 1965 White Paper and neatly encapsulated in Roy Hattersley's now famous dictum: 'without integration, limitation is inexcusable; without limitation, integration is impossible'. Good race relations were said to require a combination of stringent immigration control and firm anti-discrimination legislation supported by other positive action to counteract deprivation in the inner city and promote integration. The motivation behind this seemingly self-contradictory philosophy (Michael and Ann Dummett once described the 1965 White Paper as 'possibly the most logically incoherent Government paper ever produced') appears to have been a mixture of fear of a racialist backlash such as that which resulted in the 1958 race riots in Nottingham and Notting Hill (and lost the prospective Labour minister Patrick Gordon Walker his Smethwick seat in the 1964 election) and a genuine desire to reduce the pressure on the inner cities where so many immigrants had settled. Whatever the truth of the matter, the Labour government did make some attempt to give credence to the Hattersley equation in the late 1960s. In 1965 it not only published its White Paper, announcing even tighter immigration controls than already existed under the previous Conservative government's Commonwealth Immigrants Act of 1962, but introduced the first Race Relations Bill. In 1968 it introduced both a second Race Relations Bill and a second Commonwealth Immigrants Bill (to stem the flow of East African Asians with British passports). In May of the same year Harold Wilson announced the Urban Aid Programme as an explicit response to Enoch Powell's 'rivers of blood' speech delivered in Birmingham in April.

The educational initiatives of this period constituted a further contribution, however belated or inadequate, to the positive side of the equation. They also represented the coming together of three rather different notions of positive discrimination. First, there was the principle, originally formulated by the Plowden Report, of discriminating positively in favour of the socially disadvantaged, among whom immigrants could be grouped to the extent that they lived in deprived neighbourhoods and had unskilled or semi-skilled jobs. Second, there was the somewhat tardy recognition of the need to mount a specific policy response to the increasing numbers of immigrant children in school, many of whom spoke little or no English and came from rural and culturally different backgrounds (a recognition overtly present in Section 11 of the 1966 Local Government Act). And, finally, there was the emergent commitment, evinced by the 1965 and 1968 Race Relations Acts and partly stimulated by the American experience, to counter the effects of racism on communities who by the end of the decade were more properly seen as British ethnic minorities than immigrants. This coming together was by no means free from ambiguity or tension. For example, Urban Aid was, historically speaking, a political retort to Powellism, yet its aim was unequivocally to alleviate general social need, not to combat racism or meet the special needs of immigrants. In other words, it tion) rather than with Section 11 or the Race Relations Acts. In the 1970s these strains became more acutely evident, notably in the debate surrounding the fate of Section 11.

Government policy in the 1970s

The main policy question framed by central government during the 1970s was how (or whether) to collect information, including statistics, on children of immigrant origin and how (or whether), on the basis of what had been learnt, to cater for such special needs as they could be said to have. In the earlier part of the decade the view of the Conservative government, or at least the DES, seemed to be that while immigrant children might have difficulty with English or suffer 'the shock of immersion in an entirely different culture' or 'stand bewildered between two cultures', the educational disadvantages they suffered were substantially those they shared with the indigenous children in the 'older urban and industrial areas' where so many of them lived – that is to say, 'the educational disadvantages associated with an impoverished environment' (DES, 1971). Hence in 1973 the DES ceased to collect statistics on immigrant children in school, claiming that the definition of 'immigrant' children used – those born overseas and those British-born whose parents had been resident less than 10 years – rendered the exercise virtually valueless. The DES rejected the recommendation, contained in the report of the 1972–1973 session of the Select Committee on Race Relations and Immigration, that a central fund should be established to which local education authorities 'could apply for resources to meet the special educational needs of immigrant children and adults'. Pointing out what was already available under Section 11 (itself a central fund of a sort) and Urban Aid, the DES argued that the 'pattern of special help must . . . provide for all those suffering educational disadvantage' (DES, 1974).

In 1974 the DES effectively subsumed the needs of the ethnic minorities within a broader concern for the educationally disadvantaged, when it included them on the agendas of two new institutions – its own Educational Disadvantage Unit and a Centre for Information and Advice on Educational Disadvantage (CED). The CED was opened in Manchester the following year and summarily closed in 1980, ostensibly as part of the Conservative government's cuts in public expenditure. The 1974 decision did not imply that the DES had failed to recognize, or disregarded, the 'distinct needs of different ethnic groups', rather that these counted for little when weighed against the powerful combination of universalism and individualism that dominated the teaching profession, and the teachers' unions. This influential ideology recognized only common human needs and the particular needs of individual children. Group needs were not recognized (indeed were distrusted as potentially divisive), except in the case of the socially deprived and the mentally and physically handicapped, where the evidence of educational disadvantage, and the argument for special provision, were irrefutable. The DES was sharply criticized by ethnic minority organizations, and from within the multicultural education lobby, for lumping immigrants or ethnic minorities together so crudely with the most unfortunate members of the majority community. It did rather look as though the DES's decision had been dictated by political considerations with no regard for logic or evidence. Many ethnic minority pupils certainly did come from disadvantaged homes as measured by the conventional indices listed in the Plowden Report, but a significant number certainly did not.

Under the Labour government of 1974–1979 there was something of a change of mind, although this was less apparent at the DES than at the Home Office, the government department with central responsibility both for race relations and immigration and for combating social disadvantage. The first signs of this were detectable in the 1978 White Paper on the West Indian community, which had been prepared in response to the report of the 1976–1977 session of the Select Committee on Race Relations and Immigration. Though rejecting the idea of 'special provision' in the form of a central fund, which the Select Committee had once again recommended, the White Paper conceded that 'as well . . . as sharing in the general problems of urban deprivation and unemployment, the West Indian community and other ethnic minorities have certain special problems which we call by the shorthand term "racial disadvantage" ' (Home Office, 1978a, p.4). A direct outcome of this concession was the Rampton Committee of Inquiry into the Education of Children from Ethnic Minority Groups, which was constituted in 1979 and asked to give priority to submitting an interim report on the situation of West Indian children. By the end of 1978 the Home Office appeared to have conceded the point on the desirability of a central fund too, in its proposals for replacing Section 11 of the 1966 Local Government Act.

Section 11 had long been a target for criticism from those in principle favouring a central government grant to local authorities for meeting the needs of ethnic minorities. Criticism concentrated on three issues: who Section 11 was for; what it was for; and the way it was administered. The limitation of the grant to Commonwealth immigrants seemed arbitrary, even perverse (though politically comprehensible); there was clearly a good case for including Irish and Italian immigrants, especially the latter since they not only came from impoverished rural backgrounds in the *mezzogiorno* but were culturally different and spoke no English. Also excluded were Pakistanis who arrived after 1971 (when Pakistan left the Commonwealth following the secession of Bangladesh) and Vietnamese refugees. Moreover, the two percent rule meant that the many immigrants living outside noticeably multi-ethnic areas were deprived of whatever benefits the Section 11 grant conferred. Equally restrictive was another rule which stated that the grant was only applicable to those immigrants who had been resident less than 10 years. The grant was further criticized for being limited to the recovery of expenditure on salaries. Why could it not be used for capital projects, for example, or to support voluntary organizations? But the main criticism concerned the way Section 11 was actually administered. Common sense suggested that the grant ought to have been paid in advance to local authorities in accordance with the size of their immigration population and whatever they proposed to do to meet its needs. In addition, the grant's use should, of course, have been subject to careful monitoring and evaluation. In fact local authorities had to apply for it; payment was retrospective; and there was no monitoring or evaluation at all. The result was extremely uneven take-up (and regardless of an authority's ethnic composition) and considerable confusion about what the grant was supposed to achieve. Often the grant was simply used to add to the staffing complement of multi-ethnic schools; in their investigation of six multi-ethnic authorities Young and Connelly (1981) found that several head-teachers 'were either unable to tell whether or not they had S11 teachers on their staff, or were unable to identify them' (p.107).

The Labour government attempted to meet some of these criticisms in its Local Government (Ethnic Minorities) Bill, which was presented to Parliament in 1979. It envisaged a specific grant available to authorities with ethnic minorities for programmes in education, housing and social services. The aims were '(a) to alleviate any special features of social and educational disadvantage suffered by these groups; and (b) to promote equality of opportunity and good relations between such groups and the general population' (Home Office, 1978b, p.5). However the Bill lapsed when the Conservative Party was returned to power in May 1979. The Conservative government instituted its own Home Office review of the operation of Section 11 and in 1982 issued new guidelines for local authorities which became effective in January 1983. These met a few of the criticisms that had been made: the two percent rule was relaxed; programmes to combat racism were allowed; and Section 11 posts were defined as those that involved staff spending at least 20 percent of their time with Commonwealth immigrants, or their children under 21, including Pakistanis who had emigrated from Pakistan before 1971. But Section 11 remains substantially unaltered. Its significance is that it is the 'only Government finance earmarked directly and exclusively for combating racial disadvantage' (House of Commons,

1981, p.xxiii). In 1980–1981 the Government paid an estimated £50 million to local authorities under Section 11, over 85 percent of which went towards the salaries of teachers and other educational staff, either engaged in specialist language teaching or, more often, simply working in schools with a conspicuous proportion of pupils of Commonwealth immigrant origin.

There can be little doubt that successive governments, and the DES, managed to get themselves in an unsightly tangle in the 1970s over the single policy issue of how (or whether) to discriminate positively in favour of immigrant (or ethnic minority) children in the education system. This confusion was partly a result of the change from thinking in terms of children who had recently arrived in Britain, frequently speaking no English and bearing very different cultural traditions, and who might one day return whence they came, to thinking in terms of children born in Britain of immigrant stock who were probably here to stay. But it also betrayed uncertainty over whether the educational disadvantages suffered by these children, both immigrants and British-born, could be incorporated within a general concern for the socially deprived or demanded some special provision of their own.

The collection of statistics

The confusion was particularly evident in the debate over the collection of statistics. In 1973 the Conservative government had stopped collecting statistics on immigrant children because the definition used had ceased to have any usefulness (see p.79). Why was the inadequate definition not simply replaced by a better one? After all, the administration of Section 11 clearly required statistics of some kind, and both the 1974 White Paper *Educational Disadvantage and the Educational Needs of Immigrants* and the 1978 White Paper *The West Indian Community* admitted that special provision would need statistical information. In the second half of the decade there were several tentative forays by central government in that direction, including the trial run of a question on ethnic origins for possible inclusion in the 1981 Census. In the event the only question included was the traditional one asking respondents to name their country of birth. The main reason for this decision was opposition from the ethnic minorities, who remained deeply suspicious of the use to which statistics might be put. In the case of educational statistics they were joined by many teachers, whose commitment to the dominant professional ideologies of universalism and individualism meant they were instinctively repelled by the prospect of identifying their pupils according to ethnic origin. Officially there is still no national collection of statistics on ethnic minorities, though the Home Affairs Committee of the House of Commons appears to be pressing for the inclusion of relevant questions in the 1991 Census, and a number of local authorities regularly collect statistics of their own. Unofficially national data of some kind do seem to be available. How else could the DES specify the proportion of 'non-white and non-UK born' 0–17-year-olds in each LEA, precise to the second decimal point?

The other reason for the vacillation over the collection of statistics is that it has never been clear what a more satisfactory definition of 'immigrant' or 'ethnic minority' children might be. In its 1978 document on replacing Section 11, the Labour government objected to 'Commonwealth immigrants' as too restrictive. It had in mind not so much the exclusion of other immigrants, such as the Irish or Italians, who might be thought to have some entitlement to extra resources, as the exclusion of those of Commonwealth origin who were British born and particularly those who were black. The Conservative government, in deciding to stand by 'Commonwealth immigrants' in its 1982 guidelines on Section 11, effectively rejected the claims of black British and more recent arrivals like the Vietnamese refugees.

The concept of racial disadvantage

Notwithstanding these differences of view the two governments were united in their preoccupation with West Indians and South Asians. 'Commonwealth immigrants' was as much a euphemism for black immigrants on the positive side of Roy Hattersley's equation – in this instance Section 11 – as it was on the negative side – immigration control. Little if any heed was paid to the situation of the other immigrant groups from the New Commonwealth – the Maltese, the Cypriots or the Hong Kong Chinese. This preoccupation with black immigrants and settlers was underlined by the increasing use in the late 1970s of the concept of 'racial disadvantage', an odd phrase and yet another infelicitous addition to the vocabulary of ethnic relations. Precisely what was it supposed to refer to? Neither of the two Home Office documents of 1978 (the White Paper on the West Indian community and the proposals for replacing Section 11) betrayed any sense of a necessity for definition or elaboration. 'Racial' appeared to be a straightforward misnomer for 'black' (the old confusion of 'race' and 'colour'). Had the Home Office had ethnic minorities or immigrants as a whole in mind, one would have expected them to refer to 'ethnic' or 'immigrant' disadvantage.

If my interpretation is correct, racial disadvantage could refer to one of two things – the general disadvantage suffered by black people or, more narrowly, the disadvantage suffered *exclusively* by black people, that is, as a result of the racial discrimination directed against them. The confusion of these two possible meanings is evident in the 1981 report of the House of Commons Home Affairs Committee entitled *Racial Disadvantage*:

> Racial disadvantage is a particular case of relative disadvantage within society. With the exception of racial discrimination, the disadvantages suffered by Britain's ethnic minorities are shared in varying degrees by the rest of the community . . . But the ethnic minorities suffer such disadvantages more than the rest of the population, and more than they would if they were white.
> (House of Commons, 1981, p.x)

At first sight 'racial disadvantage' here seems to mean the disadvantages experienced by 'ethnic minorities' (i.e. black people) *apart from* racial discrimination, since they are said to be 'shared in varying degrees by the rest of the community'. Yet what is one to make of the last sentence quoted? Blacks can certainly be said to suffer 'disadvantages more than the rest of the population' in the sense that they are disproportionately represented in impoverished, urban areas and undervalued forms of labour (though the usefulness of such crude generalizations has already been queried). However, it can only be claimed that they would not be so disadvantaged 'if they were white' (a doubtful assertion, to say the least) if the cause is identified in racial discrimination.

The case for positive discrimination

Setting these semantic difficulties on one side for the moment, is there in fact a good case for discriminating positively in favour of the ethnic minorities in education in the 1980s? I think we can best set about answering this question by starting from the simple egalitarianism of the 1940s – 'equal shares for all'. Egalitarian considerations suggest that ideally exactly the same amount of money should be spent, per capita per annum, on the education of each child. This principle seems to me to provide the only proper basis for the allocation of resources in a national system of education. However, egalitarian considerations also suggest that it may be necessary to breach the principle and spend more money on specific categories of underprivileged children than on the majority in order to promote equality of opportunity. It is now generally accepted that, should the effective teaching of mentally and physically handicapped children require extra money and resources, they should be allocated without demur, since such children are demonstrably at an educational disadvantage in our society. It is also now fairly generally accepted that the overwhelming evidence of underachievement among working-class children demands some kind of positive discrimination to counter it. This would probably take the form of distributing resources unequally in favour of local authorities scoring highly on indices of social deprivation and schools serving physically and economically impoverished catchment areas.

The needs of handicapped children and socially deprived areas and schools both constitute clear prima facie cases for positive discrimination. Do the needs of ethnic minority pupils constitute another? As such, emphatically not. Some ethnic minority children, of course, fall within the categories of physically and mentally handicapped, while many reside in 'educational priority areas' and attend socially deprived schools. These children will naturally benefit from whatever positive discrimination these categories, areas and schools attract. Others, like the Vietnamese or some Bangladeshis and Pakistanis, may themselves be immigrants from very different cultural backgrounds speaking little or no English. I do not think there would be much disagreement that they also constitute a prima facie case for positive discrimination, if only in the short term until they have achieved sufficient command of English to participate in the regular curriculum and have sufficiently accustomed themselves to British life. Indeed the precedent for centrally supported initiatives to meet the short-term educational needs of recent immigrants was established as long ago as 1947 with the Polish Resettlement Act.

Yet most ethnic minority children are British born and speak English perfectly well. How can positive discrimination in their favour possibly be justified? Certainly not by reference to underachievement. As we have seen from the previous chapter, the available evidence, although patchy, does not support the popular belief that ethnic minority (or, more narrowly, black) children as a whole underachieve. The performance of West Indian and Cypriot children may be a cause for concern, but in both instances the empirical picture is incomplete. Other groups, notably those of South Asian origin. (Even though, incidentally, American Orientals are no worse off ethnic minority group who experience underachievement on the scale experienced among working-class children are the Gypsies, and that is essentially a product of the cultural divorce and conflict between them and *gorgio* society. Does this mean we are to follow the American example whereby only certain designated groups benefit from positive discrimination? In the United States positive discrimination is limited to blacks, American Indians, Spanish-speaking Americans and those of Oriental origin. (Even though, incidentally, American Orientals are no worse off educationally or economically than the majority, indeed they appear to be rather successful.) It is doubtful in the extreme whether a similar limitation to educationally underachieving groups in this country – say, Gypsies, West Indians and Cypriots (assuming the evidence of underachievement among all three was incontrovertible) – would be either politically desirable or practically feasible; nor, of course, whether it would be acceptable to the groups themselves.

The other approach to justifying positive discrimination in favour of pupils from the ethnic minorities has been to appeal to the concept of special educational needs. However, they do not have special educational needs in the sense that the blind or deaf do. The only needs found among them and not among the majority are those associated with learning English as a second language; and they affect only some ethnic minority pupils. It has been claimed that there are special educational needs associated with the elusive phenomenon of 'racial disadvantage'. In this context 'racial disadvantage' cannot refer simply to the educational disadvantages suffered by the ethnic minorities, for they are already covered by initiatives of the EPA variety. It must refer instead to those suffered as a result of racial discrimination in the education system and the wider society. If so, the claim is a decidedly weak one. There is little evidence on how, or whether, racism impinges upon the educational prospects of children from the ethnic minorities; in so far as it is a problem, the experience of both Jews and South Asians suggests that it is not insurmountable. It would seem strange to base educational policy, involving the distribution of resources, on conjecture rather than hard facts.

In sum, I believe there is a good case for positive discrimination (similar to Section 11 but appropriately amended) to assist children, including those born in Britain, whose poor grasp of English prevents them from participating fully in the regular curriculum, and recent arrivals, like the Vietnamese, from very different cultural backgrounds. The needs of such children would, of course, be short term. Positive discrimination in their favour would also require both a statistical exercise, to ascertain how many there are and where they are, and monitoring and evaluation of schemes undertaken to meet their needs and in receipt of extra funds. What I think is quite wrong is the present arrangement (not only under Section 11 but under the new system for allocating the rate support grant as well) whereby local authorities and schools may receive extra staff and resources simply because they have a certain proportion of pupils from the ethnic minorities. An arrangement of this sort presupposes that to belong to an ethnic minority and attend school in Britain is necessarily to be at an educational disadvantage. The evidence cited in the previous chapter does not support this presupposition.

Meeting special cultural needs

The kind of positive discrimination I have had in mind so far is that advocated by the Plowden Report: the provision of extra staff and resources to meet special educational needs and offset educational disadvantage. However, extra staff and resources can also be made available to serve two rather different causes (which may or may not have bearing on promoting equality of educational opportunity): meeting special *cultural* needs and combating racism. These two causes, which have added a further dimension to the debate about positive discrimination, owe a major part of their inspiration to two important events of the 1970s: Britain's entry into the Common Market in 1973 and the passing of the third Race Relations Act in 1976.

From a financial point of view joining the EEC meant that both central and local government could take advantage of Community funds for the education of migrant workers' children. Several authorities made applications to support ventures in developing the first languages of ethnic minority pupils while central government was able to 'claw back' much of its expenditure under Section 11 and Urban Aid. As a member state Britain became subject to any Community legislation relating to migrant workers' children. In July 1977 the Council of Ministers issued a directive on the education of children of migrant workers. Article 3 read: 'Member states shall, in accordance with their national circumstances and legal systems, and in cooperation with states of origin, take appropriate measures to promote, in coordination with normal education, teaching of the mother tongue and culture of the country of origin'. Strictly speaking the directive aplied only to children from EEC member states, but the DES has made it clear that no distinction is to be made between them and other ethnic minority children. However, it has also indicated that it does not interpret 'promote' in Article 3 as guaranteeing the right of each individual child to 'mother tongue' teaching. Up until now 'promotion' by the DES has been limited to funding research and supporting voluntary ventures with short-term grants. By the time the directive came into force in July 1981 only France, Germany and The Netherlands were judged to have implemented initiatives to the satisfaction of European Commmission officials. Britain was one of the countries 'being left behind'.

The main thrust of the 1977 directive concerned cultural maintenance – acknowledging a child's right to develop his or her first language; improving communication between migrant workers' children and their older relatives; and facilitating reintegration into the country of origin in the event of return. How far a national system of education can or should be party to the maintenance of minority cultures is a question discussed in Chapter 6. What is important to recognize here is that there is a gathering argument, substantiated by some evidence, that 'mother tongue' teaching has implications for equality of opportunity. Its inclusion in the curriculum is likely to ease the young child's transition from home to school and foster self-esteem, general linguistic development and conceptual growth.

Combating racial discrimination

The 1976 Race Relations Act was primarily a government response to the evidence gathered by Political and Economic Planning in the early 1970s on the extent of racial discrimination in Britain; its principal aim was to strengthen the law on discrimination in employment. To this end it widened the concept of discrimination to include 'indirect' discrimination (or discrimination in effect as opposed to intention). In addition it permitted 'positive' discrimination in training programmes (but not 'at the point of selection' for employment), and entrusted the new Commission for Racial Equality (CRE) with greater powers (for example the undertaking of formal investigations) than those of its predecessors under the 1965 and 1968 Race Relations Acts. The 1976 Act was very similar in its scope and provisions to the Sex Discrimination Act of 1975 and both were closely modelled on American initiatives in the field of anti-discrimination legislation. Deprived of the American tradition of legislating for social justice, and unsupported by a general Bill of Rights (despite several attempts to enact one since 1969), both Acts were almost bound, however, to be limited in their effectiveness and to impress the general public with their anomalousness. The 1974 White Paper *Equality for Women* accepted the principle that it should be unlawful to treat someone adversely 'on grounds irrelevant to that person's intrinsic qualities and qualifications'. Yet protection against discrimination on such grounds in the United Kingdom is reserved for women and the groups covered by the 1976 Race Relations Act (i.e. those distinguished by race, colour, nationality and ethnic or national origin). In Northern Ireland, discrimination in employment on the basis of political or religious beliefs was also made unlawful under the Fair Employment (Northern Ireland) Act of 1976. This means that in the United Kingdom apart from Northern Ireland it is unlawful to discriminate on grounds of religion only when the religion is ethnically or nationally based. In other words it is not unlawful to discriminate against Catholics as such.

The result of this strange discrepancy was the pantomime of the Mandla v. Lee case which engaged the courts and public attention in 1982. A Sikh boy had been forbidden to wear his turban by the headteacher of the independent school he attended in Birmingham and his father had taken the case to court alleging discrimination under the 1976 Race Relations Act. Legal disputation centred on whether Sikhs are an ethnic as well as a religious group; critical lay comment argued that this was a semantic quibble as the intention of the Act had patently been to protect groups like the Sikhs. But the essential point surely is that *all* discrimination on grounds irrelevant to a 'person's intrinsic qualities and qualifications' should be unlawful throughout the United Kingdom. Why should discrimination on grounds of social class, religion, age, handicap or whatever be allowed when discrimination on grounds of sex and 'race' (as defined by the 1976 Act) is not? One can understand sex discrimination taking precedence in legislation covering employment, since sex inequality has always been the most fundamental inequality in the labour market, but not in education, where the fundamental inequalities have always been those associated with social class.

From the point of view of education the most relevant clauses in the 1976 Race Relations Act are contained in Section 71. This imposes on local authorities a duty to ensure that the services they provide are free from racial discrimination (both direct and indirect) and to promote equality of opportunity and good relations between different 'racial' groups. The influence of Section 71 is clearly detectable behind the Labour government's lapsed Local Government (Ethnic Minorities) Bill of 1979 and the

Conservative government's revisions to Section 11 of the 1966 Local Government Act in 1982. The educational implications of implementing Section 71 have been outlined by a CRE pamphlet published in 1981. Unfortunately, in its analysis of the position of children from the ethnic minorities, this pamphlet perpetuates much of the conceptual muddle typical of government thinking in the 1970s:

> Ethnic minority groups, though disproportionately exposed to urban deprivation because of their demographic and social location, also experience forms of inequality not shared with the wider community. Minority group children are confronted with forms of disadvantage qualitatively different from those of other urban children, and policies that do not take cognisance of institutionalized racism and the ethnic dimension to educational inequality will fail to achieve their aims and will not contribute to the realisation of S71 objectives.
>
> (Commission for Racial Equality, 1981, p.20)

Such an assertion commits the elementary error of treating 'minority group children' as an undifferentiated entity. Is the phrase meant to incorporate Jews as well as Gypsies, South Asians as well as West Indians? It also repeats the myth that 'minority group children experience forms of inequality not shared with the wider community' and 'are confronted with forms of disadvantage qualitatively different from those of other urban children'. Nowhere in the pamphlet are these forms of inequality and disadvantage elucidated; nor is a single item of evidence cited to support such a sweeping claim. The actual proposals advanced by the CRE have a familiar, not to say jaded, look about them: schools and colleges developing 'an explicit and comprehensive policy on multiracial education' (evaluating curriculum and materials for ethnocentric bias, teaching about race relations, fostering minority languages, maintaining an alert eye on the 'hidden' curriculum or institutional ethos); and local authorities recruiting specialist staff, catering for special cultural needs, collecting ethnically based statistics, instituting in-service courses, providing the necessary resources and so forth.

Up to now, however, only a handful of authorities have shown any sign of mounting a significant response to Section 71; and one or two of those seem to be in danger of compounding the mistake implicit in having race relations but no overall anti-discrimination legislation on the statute book. For example, in 1982 Berkshire (ironically the object of the only formal CRE investigation in education yet completed – and examined in the next chapter) published a discussion document entitled *Education for Equality*. This had been prepared by the county's Advisory Committee for Multicultural Education as a first step in the formulation of a response to Section 71, and formed the basis for a policy on promoting racial equality and justice adopted by Berkshire Education Committee in January 1983. Where the CRE pamphlet writes vaguely of 'minority group children', this document actually defies the letter (if not perhaps the spirit) of the 1976 Act by announcing that it proposes to concentrate on black minorities, and their relations with white society, to the explicit exclusion of children of Irish, Italian, Polish, Portuguese, Spanish, Vietnamese and Hong Kong Chinese origin. The reason given for this drastic curtailment of the scope of the Act is as follows: 'Black people . . . have a distinctive historical relationship with Europe, and have distinctive experiences and concerns in Britain at the present time. In particular, they experience racism' (Berkshire Advisory Committee for Multicultural Education, 1982, p.4). If the 'distinctive historical relationship' is a reference to colonialism, then the Irish, Vietnamese and Hong Kong Chinese should also be included. As for the second sentence, that seems to imply that other ethnic minorities do not experience racism, which is manifestly untrue, unless of course 'racism' is a misnomer for 'colour prejudice', in which case it is tautologous. To be fair, the policy statement eventually adopted by the Education Committee in 1983 brings Berkshire back within the letter of the 1976 Act. It rescinds the discussion document's exclusion of other ethnic minorities, though it appears to persist with the fiction that racism is essentially something done to blacks by whites. What it does not do, however, is to correct the discussion document's paradoxical failure (given its title) to locate the position of ethnic minorities within the context of long-established educational inequalities. There is a passing reference to gender inequality but no indication at all that social class might have any bearing on the subject under discussion. Of the few authorities displaying an interest in Section 71 only ILEA has signified its intention to complement initiatives aimed at promoting equal opportunities for ethnic minorities with other initiatives designed to counteract the educational effects of inequalities related to gender and social class.

Local authority policies

Local authority performance in discriminating positively in favour of ethnic minority pupils, whether to foster equality of opportunity or meet special cultural needs, and more generally in the field of multicultural education (combating racism and so on), has been systematically (but not in all cases

comprehensively) reviewed on a number of occasions over the past 20 years. The researchers' findings have been supplemented by the DES's own surveys and by those studies of ethnic relations in particular cities and localities that have included education in their brief. They reveal, as one might expect from a decentralized system in which headteachers and schools enjoy 'customary autonomy', marked variations in policy and practice between different authorities and a pronounced tendency towards *laissez-faire* and 'inexplicitness' in policy formation. 'Most of our LEAs', write Young and Connelly (1981), 'had little that could be described as a broad policy or strategy for education in a multi-racial society' (p.103). On the other hand, and partly as a result of pressure from central government, most multi-ethnic LEAs do more than they did, say, 15 years ago, to meet the needs of ethnic minorities and promote multicultural education. It is widely assumed that this is a good thing, that more special provision means better provision.

Action to foster equality of opportunity, within the existing framework of legislative and financial arrangements, may include: the collection of statistics on the distribution and performance of ethnic minority pupils; the recruitment of staff to teach English as a second language through use of Section 11 of the 1966 Local Government Act; capital projects, like the construction of language centres, as part of the Urban Aid Programme or its successors; and the recruitment of staff from the ethnic minorities. Special provision to meet cultural needs may include taking advantage of EEC funds to make arrangements for the teaching of minority languages, and financial and strategic support for ethnic minority initiatives such as supplementary schools and religious and language classes. Both kinds of provision may be further assisted by steps taken to promote multicultural education, such as the appointment of advisers (and other categories of specialist staff), the establishment of resource centres and the funding of curriculum and research projects. Other steps include the dissemination of advice and information to schools through policy statements and guidelines on such matters as combating racism and evaluating materials for ethnocentric bias.

The authority that has done more than any other in these directions is ILEA. This is perhaps as it should be, since it is almost certainly the most multi-ethnic authority in the country, not so much in overall proportions (the London Borough of Brent has long claimed that honour) as in the diversity of the ethnic groups represented. In 1977, deriving support from contemporary initiatives like the 1976 Race Relations Act and the 1977 EEC directive on the education of children of migrant workers, ILEA became the first education authority to commit itself publicly to a policy on multi-ethnic education. A document bearing that title defined the authority's objectives as ministering to 'the specific needs of each pupil having regard to his (sic) ethnic or cultural attachment' and promoting 'within each pupil an interest in and a respect for the cultural heritage of his (sic) fellows'. Having summarized existing provision in ESL teaching and projects undertaken in multi-ethnic curriculum development, the authority expressed an overt commitment to equality of opportunity. ILEA announced that it would radically reappraise its policies, recruit a specialist inspectorate and administrative team, fund a 'major resource bank of curriculum resources for multi-ethnic schools', and explore the question of the further recruitment of ethnic minority staff and 'the possibilities of providing positive teaching against racism' (ILEA, 1977, pp.4–5). In a progress report published two years later the authority found encouraging signs of development (in language work, curriculum development, in-service training and support for supplementary education), pockets of resistance in schools and 'no grounds for complacency'. On the question of recruiting ethnic minority staff, it noted that 'positive discrimination' in training was permitted by the 1976 Race Relations Act and declared that 'ways are being explored of providing special courses of preparation for professional training for those without the normal qualifications' (ILEA, 1979, pp.2–3). It also repeated the 1977 document's promise of action to combat racism. This was eventually fulfilled in 1983 with the publication of its *Policy for Equality* which laid particular stress on the need to 'unlearn and dismantle racism'. In the same year the authority stipulated that all schools would be expected to draw up anti-racist policies and implement curriculum changes to give every subject a multi-ethnic dimension.

It follows from what has been said about central government policy on positive discrimination that I find local authority initiatives to promote equality of opportunity for ethnic minorities unexceptionable only insofar as they are limited to children who actually are immigrants and/or cannot speak English well enough to participate fully in the regular curriculum, and provided they are not separatist. Since the Bullock Report made its point in 1975 about not cutting ESL work off from 'the social and educational life of a normal school', the trend has been firmly away from segregating children in need of specialist language teaching in separate centres, units or withdrawal groups towards incorporating them into everyday classwork as often as possible. Twenty years ago it almost seemed self-evident that a demonstrated need for ESL teaching required some form or degree of segregation for the children concerned. It does not seem so self-evident now.

Local authority initiatives to meet special cultural needs among ethnic minorities are discussed in Chapter 6. However, to the extent that programmes designed to develop competence in minority languages can be justified by reference to equality of opportunity rather than cultural maintenance, they too perhaps should fall into the unexceptionable category. Anti-racist initiatives undertaken by local authorities are discussed in Chapter 7, but mention must be made here of the gathering momentum of initiatives in multi-ethnic education as a whole. A not insignificant number of multi-ethnic authorities have devoted resources to the recruitment of advisers in multicultural education, and other types of support staff, together with the establishment of special resource centres and the funding of curriculum and research projects. One can appreciate how these initiatives may have been politically necessary in the past, as a way of challenging prevailing inertia. Moreover, it goes without saying that all schools should develop multi-ethnic curricula and resources and be culturally sensitive in their other policy decisions. But it is debatable whether in the 1980s, and at a time of public expenditure cuts, multi-ethnic education continues to justify either institutional segregation or financial favouritism. It could also be argued that, just as constant talk of the 'special needs of ethnic minority pupils' encourages the dangerous myth that they are a different subspecies, so the institutional segregation of multi-ethnic education impedes its integration into mainstream educational debate and decision-making. Such segregation seems to foster the mistaken view that multi-cultural concerns are separate from, instead of part of, a more general concern to promote accurate and rational curricula and sensitive policies for school organization and administration.

In authorities suffering acute social deprivation, multi-ethnic initiatives can also be criticized as a diversion from more pressing problems. For example, in 1983 ILEA announced that it intended to allocate the bulk of the £300,000 earmarked for in-service training in the coming academic year to courses on multicultural education and combating racism. Non-teaching staff as well as teachers would be expected to attend these courses. One cannot help feeling this money would have been better spent on examining ways of improving the quality of education in urban schools. The fundamental problem confronting ILEA, and other urban multi-ethnic authorities, is massive social class underachievement, not racism.

Turning, in conclusion, to the epigraph from the 1981 Scarman Report which heads this chapter, I have tried to argue that in education there are no good grounds for positive discrimination in favour of ethnic minorities as such. However, there is a clear prima facie case for allocating extra staff and resources to meet the short-term needs of children who are themselves immigrants and/or have difficulties with English because it is not their first language. In the absence of elucidation of the vague concept of 'racial disadvantage' and firm evidence to substantiate it, this seems to me the only tenable position to hold. My argument in this chapter has concentrated on the *principle* of positive discrimination. Whether the redistribution of resources in favour of disadvantaged areas, schools and pupils is ever likely to make much impression on deep-seated inequalities in outcome – whether education can ever, in Basil Bernstein's famous phrase, 'compensate for society' – is another question altogether; and so indeed is the effectiveness or otherwise of the relatively modest and limited schemes so far attempted.

CHAPTER 5

INTEGRATION OR SEGREGATION?

> The presence of immigrant children in a school provides one of the best means of demonstrating and assisting the acceptance of immigrants as equal members of society. If Britain is becoming, at least to some extent, a multi-racial community, the school, as a microcosm of the community, can be a multi-racial society. If, as we have suggested, it is one of the purposes of education to widen the horizons of immigrant children, the presence of immigrant children in a school should widen the horizons of other children.
>
> (Commonwealth Immigrants Advisory Council, 1964)

The second major policy question confronting central and, more particularly, local government is that of integration or segregation. Specifically, should a deliberate effort be made to ensure that wherever possible ethnically integrated rather than ethnically segregated schools are the norm in multi-ethnic towns and cities? Strangely, this question has never attracted the same degree of attention as positive discrimination, apart perhaps from a brief period in the mid-1960s (see below) when a handful of local authorities followed central government advice on the need for dispersal to avoid 'undue concentrations of immigrant children'. One could be forgiven for imagining that the issue was now dead. I find this neglect odd because integration has proved to be the dominant ideology in so many recent educational debates (on comprehensivization, mixed-ability teaching, coeducation, provision for children with 'special educational needs', the teaching of ESL). Moreover, a tendency towards ethnic segregation is clearly discernible in many areas.

Just as 100 years ago a number of board schools in London's East End had a majority of Jewish pupils, so there are now a far greater number of urban schools around the country drawing most of their pupils from the ethnic minorities. It is by no means uncommon for the proportion to reach 80 or 90 percent. I carried out research in an infant school in a Lancashire mill town in the mid-1970s where the proportion eventually reached 100 per cent: all the children in the school were of Pakistani parentage. Equally, it is possible to find voluntary-aided and selective schools in some inner-city areas whose pupil populations could scarcely be claimed to reflect the ethnic composition of the communities surrounding them – all-white islands, it might be said, in a multiracial sea. In addition there are, of course, many more suburban schools in multi-ethnic authorities where ethnic minorities either constitute a tiny fraction of the pupil population or are not represented at all. Setting practical considerations on one side, it has to be asked, as a matter of urgency, whether this is right. Is this state of affairs consonant with the kind of multi-ethnic society we should like to see in Britain?

Ethnic segregation in education is essentially a very visible manifestation of social class segregation, whose resilience I commented on in Chapter 2. It is a product of residential segregation between different ethnic groups and adherence to the neighbourhood principle of school allocation among local authorities. It should be added that, in the case of ethnic minorities, residential segregation reflects not just social class position (or, for those who have settled since 1945, the influence of the circumstances of their migration) but also the effects of a combination of their own preferences for living close together and discrimination directed against them in the housing market and the wider society. However, the main point is that ethnic segregation at school has, like social class segregation, all too often been thought to have some kind of inevitability about it, and for similar reasons. Yet 20 years ago there was one striking, if unsuccessful, attempt by central government to intervene in the cause of integration, though the immediate occasion for action was not integrationist zeal but indigenous protest.

Dispersal in the 1960s

In the autumn of 1963 white parents of children attending two primary schools in Southall protested vigorously about the proportions of Asian children attending them. The Conservative Minister of Education at the time, Sir Edward Boyle, felt obliged to make a hurried visit which resulted in the proportion of immigrant children in Southall schools being limited to 30 percent. He commented in the House of Commons in November:

> If possible, it is desirable on education grounds that no one school should have more than about 30 percent of immigrants . . . I must regretfully tell the House that one school must be regarded now as irretrievably an immigrant school. The important thing to do is to prevent this happening elsewhere.
>
> (Quoted in Rose et al., 1969, p.268)

This was the beginning of an official policy on the dispersal of immigrant children that was confirmed by the incoming Labour government of 1964 and eventually formally adopted as a recommendation in Circular 7/65, *The Education of Immigrants*, and in the White Paper, *Immigration from the Commonwealth*, published in August of the same year. The recommendation, entitled 'Spreading the children', read as follows:

> Experience suggests . . . that, apart from unusual difficulties (such as a high proportion of non-English-speakers), up to a fifth of immigrant children in any group fit in with reasonable ease, but that, if the proportion goes over about one third either in the school as a whole or in any one class, serious strains arise. It is therefore desirable that the catchment areas of schools should, wherever possible, be arranged to avoid undue concentrations of immigrant children. Where this proves impracticable simply because the school serves an area which is occupied largely by immigrants, every effort should be made to disperse the immigrant children round a greater number of schools and to meet such problems of transport as may arise. It is important for the success of such measures that the reasons should be carefully explained beforehand to the parents of both the immigrant and the other children, and their cooperation obtained. *It will be helpful if the parents of non-immigrant children can see that practical measures have been taken to deal with the problems in the schools, and that the progress of their own children is not being restricted by the undue preoccupation of the teaching staff with the linguistic and other difficulties of immigrant children.*
>
> (DES, 1965a, pp.4–5)

It is this concluding sentence which has convinced critics that the dispersal policy was basically a panic reaction (and as such in keeping with the overall immigration policies of both Conservative and Labour governments) designed to appease the anxieties of whites. For, despite Sir Edward's remark about dispersal being desirable 'on education grounds', and the circular's awareness that ability to speak English might be one of them, the recommendation was for the dispersal of immigrants *as* immigrants.

Critics of government performance on race relations during the 1960s have found it predictable that the Circular 7/65 recommendation should have been incorporated virtually unamended into the 1965 White Paper, since the two documents were inspired by the same race relations philosophy.

According to this philosophy, harmonious race relations required an alliance between restrictive immigration control, anti-discrimination legislation and other 'positive' measures to promote integration. The mistake the critics have made is to interpret the recommendation on dispersal exclusively in terms of appeasing white anxieties. Although an important factor in determining official thinking, this was not the only one; equally important were idealistic considerations of an integrationist and egalitarian kind.

The second report of the Commonwealth Immigrants Advisory Council (CIAC), which was in draft form at the time of the Southall episode, also expressed dismay at the 'creation of predominantly immigrant schools'. The council had been set up by the previous Conservative government to advise the Home Secretary on matters relating to the welfare and integration of immigrants. It recommended that catchment areas should be adjusted, and if necessary immigrant children should be dispersed round a number of schools, to secure ethnically balanced intakes. But the reasons put forward in support of its position were not limited to concern for native sensitivities. It identified three reasons for regarding the concentration of immigrant pupils with dismay: first, the overall educational progress of the school was likely to be affected for the worse; second, immigrant children would not receive such a good introduction to British life; and, finally, the chances of the school becoming a microcosm of a multiracial society, in which children from different backgrounds worked and played together as equals, would be severely diminished.

Though strictly speaking a piece of advice to government and not a statement of government policy, the CIAC report's subsequent endorsement in Circular 7/65 has resulted in it being regarded, reasonably enough, as the official expression of the Labour government's policy position. The mistake made by critics of the government has been to interpret the report and the circular exclusively with reference to immigration policy, ignoring the influence of the integrationist 'bussing' campaign in the United States and of the Labour government's integrationist policies on education. 1965 was not only the year of Circular 7/65 and the White Paper on Commonwealth immigration but the year of DES Circular 10/65, which laid down guidelines to local authorities on the establishment of comprehensive schools. This circular was infused by the same spirit as the CIAC report. A comprehensive school, it stated, 'aims to establish a school community in which pupils over the whole ability range and with differing interests and backgrounds can be encouraged to mix with each other, gaining stimulus from the contacts and learning tolerance and understanding in the process' (DES, 1965b, p.8). In other words, if it is possible to interpret the Labour government's intervention on dispersal, like its volte-face over immigration control in 1964–1965, as a capitulation to white racism, it is also possible to interpret it as part of a broader commitment to integration in education.

In the event most local authorities chose to ignore the advice of central government. Bradford had decided to implement its own dispersal scheme even before the Southall controversy, and a few other authorities followed in its footsteps. But, taking their cue from the two largest LEAs – ILEA and Birmingham – the overwhelming majority disregarded the Circular 7/65 recommendation. At the end of the 1960s the DES's own survey found no dispersal in two-thirds of the 64 areas with significant numbers of immigrant pupils and only 'marginal' dispersal (i.e. catchment area adjustment) in most of the remainder. 'In only 11 areas is dispersal practised as a matter of policy, entailing the daily movement of children by coach' (DES, 1971, p.18). Of those authorities which did disperse, a few moved children of infant and junior, as well as secondary, school age, while several had predictable problems over who counted as 'immigrants'. Some dispersed all immigrant children irrespective of proficiency in English, whereas others dispersed only 'coloured' immigrants (i.e. included West Indians but excluded Italians). In the view of the government's critics this was at least in keeping with the real reason behind the whole recommendation for dispersal since the grounds were 'racial' not educational.

By the end of the 1960s central government had changed its mind. In 1969 Edward Short, the Labour Minister of Education, conceded that 'to impose dispersal by legislation or by regulation in the centre regardless of local circumstances would probably create far more discord than harmony . . . there will inevitably be schools with a very high proportion of immigrant children on the roll' (quoted in Hiro, 1973, p.360). Noting that most local authorities had not accepted the advice of Circular 7/65, and that dispersal on 'racial' grounds was against the 1968 Race Relations Act, the DES survey anticipated that, 'as the number of new immigrants declines, and as the children of immigrants by degrees have less linguistic and cultural difficulties, the educational arguments for allocating children outside their neighbourhood will tend to diminish and disappear'. While acknowledging that it was ultimately for the local authorities to decide, it argued that 'no policy affecting groups or categories of children should be allowed to override the reasonable wishes of individual parents in the matter of choice of school' and that 'the "bussing" of infant and young junior children should not be undertaken unless there is a compelling need to do so' (DES, 1971, pp.20–21).

The continuation of 'bussing' in the mid-1970s in a few authorities (Blackburn, Bradford and Ealing) attracted controversy and investigations by the Race Relations Board. American researchers were puzzled how 'bussing' could be 'liberal' in the United States and 'illiberal' in Britain – the answer being, of course, that two-way 'bussing' on American lines was politically inconceivable in Britain since it was not a matter of integrating black and white natives, as in the United States, but of integrating white natives and black immigrants. However, dispersal policy (at least so far as deliberate 'bussing' and central government intervention were concerned) appeared finished and discredited by the end of the decade.

Secondary school allocation

Where the issue of dispersal lived on, sometimes overtly and sometimes covertly, was in local disputes about secondary school allocation which ensued from comprehensivization in many authorities in the 1970s. The definition of catchment area boundaries became the subject of political wrangling, community action and parental indignation around the country. It was not unknown for middle-class parents to move house in order to ensure that their children were allocated to a 'good' comprehensive school. For many parents, and indeed some teachers, 'bad' comprehensive schools were distinguished by, among other things, a high proportion of pupils from working-class backgrounds and from the ethnic minorities. In Bedford, where I undertook research in the late 1970s, seemingly endless and unresolvable dissension surrounded the allocation of children to upper schools after comprehensive reorganization. Initially children in one of the town's conspicuously multi-ethnic working-class areas, Queen's Park, were deprived of a neighbourhood upper school and dispersed (*de facto* 'bussed') elsewhere. This arrangement was criticized from within the area for disrupting community spirit and creating unnecessary inconvenience, and from outside the area for lowering the standards of the schools to which the Queen's Park children were sent. Whereupon the local authority built a new upper school between Queen's Park and a largely middle-class commuter village on the town's edge and allocated the Queen's Park but not the village children to it. This led to further charges of 'ghettoization' and racialism. Worse was to come. When, in the early 1980s, the authority had to face up to the implications of falling rolls, it was the new Queen's Park upper school, by now the most multi-ethnic in the town, which was identified for closure.

Bristol (later Avon) was another authority which came under attack for failing to provide a satisfactory secondary school education for the multi-ethnic inner city. It will be remembered from Chapter 2 that Bristol instituted a comprehensive system in the mid-1960s which involved dividing the city into catchment areas resembling the segments of an orange. The object was to ensure that as many schools as possible had socially balanced intakes. The St Paul's area was left without a secondary school of its own, its children being dispersed to a variety of suburban comprehensives. After the riot in St Paul's in the spring of 1980, the local NUT castigated what had originally been considered a socially enlightened policy of school allocation as 'unofficial bussing': 'It is no wonder that some children suffer a crisis of identity and confidence in secondary schools when the group with which they have gone through primary school is broken up and scattered to many parts of Bristol' (Avon, NUT, 1980). Liverpool, like Bristol, a city with a comparatively small and highly concentrated black population, came in for criticism in the same year for closing an inner-city multi-ethnic comprehensive school, because of falling rolls, and dispersing its pupils to schools in neighbourhoods notorious for the prevalence of right-wing racialism.

Unfortunately, from the point of view of trying to clarify the issues and principles at stake, none of these disputes has been adequately written up, either descriptively or analytically. Instead they remain shrouded in allegations, innuendoes and half-truths. Even local press coverage has been fragmentary and less than enlightening to the uninitiated, unused to reading between the lines of official pronouncements. One dispute which has been written up, though not adequately, is the controversy engendered by Berkshire's system of secondary school allocation in Reading in the late 1970s. This became the first (and so far solitary) subject of a formal CRE investigation in the field of education under the 1976 Race Relations Act. That Reading and Berkshire should have been singled out in this way seems to be a curious accident of history. Reading is not noted for urban deprivation, educational disadvantage or poor race relations; nor has Berkshire proved particularly remiss in its response to the presence of pupils from the ethnic minorities. The proportion of the town's population who belong to the ethnic minorities has been estimated at 16 percent, which is a good deal less than other towns and authorities of a similar size, such as Bedford where the proportion approaches one-third.

The CRE embarked on a formal investigation after receiving allegations that a zoning system introduced in 1978 for allocating secondary school places in Reading was racially discriminatory, in the sense intended by the 1976 Act. It was alleged that the new system would lead to a high concentration of ethnic minority pupils in two schools which had been assigned all three of the town's 'social priority' primary schools as 'feeders'. This system replaced an earlier one which had been based on the report of a headteachers' working party in 1976, and attempted to create a set of comprehensives with academically, socially and ethnically balanced intakes while retaining the two existing grammar schools. One gets the impression from the CRE's report of its investigation that this largely popular system was replaced in 1978 because of parental pressure from middle-class neighbourhoods. Following widespread protests, the local authority altered the 1978 system of allocation the next year with the result that children from the three 'social priority' schools were no longer allocated exclusively to the two secondary schools where pupils from the ethnic minorities were also concentrated. Nevertheless the CRE pressed on with its investigation of the original complaint and eventually (no less than four years later) exonerated the authority on the ground that ethnic minority pupils had not been disadvantaged by being concentrated in these two schools since they had broad curricula and good entry and pass rates in 16+ examinations.

The CRE report on Reading is singularly uninformative on the cut and thrust of debate in the town. Where it is revealing, albeit patchily and sometimes unconsciously, is on equality of opportunity. For example, ethnic minorities in the late 1970s were not only concentrated in schools with high proportions of low-achieving pupils but were themselves susceptible to underachievement. In 1979, 12 percent of white boys were admitted to grammar school, compared with four percent of Asian boys, two percent of West Indian boys, 13 percent of white girls, 11 percent of Asian girls and four percent of West Indian girls. That same year the median scores of both West Indian and Asian pupils on NFER tests taken at transfer to secondary school were found to be substantially below those of their white peers. During the period of the investigation there was a marked tendency for West Indian pupils to be assessed as in need of remedial help, to be entered for fewer 16+ examinations and for CSE rather than O-Level, and to be under-represented on A-Level courses despite a good staying-on rate.

Far more striking, however, is the evidence of general inequality of opportunity. Although there was no attempt to control for social class in the analysis of entrance figures for grammar school and public examinations, there was in the case of the NFER tests. The LEA's own report of the NFER findings concluded that 'social background' was of 'greater significance than ethnic origin', as 'the difference in median scores between indigenous pupils entitled to free school meals and those who were not was greater than the difference between white indigenous and ethnic minority pupils'. The CRE report also supplies evidence of wide variations in both the academic intakes and the academic policies of different secondary schools. Perhaps the single most remarkable finding is that one secondary school (not the object of the investigation and with only six percent of pupils from the ethnic minorities) entered no candidates at all for five or more O-Level examinations. What the report, in effect, bears out is both the absurdity of the Reading investigation and the inherent absurdity of any investigation into discrimination or inequality of opportunity which necessarily limits its brief to the prospects of only one category of pupil.

The basis for the original complaint in Reading was not that ethnic minority pupils were being sent to bad schools or schools which discriminated against them but that they would be highly concentrated in two secondary schools with a large number of children from the three 'social priority' primary schools. Many of these children were likely to be in need of remedial attention. The three primary schools also included a disproportionate number of children from the ethnic minorities. The implication of the charge was presumably not that children from the ethnic minorities were going to school with one another (in the first and only year of the scheme's operation they accounted for 34 percent of the pupils at one of the secondary schools involved and 28 percent at the other). Rather, it was that those children who were neither socially deprived nor underachieving were going to school with children from a variety of ethnic backgrounds who were either one or the other or both. In other words, the complaint was motivated by precisely the same kind of social and academic snobbery as had resulted (or so one infers from the CRE report) in the abandonment of the 1976 system of allocation. If there was a case for a formal investigation in Reading in the late 1970s (but not by the CRE which is hampered by its terms of reference under the 1976 Act), it was into academic standards in a town not noted for urban deprivation or social disadvantage and into the policies of secondary schools on examination entrance. Also, how or why did the 1976 system of secondary school allocation, which appeared to be both egalitarian and integrationist, come to be abandoned in favour of the 1978 system, which was neither? (CRE, 1983).

Religious segregation

The settlement of ethnic minorities from Europe and the New Commonwealth has added another dimension to the debate about religious segregation in education. Their presence has vividly highlighted the divisive effects of the 'dual system' of educational provision. The headteacher of a Glasgow secondary school, addressing a meeting I attended in the city in 1980, told his audience that whereas Chinese and Pakistani children were 'bussed' into his school's catchment area Catholic children were 'bussed' out. As a result the Asian children, no matter what their actual religious affiliation, had been drawn in on the Protestant side of the cultural and social rift dividing the city, since they went to a school which, albeit notionally non-denominational, was effectively Protestant in ethos and values. A Pakistani boy had even been caught scrawling on a wall 'FTP' ('Fuck the Pope').

The main complaints of the ethnic minority lobby have been that voluntary-aided schools have all too often effectively excluded Asian and West Indian pupils and been complicit in manoeuvres by white parents to avoid their children attending multi-ethnic schools. Voluntary-aided schools favouring their own faith in selection procedures will naturally not have many Hindu, Muslim or Sikh children or children from the Christian Pentecostalist sects to which many West Indians belong. The consequence in some multi-ethnic authorities has been racial segregation on top of religious segregation – majority black county schools and majority white voluntary schools within a stone's throw of each other. Not only does the Roman Catholic upper school in Bedford not have more than a handful of black pupils, but, according to a priest at the Italian mission in the town whom I interviewed in 1980, those Italian parents who opt for it (approximately one-third) do so to forestall close contact between their children and black children rather than for religious reasons. There is also evidence that some voluntary-aided schools, theoretically comprehensives, are taking advantage of their independence in admissions policy to select children on the basis of 'ability' as well as religious affiliation.

There have been other cases of voluntary schools with comparatively 'open' admissions policies trying to preserve their original function despite a radically transformed intake. A *Guardian* columnist in 1982 was much amused by a *Times Educational Supplement* advertisement for a headship in the East End of London which read: 'The roll is largely Muslim. Strong Church of England links and a regular communicant preferred'. The following year another advertisement for a headship in the same journal, this time for Liverpool's only Jewish voluntary school (almost half of whose pupils are not Jewish), sought 'a dynamic person of the Jewish faith capable of fostering the Jewish life of the school and sympathetic to the opportunities created by the diversity of the school's intake'.

The whole issue of voluntary schools and the ethnic minorities attracted national publicity in the late 1970s when the London Borough of Ealing decided to sell an existing multi-ethnic comprehensive school to the Church of England on the grounds that there was no Anglican secondary school in the borough and that there was sufficient parental demand for one. Rumour had it that the parents concerned were primarily motivated by a desire to avoid their children attending schools that were both comprehensive and multi-ethnic. The Secretary of State for Education and Science approved Ealing's decision in 1980; the Diocese of London paid the borough £1.8 million (85 percent of which was refunded by the DES); and the school was then redesignated a Church of England voluntary school. The Sikh community in Southall responded by putting in a bid to Ealing Borough Council for a voluntary school of their own. They were no more successful than Muslim and Hindu groups who had made similar bids elsewhere.

Further controversy arose in 1983 when a Muslim group in Bradford, the Muslim Parents' Association (MPA), put in a bid for no less than five city schools (two first, two middle, one upper) to become Muslim voluntary schools. The principal justification given was the need to educate Muslim girls separately and within the conventions of Islamic morality. How much support for the bid existed among the Muslim community as a whole appeared debatable. It was certainly anathema to most Bradford teachers who feared that acceding to the MPA's demands would imperil race relations in the city, expose pupils to a reactionary pedagogy and authoritarian discipline, and restrict the educational opportunities of girls. The staff at one of the five schools (Bradford's surviving upper school for girls with 40 percent Muslims on roll) threatened to resign if it became Muslim, while a sixth-form Muslim girl wrote to the *Times Educational Supplement* stating that she and a majority of her schoolmates were strongly opposed to the MPA proposal because it would militate against 'racial harmony' and disadvantage Muslim girls educationally. The MPA's bid eventually foundered, mainly because it failed to capture the support of the city's Council of Mosques, but it was instrumental in persuading the education committee to retain the two remaining single-sex schools. Furthermore, the authority has gone out of its way to impress upon schools the importance of cultural sensitivity in such matters as morning assembly, religious education, girls' PE and school dinner menus.

It is clear from the Bradford controversy that the debate about religious segregation concerns not just the social effects of separatism but the nature of the education provided in religious schools. Secularists and humanists have long complained that voluntary schools are both socially divisive (in exacerbating strife between Protestants and Catholics in cities like Belfast, Glasgow and Liverpool) and engaged in the indoctrination of the young. Their very *raison d'être* is to teach their pupils to be good Anglicans, Methodists, Catholics or Jews, rather than (say) encouraging them to form their own opinions in matters of religion and morals. Most humanists and secularists object equally to compulsory religious worship and instruction in county schools. Their dream is of a sharp divorce between state and religious schools with the latter belonging, as in the United States and most of Western Europe, to the independent sector, and religion only admitted to the state curriculum as a subject to be taught, and thought, *about*.

The indoctrination charge frequently levelled against the voluntary-aided schools can be illustrated through the following excerpts from the publicly declared aims of some of the 20 voluntary-aided Jewish schools:

> The centrality of Israel as a vital part of our heritage will be instilled in all the pupils, and, hopefully, they will be imbued with a love of the country.
>
> As the only Jewish school in the Midlands we feel a special responsibility for promoting Jewishness, the Hebrew language and a love for Israel.
>
> The love, knowledge and practice of the heritage of orthodox Judaism is taught as well as an identification with the Jewish life of modern Israel including spoken and written Hebrew.
>
> The school's policy is to give the pupils an understanding and knowledge of their religious and cultural heritage . . . [by] involving them in an active daily participation in a living Judaism, associated with Israel.
>
> (Jewish Educational Development Trust, 1981)

These excerpts present examples not only of religious indoctrination (teaching the 'love, knowledge and practice of the heritage of orthodox Judaism') but also of political indoctrination (instilling the 'centrality of Israel as a vital part of our heritage'). They raise two important questions: first, is it right that public money should be used to subsidize the furtherance of Judaism and Zionism? Second, are the kind of aims stated here compatible with the liberal ideals of rational discussion and freedom of conscience which we like to believe are at the heart of state education in a democracy?

Any attempt to dismantle the dual system would be fiercely resisted by the Christian churches and the Jewish organizations. Its importance to the Catholic Church was firmly underlined when Pope John Paul went out of his way to declare the Church's commitment to segregated schools in Scotland during his visit in the summer of 1982: 'The cause of Catholic education is the cause of Jesus Christ and of his gospel at the service of man . . . Worthy of special mention, I feel, are the statutory provisions of the Education (Scotland) Act 1918, whereby Catholic schools are a constituent part of the state system with essential guarantees covering religious education and the appointment of teachers'. To some extent apologists for voluntary schools feel they are justified by history; by the fact that the Churches and religious societies shouldered the task of educating the nation's young long before the state decided to intervene in the late nineteenth century. They have also argued from the premise of cultural maintenance, or that secularization would mean more not less segregation. However, the case for voluntary schools rests primarily on appeal to the principle of parental rights – to, for instance, Article 26(3) of the Universal Declaration of Human Rights which states: 'The parents have as a priority the right to choose the kind of education to be given to their children'. Whatever the merits of the apologists' case (see below), there can be little doubt that they are on the defensive; and understandably, since it is hard to see how the dual system can survive in its present form in an ethnically diverse, multi-faith society. Considerations of logic and justice strongly suggest that, if there are to be voluntary schools for Christians and Jews, then there should be voluntary schools for Hindus, Muslims and Sikhs as well. There seems to me to be four possible developments.

The first is the secularists' dream – the replacement of the dual system by a wholly secular system of state education as found in the United States and much of Western Europe. This would mean existing voluntary schools closing or becoming county schools or joining the independent sector. Alternatively the dual system could actually be extended to allow for the establishment of Hindu, Muslim and Sikh voluntary schools. This would, of course, involve not only further religious segregation but further racial segregation too. It would also result in further pressure on county schools in multi-ethnic areas already resentful of voluntary-aided schools which at a time of falling rolls operate outside the local authorities' attempts to rationalize by maintaining normal levels of intake. The third and fourth possibilities are urged by religious educationists anxious to preserve a role for the churches and religious organizations yet apprised of the need for change. The more modest of the two proposals involves those voluntary-aided schools accepting pupils primarily on the basis of religious affiliation. They should be obliged to alter their admission policy so that they become 'a service *by* the Church, rather than *for* the Church . . . admitting children of all religions and none on some criterion of service to those most in need, regardless of belief'. The more radical suggestion is the establishment of multi-faith voluntary-aided schools in appropriate areas. These would be schools 'where people of different faiths got together to run a school jointly, sharing in the necessary financial support . . . and with joint responsibility for admissions. Religious instruction and prayers would be arranged separately . . . Many subjects would be taught jointly' (Dummett and McNeal, 1981, pp.20,23). In fact there already are half a dozen ecumenical schools in existence run jointly by the Anglican and Catholic authorities.

The case for integration

So, then, to the question of the chapter: integration or segregation? I have always been a staunch supporter of integration, my attachment to the principle deriving from my own education. I was born and attended one primary and two secondary schools in Liverpool, a predominantly working-class city with a large Catholic population and, even during my childhood, conspicuously multi-ethnic. Yet, if my memory serves me right, none of my three schools had any working-class, Catholic or handicapped children to speak of, and both the secondary schools were single sex. Nor were there any Liverpool blacks or other ethnic minorities apart from a small group of middle-class Jewish children in one of the secondary schools who had separate assemblies and were excused religious instruction. At the time I vaguely thought this exclusiveness was wrong. Now I feel it was both wrong and to some extent avoidable. Approaching the question another way, it is possible to enunciate a principle which states that children should, wherever possible, attend common schools and not be artificially divided by 'ability', handicap, sex, religion, 'race' or ethnicity. Integration is, it might be said, the natural order of things. Although arguments from 'nature' are notoriously suspect in philosophy, I think it would be widely agreed that in this case a belief in the natural order of things has a certain inherent strength, or at any rate that interference with it requires a particularly cogent justification.

We have seen that three of the officially sanctioned forms of segregation – by 'ability', handicap and sex – are in retreat precisely because the original reasons advanced to justify them have failed the test of time, or else because more cogent reasons can be deployed in support of integration. Segregation for handicapped children has not meant, as was originally hoped, that their special needs have been more successfully met. If anything, it has meant the denial of equality of opportunity and has contributed to social isolation and stigmatization. That is why just about everyone now accepts that children with special needs should, so far as possible, both attend ordinary schools and engage in ordinary school activities alongside other children. The exception here is the sharp difference of opinion between deaf adults, represented by the British Deaf Association, and parents of deaf children. The parents, 90 percent of whom are not deaf, favour integration so that their children can learn to speak the same language as themselves and participate in the common culture. On the other hand deaf adults, mostly educated in special schools and living in deaf communities with their own system of communication, are hostile; they argue that integration will foster 'oralism' to the detriment of sign language, hence condemning deaf children to illiteracy and underachievement, and threaten the survival of deaf culture.

No such exceptions complicate the debate about segregation by 'ability' (of which segregation for handicap is in a sense a part), whether between or within schools, though integrationists have been rather more successful in promoting comprehensivization than mixed-ability grouping. The argument is identical for both, however; namely, that segregation has proved socially divisive and inegalitarian, labelling the majority of children 'academic failures' at an early age. Proponents of sexual segregation in education have also lost the argument irretrievably. Single-sex education was essentially a product of restrictive attitudes towards relationships between the sexes; its demise became predictable with the change in attitudes after the Second World War, and its fate was sealed by wholesale comprehensivization and falling rolls. Recent renewed support for separation on egalitarian grounds by an alliance of conservatives and feminists carries little conviction. Sexism is certainly an important issue in schools, as in society at large, but girls have always shown themselves, academically at least, more than able to hold their own, as the evidence summarized in Chapter 2 makes plain. Moreover, evidence from the National Child Development Study (NCDS) has confirmed the finding of other research that single-sex education does not produce better academic results for girls. In so far as single-sex schools do secure better results, it is because they are selective not because they are single sex. The NCDS evidence also reveals that, notwithstanding the sexist pressures, girls in mixed schools enjoy school more, would not want to switch to single-sex schools, get on better with boys and are more likely to be happily married.

Religious segregation differs from the other three forms of official segregation in exchanging the issue of equality of opportunity for the issue of indoctrination. It, too, is deeply divisive, as is evident from the experience of Northern Ireland, Scotland and English cities with large Catholic populations. In addition, it institutionalizes a view of education directly contradictory of that which ought to prevail in a democracy. In theory voluntary-aided schools are fundamentally engaged in the preservation of religious faith; their aim is to encourage children to accept a body of doctrine on matters of religion and morals (and, in the case of some Jewish schools, politics), not to arrive at their own opinions in the light of logic, evidence and consideration for others. Although historically one understands how this state of affairs has come about, it does seem extraordinary that the Anglican, Catholic and Jewish authorities should be permitted to indoctrinate their young at the public expense. The argument from history is, of course, no argument at all. The fact that religious bodies played a major role, frequently *the* major role, in educating the nation's young in the past is no justification for them continuing to do so in the future. Nor is the argument appealing to parental rights quite so unassailable as those manipulating it appear to believe. Under British law (the 1944 and 1980 Education Acts) parents are entitled to expect that their children will be educated in accordance with their wishes. Though there are obviously difficult issues to resolve in respect of how far parental wishes should determine the content of the curriculum and other aspects of school policy, I think it would be generally accepted that increased parental involvement in school life is a good thing. Many people also take it as axiomatic that deciding which school one's children should attend is a fundamental parental right. The weakness of this argument is its assumption that parental rights are the only ones involved or at least that they should prevail in the event of conflict. Little is heard of the 'rights' of the other group of consumers, the children themselves, or of the 'rights' of society as a whole.

Let us suppose, for the sake of argument, that it has been established that the majority of Muslim parents in a local authority are in favour of Muslim voluntary schools but the majority of Muslim pupils are opposed to them. It is not clear to me why the views of the parents should carry more weight than those of the pupils, when it is the lives of the latter which are directly affected and when good grounds exist for querying the social desirability of religious and ethnic segregation. There is a long tradition of utopian thought actually opposed to parental control over education. Jonathan Swift's Lilliputians were of the opinion that 'parents are the last of all others to be trusted with the education of their own children', and so was Plato in his *Republic*. There have also been a number of experiments of a socialist kind (for example, in the Israeli *kibbutzim*) to increase the community's control over the education of the young at the expense of parental discretion. To most people such views and measures now appear extremist. Quite apart from the matter of rights, it seems foolhardy to try to educate children in disregard or defiance of their parents' wishes. However, although there is a strong case, both moral and practical, for respecting and, wherever possible, satisfying the wishes of parents, I cannot see why they should have 'priority', as they do under Article 26(3) of the Universal Declaration of Human Rights. After all, parental motivation for wanting a child to attend one secondary school rather than another has all too often been shown up as snobbish or narrowly instrumental. The purpose of a public system of education is not, primarily, to meet parental demands (that is what the independent sector is for) but to educate children in the public interest; and religious segregation is emphatically not in the public interest.

Dismantling the dual system would, of course, be a major political and strategic undertaking; it would certainly mean a protracted and bitter struggle with the Anglican authorities and the almost equally influential Catholic and Jewish establishments. This should not, however, deter those of us committed to the secularization of public education in Britain. In a sense the time was never more opportune, with church and state dithering over how to respond to demands from the new religious minorities. Moreover, we owe it to the memory of John Stuart Mill and the other Victorian liberals and radicals who fought so assiduously for a genuinely public system of statutory education and were eventually fobbed off with such a disastrous compromise. Nor would secularization lead, as apologists of religious segregation have sometimes asserted, to more rather than less segregation. No doubt there would still be Catholic parents (with the money to afford it) persuaded of the 'benefits' of sending their children to Ampleforth, Downside and the like, and Jewish parents persuaded of the 'benefits' of Carmel College (all well-established institutions in the independent sector). However, most Catholic and Jewish parents, along with most Muslims, Hindus and Sikhs, would surely recognize that they had nothing to lose from a wholly and genuinely secular system, in which neither religious worship nor religious instruction had a place. The only loss would be the 'right' to indoctrinate their children at the public expense – a 'right', I would submit, to which no one is entitled, since it is incompatible with education in a liberal democracy.

I have based my adherence to the integration principle so far partly on appeal to the 'natural order of things', maintaining that any interference with it requires a particularly cogent justification. However, it has to be admitted that, were the four kinds of formal segregation to be dismantled overnight, the natural order of things would still leave considerable *de facto* social and ethnic segregation. In Chapter 2 I noted that social class segregation survived widespread comprehensivization in the 1960s and 1970s because of residential segregation between the classes and acceptance of the neighbourhood principle in school allocation. At the beginning of this chapter I commented on the emergence in many local authorities of ethnic segregation, a product not only of the social class position of ethnic minorities but also of a combination of their own preferences and discrimination in the housing market and society at large. To repeat the question I posed there – is this state of affairs consonant with the kind of multi-ethnic society we should like Britain to become? My answer is 'no'. The problem is what to do about it. At primary level there is, regrettably, very little that can be done, since it is almost universally accepted that children of that age should attend neighbourhood schools preferably within walking distance of home. On the other hand, between the ages of 11 and 13, when children transfer to secondary school, they have traditionally often had to travel longer distances by bus or bike; and it is widely acknowledged that this may be beneficial, resulting in an increase in independence and in the range of social contacts.

At present roughly half the LEAs allocate to secondary schools clearly demarcated catchment areas or 'feeder' primary schools. The other half operate a system of parental choice whereby parents rank the various secondary schools in order of preference. Under the second system, parents are only denied their first choice when demand exceeds supply of places, in which case objective criteria of some sort – proximity, family connection and so forth – are applied. Since 1979 the Conservative government has been firmly wedded to what it calls 'unlimited' parental choice; the local appeals tribunals set up under the 1980 Education Act are intended to facilitate this process. However, even before the 1980 Act well over 90 percent of parents were quite satisfied with the secondary schools their children were allocated to, whichever system their particular authority operated. The retention of some degree of selection in one-third of local authorities (not to mention the existence of voluntary schools) has, however, both impeded catchment area allocation and interfered with parental choice. I can see the attraction of allocation according to parental choice (in many ways it seems the simplest solution), but my own preference is for the catchment area system of allocation. I do not, however, favour the neighbourhood principle but the system operated by Bristol in the 1960s, and in Reading between 1976 and 1978, to try and ensure socially, ethnically and academically balanced intakes. This was also the solution advocated by Circular 10/65; it urged local authorities 'to ensure, when determining catchment areas, that schools are as socially and intellectually comprehensive as is practicable' (DES, 1965b, p.8). No other solution satisfies integrationist as well as egalitarian considerations. Local authorities adopting such a system would, of course, be under an obligation to try and ensure that their schools were also as equal as possible in other respects – facilities, resources and staff quality. Otherwise pupils allocated to inferior schools, and their parents, would have good cause for complaint. It has been estimated that something like 80 percent of the differences between schools' examination performances can be attributed to the academic and socioeconomic composition of their pupil populations, but the remaining 20 percent, for which the schools themselves are directly responsible, obviously remains critical so far as conventional measures of scholastic success and failure are concerned.

This does not mean I am advocating another central government initiative along the lines of Circular 7/65, though it is worth noting that dispersal (contrary to what has frequently been alleged) was initially popular with the South Asians whom it mainly affected, since it resulted in their children attending 'better' schools than they would otherwise have done – protests against 'bussing' were a feature of the 1970s not the 1960s. Apart from the unlikelihood of any government attempting any such thing, there is no guarantee that local authorities would be more amenable to a central recommendation now than they were 20 years ago. Resistance might emanate from the Left as well as the Right. Community educationists have long argued for the importance of neighbourhood schools, especially in socially deprived areas, both to increase parental and community involvement in formal education and to develop in children 'a critical and constructive understanding of the environment in which they live' (Hargreaves, 1982, p.120). It even became fashionable in radical circles about 10 years ago to claim, in the interest of promoting black 'consciousness' and black solidarity, that there was nothing inherently wrong with an all-black school; it was disadvantaged all-black schools that were unacceptable. All-black schools deliberately created as part of segregationist policy would, of course, like all-white schools, infringe the 1976 Race Relations Act, and rightly so. All-black schools, and all-white schools in multi-ethnic areas, are totally unacceptable, and for the same reason that all-Catholic and all-Protestant schools in Belfast, Glasgow and Liverpool are totally unacceptable. They are likely to prove breeding grounds for interethnic prejudices, myths and hostility and militate against the evolution of a harmonious multi-ethnic society in Britain.

I can see the force of the community educationists' general argument in relation to primary education; but with the advent of transfer to secondary school it runs the serious risk of becoming a narrow and retrograde doctrine, defining 'community' in an arbitrarily restricted way, shackling children instead of liberating them. Children should be encouraged to spread their wings, socially and intellectually, not to turn in on the cul-de-sacs of their own neighbourhoods. Needless to say, 'ghettoization' represents a prison for the middle-class child as much as the working-class child, the white as much as the black child. It is to be hoped that local authorities give a proper hearing to the integrationist case, especially now when so many are reviewing their provision for secondary education in the light of falling rolls.

I have hesitated to pronounce on two specific issues in this chapter: the difference of opinion, referred to earlier, between deaf adults and the parents of deaf children over the future education of deaf children; and the future education of Gypsy children. Because of their nomadic way of life, and their traditional hostility to formal education, Gypsies are the only ethnic minority with a prima facie case for segregation in education. There appears to be an unresolved debate among them whether Gypsy children should be taught on site by fellow Gypsies, in the interests of cultural maintenance, or off site in ordinary schools by *gorgios*, in the interests of integration and equal opportunity. The whole question of education and cultural maintenance is examined in the next chapter.

CHAPTER 6

THE LIMITS TO PLURALISM

> A national system of education must aim at producing citizens who can take their place in society properly equipped to exercise rights and perform duties which are the same as those of other citizens. If their parents were brought up in another culture or another tradition, children should be encouraged to respect it, but a national system cannot be expected to perpetuate the different values of immigrant groups.
>
> (Commonwealth Immigrants Advisory Council, 1964)

Current orthodoxy appears to favour central government, local authorities and schools developing 'pluralist' policies towards the cultures of ethnic minorities. That Britain is a 'plural' society, in the sense of being both ethnically and ideologically diverse, is a simple fact. Whether it is also a 'pluralist' society, or can or should be such a society, is a matter of dispute, as is the interpretation of the concept of 'pluralism'. I think it would probably be agreed that pluralism involves adopting a position of support for ethnic and ideological diversity and for ethnic minority rights. Dispute has focused on the extent to which support is either feasible or desirable.

It would probably be further agreed that Britain is a pluralist society in so far as it is not a totalitarian state, guarantees a number of fundamental freedoms and has enacted anti-discrimination legislation to support the rights of women and ethnic minorities. On the other hand that pluralism is limited in several salient respects. Our Westminster model of parliamentary democracy, for example, has proved a poor reflector of the country's plurality; not just in the survival of a non-elected chamber, but in the political, social, ethnic and gender composition of the House of Commons. Moreover, when democracy itself is felt to be under threat, governments have not hesitated to restrict fundamental freedoms. I referred in Chapter 1 to the internment of Italians during the 1939–1945 war. The proscription of Irish terrorist organizations in the 1970s breached the principle of freedom of association, while the freedom of the media to report events of public importance was severely curtailed during the Falklands War of 1982.

In Chapter 4 I criticized the arbitrary narrowness of British anti-discrimination legislation, and the fact that the whole population is not protected by a Bill of Rights. From the viewpoint of minorities, it has been argued that there are other gaps in the statute book. Given that the United Kingdom has ratified Article 4 of the International Convention on the Elimination of All Forms of Racial Discrimination, which requires that states should 'declare illegal and prohibit organisations . . . which promote and incite racial discrimination', ethnic minorities might have been entitled to expect that racialist (as well as terrorist) organizations would be proscribed. In contrast, some of the law's proscriptions, while historically explicable, appear to penalize minorities unnecessarily. Marijuana smokers have been criminalized when their particular predilection is almost certainly less harmful than the (socially sanctioned) consumption of tobacco and alcohol; and I cannot think of a good reason why the age of consent for homosexual lovers should be higher than that for heterosexual lovers. All in all, Britain does not seem to be as pluralist a society as (say) the United States (not itself beyond reproach, of course), either in the defence of fundamental freedoms or in the protection of minority rights. But the United States has both a written constitution and civil rights legislation to advance these causes and is unencumbered by a constitutional monarchy and an established church which have constrained them. In Britain Catholics, Jews and Protestant non-comformists have all had to struggle to secure political and religious emancipation.

I do not propose to get embroiled in any of the specific issues mentioned above, though I shall have something to say about the proscription of racism in the next chapter. Nor is my main point that Britain is less pluralist than it should be; rather, that there is bound to be a limit to how pluralist it or any society can ever be. One explanation for this is the tension within the pluralist philosophy between libertarianism and proscriptiveness. Maximizing human freedoms is not wholly compatible with protecting minorities from discrimination. Achieving the latter may mean sacrificing the former; and vice versa. Hence, it has sometimes been claimed that the freedom of racists to express their racism and the right of ethnic minorities to protection from its effects are mutually exclusive.

The most widely accepted view on liberty, classically expounded by John

Stuart Mill in his essay of that title, is that people should be free to do as they wish provided their actions do not intefere with other people's right to do likewise or cannot be shown to be contrary to society's best interest. In the previous chapter I queried the right of parents to have the final word on the choice of secondary school, both because their wishes might not coincide with their children's and because 'unlimited' parental choice could lead to an even more inegalitarian and divided society. The other main way of explaining the limits to pluralism is to say that each society develops an agreed core of values which it will normally want to see embodied in legislation, perhaps a constitution and certainly in its social institutions. Although a degree of value tension and value conflict may be tolerated and accommodated (a liberal democracy will regard that as one of its strengths), direct contradictions of, or threats to, those core values often cannot. Bhikhu Parekh (1974) made the point in relation to immigration more than 10 years ago: 'British society, like any other society, has a certain definite conception of the good life to which its members subscribe and which influences the way they live . . . [it] is entitled to insist that every one of its members, immigrant as well as native, must conform to . . . [those] basic, minimal, values . . . that it regards as constitutive of its conception of the good life'. Parekh therefore went on to argue for 'modified' rather than 'full-blooded' pluralism, that is to say, for 'pluralistic integration within the framework of a generally accepted conception of the good life' as the 'ideal governing Britain's relations with her immigrant population'. This was to be accompanied by the realization of equality of opportunity and some redefinition of what it means to be British (Parekh, 1974, pp.220–231).

'Full-blooded' or 'modified' pluralism?

The argument from a core of 'basic, minimal values' combines a mixture of pragmatic and moral considerations. 'Full-blooded' pluralism founders both because it is impractical and because some of the practices and customs of ethnic minorities may prove to be morally wrong when measured against those values. This assumes, of course, that the core of values is itself valid, which ultimately must be a matter of opinion. Parekh's argument was based on the belief that the 'conception of the good life' which had developed in Britain more or less represented a triumph for reason and humanity. He expected immigrants to conform to it for the same reason that he would expect natives to conform to it – not because they were newcomers or in a minority but because it was a morally sound one.

'Modified' pluralism means that some traditions of the ethnic minorities may be the subject of legal proscription, official discouragement or moral disapproval. During the colonial period the British authorities oscillated between a policy of *laissez-faire* towards indigenous cultures, and attempts to extirpate practices they deemed uncivilized. A famous example of moral intervention was the decision by Lord William Bentinck, Governor-General of India between 1828 and 1835 and a Benthamite radical, to suppress the Hindu practice of *suttee*, the immolation of widows on their husbands' funeral pyres. Some might say that his decision was a flagrant piece of cultural imperialism on the part of an alien and oppressive regime which had no right to be in India in the first place, and ought at the very least to have respected the Hindu customs which prevailed at that time. Bentinck would probably have retorted that the political circumstances were irrelevant; *suttee* offended against universal moral law and had therefore to be stopped. It was on this ground that he later suppressed *thugee*, the ritual murder and robbery carried out by the followers of the goddess Kali.

Another cultural practice which led to conflict between the British colonial authorities and indigenous peoples, though this time in Africa, has by an ironic twist of history recently reappeared in Britain. In 1982 the national press revealed that circumcision and infibulation were being carried out on African women and girls in private clinics in Harley Street. The subsequent outcry was of the unanimous opinion that if this barbarous custom was not against the law, it should be. No voices were raised in defence of the right of ethnic minorities to retain traditional customs. Nor did anyone make the point that the women and girls involved presumably underwent the operations of their own free will, for in so far as they did, it can only have been as a result of the same degree of social pressure as drove Hindu widows onto the funeral pyres before Bentinck intervened. In any case the fact that an action is freely undertaken is not a sufficient guarantee (though it is a necessary one) of its moral acceptability. There may be room for disagreement, for example, over the precise year at which the age of consent, whether homosexual or heterosexual, should be fixed, but paedophiles are alone in arguing that provided children give their consent it does not matter how young they are.

More controversial have been the instances of conflict between British values and South Asian communities over marriage and the role of women. At the very moment when British society has been struggling to meet demands for equality and justice from a rejuvenated 'women's movement', it has found itself also required to respond to newly settled cultures with long-established traditions of *purdah*, arranged marriage and the overall subjugation of 'the second sex'. The education system and the social services, based on a core of liberal and humanitarian values and sensitive of their self-proclaimed image as 'caring' institutions, have been faced with a number of intractable cases involving girls in South Asian families. If we take the much publicized example of a girl running away from home, even asking to be taken into care, rather than submit to an arranged marriage, their sympathies are probably with her; in their eyes she may be legitimately asserting her individuality against a repressive regime. Were they to take her side actively, however, they would risk being accused of assimilationism or ethnocentricism (presumptuously intervening to support an Indian girl against her parents when they would not if she were English). Were they, on the other hand, to side with the parents or remain aloof, they might lay themselves open to the criticism of professional negligence, not to mention helping to perpetuate a reactionary tradition. Moral considerations of a more utilitarian kind might suggest that intervention would be unlikely to bring beneficial results for the girl or anyone else, and that provided she was not actually being harmed, the most appropriate policy could be to leave well alone.

Whatever the solution to these difficult dilemmas, the general point is that, although most people no longer share Lord William Bentinck's faith in something called universal moral law, we continue to believe in a clear distinction between right and wrong, even if we might not always agree whether a particular practice belongs to one category or the other. Our commitment to liberal democracy is founded on a core of 'minimal values' which we feel ourselves entitled to use as touchstones for judging the moral acceptability of all cultural practices. It is important to stress that this is not a ploy for interrogating or excoriating only the cultures of ethnic minorities; nor is it intended to imply that debate and development on such issues as equality for women and more freedom for girls are not taking place within them. It is as much a demand for regular self-appraisal on the part of the ethnic majority. It is equally important to recognize that the agreed core of values, 'the conception of the good life', must itself be open to review and revision, hence Bhikhu Parekh's point about redefining what it means to be British.

'Full-blooded' pluralism is characterized by the belief that the cultures of ethnic minorities should be maintained and fostered irrespective of the content of specific customs. The current popularity of the notion that these cultures should be exempt from critical comment, official disapproval or legislative interference appears to be due to a wish to compensate for the depredations of ethnocentricism which ethnic minorities, as relatively powerless communities, have all too often had to contend with in the past. But the real theoretical basis for pluralism is philosophical and moral relativism.

Relativism is distinguished by two related tenets: that all cultures are equally valid and can only be properly understood and appreciated from within their own framework of 'rationality'. Relativism specifically rejects any belief in what Paul Zec (1980), in a valuable article on multicultural education and relativism, has called 'transcultural criteria of rationality' and 'right conduct' (in other words, an agreed core of minimal values) against which all cultures can be described, interpreted and judged. The logical outcome of relativism in education is, as Zec points out, ethnic segregation: 'to accept relativism is to accept the view that in a multicultural society the only choice is between on the one hand the maintenance through education of a dominant culture (which is undesirable because elitist, anti-democratic etc.) and on the other hand the institution of separate but equal educational programmes for the transmission of their culture to co-existing cultural groups (which is also undesirable because it smacks of apartheid)'. Furthermore, although the attempt to divest oneself of cultural persuppositions and see matters from another culture's point of view may well be a sound prerequisite to moral judgement in interethnic contexts, it cannot of itself provide a basis for either judgement or action. Indeed, relativism appears to debar both.

For my part, I believe that certain cultures, and certain cultural practices, are better than others, and that this can be substantiated by reference to 'transcultural criteria of rationality' and 'right conduct'. In other words, some cultures can be shown to be more liberal, more rational, more egalitarian and more humane, rather in the way that the journal *New Internationalist*'s monthly profile evaluates countries on a five-point scale (from excellent to appalling) by reference to their performance on such indices as income distribution, the extent of freedom and the position of women. Relativism is particularly inappropriate as a theoretical basis for a public system of education. State schools could never be value-free even if they wanted to be. Their curricula and other institutional arrangements are bound to be predicated on certain values – those held to be so vital that they cannot be left to chance. Paul Zec (1980) rightly insists that 'a non-ethnocentric, non-imperialist education for *all* in a multicultural society' must be inspired by faith in 'transcultural criteria of rationality' and 'right conduct', and that therefore only a 'weak' (as opposed to 'strong') form of relativism – roughly equalling objectivity plus empathy – makes any sense (Zec, op.cit., pp.77–86).

Pluralism and assimilation in education policy

A good example of 'full-blooded' pluralism in education is the response of the London School Board to the increased numbers of Jewish children in the school-age population at the end of the last century (see Chapter 2). When the proportions of Jewish children in an elementary school reached a certain point, the school board handed it over to the Jewish community so that it could be 'run on Jewish lines'. This did not mean that the London School Board subscribed to pluralist philosophy. Its policy was more likely to have been dictated by practical exigencies or may simply have reflected early confusion about what the new elementary schools were for. But the effect was the same as if it had – the emergence of a separate Jewish subsystem of educational provision. The dual system inaugurated by the 1870 Education Act was also pluralist policy of a kind since it enabled religious minorities (including Anglicans, for that is what they have since become) to further the preservation of their faiths at the public expense; its effect was likewise divisive. On the other hand central and local government response to the children of European and New Commonwealth immigrants who began appearing in school in the 1950s and early 1960s was patently not pluralist. There was never any suggestion of following the example set by the London School Board over half a century earlier.

Precisely what government policy was, and how it is best characterized, remain matters for disagreement. Most of the local education authorities affected confined their arrangements to the teaching of English as a second language and to the introduction of immigrant children to British life. Central government attempted to assist them, after almost a decade of *laissez-faire*, by making available extra funding and resources (see Chapter 4). There were no policy pronouncements, however, and no statements of educational philosophy until 1963 when the 'immigrant schools' controversy erupted in Southall. Since then a myth has grown up that government policy in those early years was 'assimilationist', in that it expected immigrant children to renounce their distinctive ethnic identities and become culturally British; in other words, that it was the very reverse of pluralist. Strangely enough, government critics, to support the 'assimilationist' charge, have seized on a passage in the Commonwealth Immigrants

Advisory Council's 1964 report which says nothing about assimilation as a desirable aim and which I have chosen as an epigraph for this chapter because it succinctly expresses the limits to pluralism. The key clause – 'a national system cannot be expected to perpetuate the different values of immigrant groups' – has been widely, and quite illogically, interpreted as urging that schools should try and anglicize immigrant children. In fact, it meant exactly what it said: that 'a national system cannot be expected' to teach Muslims to be good Muslims, Hindus to be good Hindus or Sikhs to be good Sikhs. Nowhere did central government mention assimilation as a desirable goal (except in Circular 7/65 where it referred to social integration not cultural conversion). It was even cautious about integration to the extent that such an objective might have implications for cultural affiliation and conflict with the wishes of immigrant parents.

Central government's first piece of public advice on the education of immigrants, contained in Ministry of Education Pamphlet 43 *English for Immigrants*, published in the previous year to the CIAC report, warned schools against trying to impose 'the kind of conformity that a too narrow interpretation of "integration" ' would involve (Ministry of Education, 1963, pp.5–6). Quite apart from this, the CIAC report and Pamphlet 43 were absolutely right on most of the major issues raised by the presence in British schools of increasing numbers of immigrant children from different cultural backgrounds. A national system of education cannot, and should not, pretend to 'perpetuate the different values' of ethnic minorities, though it is only fair to add that this is precisely what the 'dual system' has permitted religious minorities to do for over 100 years.

In the early years of European and New Commonwealth immigration assimilationism, in the sense of attempted cultural anglicization, was in fact rampant among headteachers and in staffrooms around the country. Evidence of this was provided by several local studies undertaken at the time. 'You can't tell which is which', a headteacher told Elspeth Huxley during her visit to Bedford schools in 1964, 'we're turning them all British' (Huxley, 1964, p.224). In her research in Sparkbrook, Birmingham, Jennifer Williams found the assimilationism more broadly based, including social class as well as cultural values. She summarized the school's role (excluding the Catholic voluntary sector) as that of a 'socializing, anglicizing, integrating agency', with the teachers identifying their task as instilling 'a certain set of values (Christian), a code of behaviour (middle class) and a set of academic and job aspirations in which white collar jobs have a higher prestige than manual, clean jobs than dirty . . . and interesting, responsible jobs . . . than just "good money" jobs' (Williams, 1967, p.237).

Further examples of assimilationist views were yielded by the Townsend and Brittan investigation into teachers' opinions in the early 1970s. One headteacher declared: 'I believe our duty is to prepare children for citizenship in a free, Christian, democratic society according to British standards and customs' (Townsend and Brittan, 1973, p.13). Such expressions of opinion were all too often accompanied by gratuitous acts of ethnocentricism. Traditional dress and ornaments and minority languages were banned from school premises; parental wishes were ignored; religious sensibilities were flouted. Although the teaching profession appears now to be turning against the assimilationists, isolated acts of ethnocentric arrogance or insensitivity are by no means uncommon. A few years ago a copy of a letter came into my possession written (in 1977) by the irate headmaster of a Church of England junior school to a Muslim parent. The headmaster's complaint was that the parent's daughter was still coming to school in trousers despite instructions to the contrary. He threatened to exclude her from school unless she started to attend 'dressed in the proper uniform' and he took the opportunity to arraign Islam for its discriminatory treatment of women – 'Christians, unlike Muslims, believe in the equality of women with men in the sight of God'. The direct intervention of the DES was needed to settle the matter in the family's favour.

On the whole LEAs have been careful to distance themselves from the assimilationism and ethnocentricism of many of their teachers. In 1967 the Bedford Borough Education Officer was at pains to stress that, like the central government documents of 1963–1965, the aims of borough policy were to do with equality not cultural assimilation:

> The word 'integration' is to be approached with caution, since it is emotive and has dangerous undertones. It was never the prime objective of the Borough teachers. Their job was to give the immigrant children adequate tools for learning, so that they could be educated like all the other children with skill, devotion and respect and in accordance with their 'age, ability and aptitude'.
>
> (Walker, 1966–1967, p.329)

However, it is only recently that some LEAs, prompted by major initiatives like the 1976 Race Relations Act and the 1977 EEC Directive on the Education of Migrant Workers' Children, have begun to take positive action to try and ensure that the special cultural needs of ethnic minorities are met in their schools. One of these is the City of Bradford. In 1981 Bradford Metropolitan Council approved a policy statement on race relations which recognized 'that Bradford has both a multi-racial and multi-cultural population and that all sections of the community have an equal right to the maintenance of their distinctive identities and loyalties of culture, language, religion and custom'. The statement affirmed that 'so far as is compatible with individual needs, the provision of services will at all times respect the strength and variety of each community's cultural values'. The following year the Directorate of Educational Services stated four aims for education in Bradford: 'to seek ways of preparing all children and young people for life in a multi-cultural society; to counter racism and racist attitudes, and the inequalities and discrimination which results from them; to build on and develop the strengths of cultural and linguistic diversity; and to respond sensitively to the special needs of minority groups'. It also issued a memorandum prescribing rules of procedure on matters of cultural and religious differences which it expected headteachers and their staffs to follow. This laid down that schools should make absolutely clear to ethnic minority parents, using written translations and interpreters where necessary, the nature of their rights with regard to the withdrawal of their children from religious assemblies and religious education, and from school for religious festivals, and to special provision for religious instruction in their own faith during school hours whether in school or not. It further stipulated that pupils should be permitted to wear traditional dress (albeit in school colours where a uniform existed) and religious jewellery (except when considered dangerous, as in PE lessons); and that allowance should be made, if required, in PE, swimming and dance for separate lessons, and for fuller clothing than normal, for girls.

More controversially, the memorandum announced that the authority was considering introducing *halal* meat dishes in addition to existing vegetarian options in certain schools (City of Bradford Metropolitan Council, 1982). After consultations with the RSPCA, and despite receiving protests from animal rights groups, the authority decided to press ahead with the experiment in 10 schools in 1983. The chairman of Bradford's race advisory group remarked, with some complacency, that he had seen 20 sheep slaughtered in the orthodox Islamic way (i.e. their throats had been cut while they were alive and conscious) and they had been dead in 'under half a minute'. 'We have equipped our public abattoir with an Islamic slaughtering unit. We have 50,000 Muslims in the city and they have complete rights over ritual slaughter. They do pay their rates' (*Times Educational Supplement*, 12 November 1982).

Setting the question of *halal* meat for the moment on one side, Bradford's initiatives appear to be unexceptionable, combining, as they do, worthy objectives with publicity for parental rights under the law and sensible compromises on possible points for conflict. Moreover, the spirit pervading the city's policy is unwaveringly integrationist. Segregation and withdrawal are only recommended as last resorts; the authority remains convinced 'that, with sensitivity and a sympathetic understanding of cultural and religious issues, the educational needs of ethnic minority children can be met within the one educational system and within the framework of a common school curriculum'. The only ground for criticism might be timing. Bradford has had a 'multi-racial and multi-cultural population' for at least 20 years. Why did it take so long for a memorandum prescribing procedures on ethnic differences to appear? The answer does not seem to be, as one might have expected, the traditional reluctance of the LEA, under the British decentralized system, to be seen as telling individual headteachers and their staffs what to do. Bradford has long had a reputation for being a relatively prescriptive authority, and had policies on 'immigrant education' almost before any other. It was the first to implement dispersal in the early 1960s, in the interests of integration and equal opportunity, and the last to abandon it, in 1979. The memorandum represented not so much the introduction of official policy where previously there was none as a radical shift in policy direction, from integrationism to pluralism. The reason for the shift, at least in part, was the need to head off increasing Muslim demands for single-sex education and/or their own voluntary-aided schools (see Chapter 5). The memorandum certainly reads as having been addressed to the religious sensibilities of South Asians, and of Pakistani Muslims in particular.

Besides being long overdue, the Bradford memorandum appears to me to be open to criticisms of a different kind. It could have the unfortunate effect of placing South Asian pupils in a privileged position in relation to other pupils, and rather implies that religious sensibilities are more important than other kinds of sensibility. If I were a parent in Bradford, I would expect my children to have vegetarian options available at lunchtime (whether there were South Asians present in school or not) and to be informed of the right of withdrawal, on grounds of conscience, from religious worship and instruction. I would also want to press the authority on another issue. Many schools do not allow girls to wear trousers, or any pupil to wear jewellery, ornaments or headgear in the classroom. Is the implication of the memorandum that such rules should stand but be waived in the case of those who can, like Sikhs in respect of motorcycle helmets, produce a religious justification for not obeying them? If so, pupils brought up without benefit of religion (or having lapsed) would have good cause for complaint. I once taught in a school which forbade girls to wear trousers, and only grudgingly permitted female staff to do so, but made a blanket exception for all South Asian girls. Needless to say, this was an unpopular policy which created a good deal of resentment.

As for the decision to provide *halal* meat dishes in certain schools, it is hard not to be puzzled by it. Political considerations apart, there seems to be no reason for such a controversial concession to religious sensibility (the authority can hardly have been surprised by the level of protest), since Muslim children could either bring their own packed lunches or eat the vegetarian options already on the lunch menu.

Ours is at present a largely carnivorous society which has always accepted the ritual slaughter of animals in the preparation of *kosher* meat for Jews. So there can be no question of proscribing it for Muslims for the foreseeable future. However, it is also generally felt that if animals are to be killed for meat there are more humane ways of doing it. For the Bradford Metropolitan Council to have taken such a step, when it was neither necessary for Muslims nor welcome to many non-Muslims, was an act of curious insensitivity. At a time of increasing concern for animal rights – with teachers and pupils participating in various protest campaigns and rejecting lessons in animal dissection (one wonders if Bradford has drawn attention to children's rights in respect of the latter) – they appear to have gone out of their way to approve a cultural practice which many people regard as inhumane. They have since made another mistake, again under pressure from Muslim demands, by reneging on their commitment to a fully coeducational school system, even though these demands are unlikely to outlive the immigrant generation of Muslims in the city.

More generally, the Bradford memorandum illustrates the invidiousness of the 1944 Education Act's injunctions on religious worship and instruction. It was a Schools Council working paper on religious education which pointed out that there was 'something wrong with an aspect of the curriculum when it is expected at the outset that some parents and teachers will wish to opt out on *grounds of conscience*' (Schools Council, 1971, p.11). Happily a number of schools have found it possible to evade the injunctions with impunity.

Pluralism and the curriculum

Though raising important matters of principle, the aspects of school life covered by the Bradford memorandum are rather peripheral to the main business of teaching and learning. When we turn to the curriculum proper, we find the limits to pluralism even more clearly revealed. Almost everybody now agrees that the curriculum of all schools, irrespective of their ethnic composition, should reflect society's cultural diversity – a point first made publicly by the Ministry of Education's Pamphlet 43 in 1963 and repeated *ad nauseam* ever since. It is also pretty well agreed that the reflection of cultural diversity will affect some parts of the curriculum more than others because certain subjects – maths, the sciences, technology – are relatively culture-free.

The development of a multi-ethnic curriculum can, however, be justified without reference to pluralism. Pamphlet 43 saw it essentially in terms of curriculum relevance and enrichment; for the Ministry the cultures of immigrant children represented new sources of material which could be tapped to add meaning, interest and variety to the arts and humanities. There are other academic grounds as well. One very respectable way of looking at the curriculum is to say that it should include, in Matthew Arnold's famous phrase, 'the best that has been thought and known in the world'. Obviously this extends beyond the narrowly British or European. A well-founded and frequently voiced complaint in recent years has been that in practice the culture-bound areas of the curriculum, such as the arts and humanities, have been restricted in their scope to what falls within a white, male, middle-class world view. Children encountering curricula of this limited type could truly be described as culturally deprived since they have been kept in ignorance of important areas of human experience and achievement. Moreover, had schools serving multi-ethnic neighbourhoods been faithful to some of our most cherished educational axioms – starting where the children are, strengthening links with parents, using the local community as a resource – multi-ethnic curricula would have emerged as a matter of course. The curriculum should be multi-ethnic, it might be said, because life is. So much is generally agreed. Disagreement centres on the aims of a multi-ethnic curriculum and what pupils and teachers should make of the new (and existing) cultural material included.

A popular aim with the advocates of 'full-blooded' pluralism is cultural maintenance. They believe schools should provide opportunities for children from the ethnic minorities to master the cultures of their parents and grandparents. This aim seems to me both unattainable and undesirable. One can see how it might be contemplated in a separate subsystem, such as that of the Jews in London 100 years ago, or for religious minorities in the denominational sector or private schools of their own. And limited opportunities of a kind are already provided within ordinary county schools. Religious minorities are entitled to separate morning worship and religious instruction under the 1944 Education Act; and a number of local authorities have made premises available to minority communities in the evenings and at weekends for supplementary classes in language and religion. In addition, some LEAs have managed to broaden the repertoire of foreign-language teaching within the curriculum to embrace Italian, Greek, Urdu, Punjabi and so on when the ethnic composition of their schools demands it.

In Chapter 5 I made plain my opposition to segregated provision, as represented by the 'dual system', and, though I am certainly in favour of broadening the repertoire of foreign-language teaching, my immediate concern here is not with optional or extracurricular activities. My concern is the common curriculum which all children experience (or should experience) in common schools. Cultural maintenance is inconceivable in an integrated context; its realization conjures up instead a nightmare of separatism – Muslims being taught to be good Muslims in one classroom, Hindus to be good Hindus in another, Jews to be good Jews in a third. It also involves a peculiar way of looking at culture. Cultures are naturally dynamic and adaptive. I do not mean they are discontinuous with their origins or histories, but that they continually shift and evolve, discarding aspects of what is established or received and assimilating aspects of what is foreign and new. It is this process of cultural transformation that schools should facilitate and encourage, not cultural maintenance.

Cultural transformation will obviously be exaggerated and accelerated in interethnic encounters, with much cultural borrowing, exchange and hybridization. Signs of it are already apparent in contemporary Britain. Aspects of the cultures of recently settled ethnic minorities have been absorbed into the mainstream (one thinks of the impact of black music on youth culture, the popularity of Chinese, Indian and Italian cuisine, and the benefit many non-Hindus have derived from yoga and meditation). The ethnic minorities themselves have acculturated with remarkable speed to a society which is ethnically different, urban and industrial (or, to be precise, post-industrial). Advocates of cultural maintenance seem to be oblivious of what is happening now and is likely to happen in the future; or perhaps it is their objection to present trends and their fear for future prospects that have impelled them to champion a rival process akin to cultural ossification. The most plausible model for the future development of (say) cultures of South Asian origin is provided by the experience of British Jewry, which has undergone considerable anglicization over the generations and would have undergone even more had it not been for the Holocaust and the creation of Israel. My guess is that in the near future South Asians will be as well integrated economically, residentially and socially as Jews now are; that they will (like the Jews) have adopted English as their main language; and that they will have approximated to British norms on freedom and equality for women. On the other hand South Asian enclaves will remain as visible in many towns and cities as Jewish enclaves still are; and the survival of South Asian cultures will be as securely guaranteed as Jewish culture now is by the strength of commitment to religious institutional life and the tendency of the majority to marry 'in' rather than 'out'.

Advocates of cultural maintenance have dedicated a good deal of energy to the question of language. Clearly local authorities and schools should do everything practicable to provide opportunities for children from the linguistic minorities to increase their understanding and control of their communities' principal languages, including entry for O- and A-Level examinations. Apart from the matter of their rights, Britain would, culturally speaking, be a poorer place, were they to die out. Unfortunately I cannot share the pluralists' hopes for the survival of South Asian and other minority languages in Britain. The example of Welsh, which has the advantage of indigenous roots, hardly inspires optimism. Despite the increase in bilingual and Welsh-only schools, and the widespread use of Welsh in official settings and the media, the proportion of adult Welsh speakers has fallen from one in two in 1901 to less than one in five in 1981. Cut off from their roots in the Indian subcontinent and elsewhere, the languages of recently established ethnic minorities seem destined for a quicker and more drastic demise. I envisage a situation in which South Asians, for example, speak English first and foremost, comprehend something of the language of worship and their sacred texts (Quranic Arabic, for example), perhaps learn 'standard' Punjabi or Gujerati at school as an alternative to French or German and to a similar level of competence, and preserve vestiges of demotic for occasional domestic or informal use. However sound these various forecasts, one thing can be confidently predicted: as a result of the process of cultural transformation, there will soon be as many ways of being a British person of South Asian descent (maybe there already are) as there now are of being a British person of Jewish descent.

The principal drawback, however, to the philosophy of cultural maintenance is not its lack of realism, though that is certainly a serious weakness, but its moral unacceptability. It conflicts with one of our most fundamental 'minimal' values – the right of each individual to self-determination – and with one of our most widely held educational aims – teaching children to think for themselves. The Bradford memorandum argued that 'all sections of the community have an equal right to the maintenance of their distinctive identities and loyalties of culture, language, religion and custom'. It failed to add that individual members of these 'sections of the community' have an equal right not to maintain them should they so choose.

Several years ago I had a long interview with a 14-year-old Sikh girl during an evaluation of the multicultural humanities course she and her classmates were following. She had just completed some work on India which she saw as supplementing the knowledge she had gained from her parents and from a visit two years previously to her 'home' village in the Punjab. She began with some unflattering observations on the Raj – 'a disaster . . . they didn't give India a chance'. However, the iniquities of imperialism were nothing, in her eyes, compared with the iniquities of Western journalists and film-makers who insisted on giving 'a bad impression' of India by confining their attention to poverty and suffering. It was a point she reverted to more than once – 'they're not all beggars there', 'India was building temples and things like that when the British were thatching roofs'. Yet her opinion of classical Indian civilization was not entirely favourable. She detected absurdities in Hinduism and Sikhism – 'all those Gods', 'miracles' and the notion of 'divine punishment'. But she reserved the full vigour of her youthful disapprobation for what she saw as the discriminatory treatment of girls in Indian families. She objected repeatedly to the restraints imposed on her personal freedom, particularly in relations with the opposite sex. 'What's so wrong about talking to a boy?' 'It's silly when you think about it. It's really stupid.' 'The parents don't trust their kids in an Indian family.' 'You've got to try and get it into your parents' head that this is a different country.' Her experience had even affected her attitude towards Mrs Thatcher's becoming Prime Minister in 1979. Although she might be only 'good for the rich people', she was at least a woman and, more important, might with a bit of luck reduce the chances of being saddled with an Indian-born fiancé (a reference to the Conservative government's proposed changes to the immigration regulations). 'They're stupid. All they want is kids.' When I queried how representative her opinions were, she retorted passionately, 'You ask any Indian girl how she feels and she'll say the same'. What sustained her was the conviction that when her generation became parents there would be sweeping (but not too sweeping) changes. 'It is going to die out', she assured me.

Secondary school teachers would probably say that these judgements were typical of any callow British adolescent – hypercritical, overstated ('stupid' runs a close second to 'boring' for popularity in the teenager's lexicon of evaluation) and abrasive. Had I been her teacher, rather than a visiting researcher, I would have wanted to question her more closely on the basis for her assessments of the record of the Raj, the Western media's images of India and the absurdity of Indian religions, suggesting perhaps that she might like to reconsider them in the light of the evidence contained in her course. Furthermore, few teachers would want to have been associated with her disrespectful comments on her parents and Indian family life. On the other hand I would not have attempted to undermine her resolve to control her own destiny, nor discouraged her from the free play of the critical mind which her judgements in their own inchoate way exemplified. Independence of thought and action, which she associated (rightly or wrongly) with growing up and attending school in Britain rather than India, is the single most important educational goal in a liberal democracy. One route to achieving that goal is encouraging children to reflect critically upon their own cultural heritage and that of others. We are by now familiar with the idea that schools should engage pupils in critical revaluation of British culture – for example, in respect of the role of nationalism and imperialism in British history. Some cultural pluralists seem to have got into the illogical position of arguing that, while indigenous British culture should be subjected to rigorous scrutiny, the cultures of immigrant or ethnic minorities should be shielded or exempted or even held up for uncritical admiration because of their relative powerlessness or their vulnerability in the face of racism. In other words, my Sikh girl should have been encouraged to deepen and extend her critical appraisal of the Raj and the Western media's presentation of India but discouraged from applying a similar exercise to her own culture and (presumably) that of other ethnic minorities.

This kind of thinking explains the zeal with which several schools have latched on to Rastafarianism as a piece of cultural exotica to compensate for putatively negative self-images among West Indian children and the dearth of 'high' culture in the Caribbean. Black radicals have been quick to condemn this as control by cooption, neither better nor worse, only more insidious, than the control by exclusion exerted by other schools. Whatever the justice in this particular charge, the atavistic obscurantism of the Rastafarian creed (a weird farrago of Old Testament history, 'back to Africa' Garveyism and marijuana-based 'alternative' living) is very much in need of critical classroom attention, as is the whole reactionary 'roots' philosophy to which it belongs. Irked by its male chauvinism perhaps or by its pseudo-mystical waffle, West Indian girls (credited by Geoffrey Driver, Mary Fuller and others with a sharp awareness of social and economic realities) appear already to have submitted Rastafarianism to the test of common sense and found it wanting.

Anxiety to compensate for racism, and hence to promote more 'positive' images of the cultures of ethnic minorities, also explains some of the bland, nervous and evasive curriculum development spawned by the movement for multicultural education. ILEA's world history package of material on India, produced in 1974, restricted mention of the caste system to a single note for further reading, while commenting on the intercommunal massacre that accompanied and followed the partition of the Punjab and Bengal in 1947 as follows: 'It is *believed* that many thousands of people *may* have died in the violent clashes' (my emphases). Zulfikar Ghose in the poem at the beginning of this book refers to Sikhs and Muslims killing one another by 'the hundred thousand'; and the Penguin *History of India*, published four years before the ILEA package, described the massacre as a 'holocaust', placing the number of dead in the Punjab alone at half a million.

The proper aim of a multi-ethnic curriculum is not, as cultural pluralists fondly imagine, to prescribe the attitudes children ought to develop towards their own and other cultures (distorting content choice accordingly). Rather the aim is to provide children with the knowledge and skills to come to a critical understanding of the different cultures impinging upon them, so that they can decide for themselves which cultures, or parts of cultures, are worthy of admiration, allegiance and adoption. A multi-ethnic curriculum should enable them to answer for themselves the fundamental question: How shall I live? It will thereby also contribute to the process of cultural transformation described above.

Behind the cultural pluralists' concern to teach children sympathetic appreciation of cultures different to their own, is a perfectly legitimate educational aim. Of a piece with getting children to stand back a bit from their own culture is dissuading them from jumping in peremptorily with judgements on others. I have already noted that knowledge of a culture, and some insight into how it looks to those brought up within it, are necessary precursors to evaluation. This is essentially what Paul Zec means by 'weak' relativism – a combination of objectivity and empathy that does not renounce belief in 'trans-cultural criteria of rationality' and 'right conduct'. The difficulty of achieving such sympathetic appreciation in practice can be illustrated by the recent history of religious education. In the early 1970s a new approach to religious studies was developed by two Schools Council curriculum projects under the guidance of Ninian Smart at the University of Lancaster. These projects rejected the traditional 'confessional' promotion of a particular religious viewpoint, associated with the 1944 Education Act. They also rejected the merely informative alternative of comparative religious education, favoured by those secularists prepared to grant religious education any kind of place in the curriculum. Instead the Lancaster projects argued that children should be encouraged to participate imaginatively and empathetically in the 'subjectivity of others', learning what it actually feels like to be a Jew, Muslim or Hindu.

This 'phenomenological' approach has an obvious appeal: it avoids both the ethnocentricism of confessionalism and the arid 'naming of parts' of comparative religious education. Yet it poses problems of its own. While working on a television programme for an Open University course, the BBC producer and I accompanied a primary school class on a visit to a local *gurdwara* – one of a series of visits to religious institutions. On entry the children were asked to take off their shoes, cover their heads and (later) to kneel and bow down before the *Granth*, the Sikh holy book. I was quite happy to meet the first two requirements but declined to do the third. Afterwards I said to the class's teacher that I thought it wrong that the children should have been obliged to perform an act of worship as part of an educational visit. The BBC producer, a trained anthropologist, dissented. She maintained both that it was part of 'knowing what it is like to be Sikh' and that every faith has a right to set conditions for the entry of non-believers into its place of worship. I asked her whether she would also, on the basis of that argument, genuflect and cross herself on entering a Catholic church. 'Certainly,' she replied. My position was that the *gurdwara's* requirement on honouring the *Granth* exceeded what Sikhs had a right to expect from non-Sikhs as a mark of respect.

The Lancaster projects were not, however, manifestations of 'strong' relativism or 'full-blooded' pluralism. In addition to empathy or 'openness to the possibility of alternatives', they identified two further conditions for objectivity in religious education – evaluative criticism and academic freedom:

> It is not sufficient to parade alternatives before the eyes of the imagination and leave it at that, as if there were no objective ways of judging their relative truth or adequacy. The special function of academic communities is to create schemes for the critical evaluation of interpretations originating in non-academic communities . . . Although the various disciplines study different aspects of experience, they are united in a common loyalty to this principle of criticism, the search for consistency and adequacy in their interpretation of the data. That search must form an integral part of religious education in schools and, at the appropriate stages, pupils should be introduced to the methods of inquiry, and the language and the thought-forms, that are used in this kind of inquiry . . . Religious education is seen by many as the induction of the young into the beliefs and practices of a particular religious community, and its goal the perpetuation of that community. Although this process may be well suited to serve the special interests of a community of faith, it cannot be the basis for public education in a society composed of the adherents of many faiths and none.
>
> (Schools Council, 1971, pp.26–27)

What this might amount to in terms of curriculum practice can be illustrated by a simple example. Let us imagine that a teacher has decided, for sound academic reasons, to make a study of Hinduism with a third-year humanities class. One aim would be that the children should become knowledgeable about the oldest of the world's major faiths – in itself an ambitious target. The teacher might also want to draw their attention to particular aspects for admiration or appreciation and encourage them towards an empathetic grasp of what it is to be a Hindu. But the most important objective would be that, when it was all over, the children should be in a position to reflect critically on what they had learned, rather than merely adopting the teacher's enthusiasms or the devotee's perspectives – an objective equally applicable to any Hindu children there might be in the classroom. Unfortunately, although Hindu parents would no doubt welcome all children acquiring greater knowledge and appreciation of their faith, I cannot imagine too many being happy at the idea of Hinduism becoming a subject for the cut and thrust of critical classroom debate, let alone of their own children joining in and possibly rejecting the ancestral religion as a result. Nor can I imagine too many Muslim parents reconciled to the prospect of their children being exposed to Hinduism in this way.

Herein lies part of the problem for cultural pluralism. Most of Britain's ethnic minorities are religiously distinct. They are also religiously based. For several of them religious faith is woven into the very fabric of their culture. It is not extricable in the sense that the Anglican faith (though not, of course, the *Authorized Version of the Bible*, the *Book of Common Prayer* or

Hymns Ancient and Modern) is extricable from English culture. Generations of emotional investment are at stake. Because of a quirk of history, religion is enshrined in the school curriculum in Britain; religious worship and instruction are indeed the only two obligatory ingredients. They sit uneasily there, which is why so many schools have twisted and turned to adapt them to the aims of liberal education and to the realities of life in a multi-ethnic and largely secular society. The development of a multi-ethnic curriculum would be an altogether more straightforward business if we could somehow be disembarrassed of both.

The idea that religion has no place in the state school curriculum was one I encountered from a group of teachers in Poona, India, during a visit in 1979. When I asked them what they were doing to educate pupils for life in their particular multi-ethnic, multi-faith society, they recoiled with a mixture of horror and embarrassment as though the question were an indelicate one. Those who spoke were unanimous and emphatic that the school's business, apart from imparting knowledge and skills, was to encourage integration and national unity. The fostering of separate cultural identities was the business of the home and religious institutions. This was exactly the philosophy that prevailed when I was teaching in Kenya in the 1960s – preserving or promoting the cultural neutrality of the school in the interests of wider unity. It was also endorsed by the first Minister of Education in independent Zimbabwe. On taking up office in 1980 he commented: 'It is necessary for the people of Zimbabwe to evolve a Zimbabwean culture which transcends ethnic or regional barriers'. This particular brand of assimilationism has an understandable appeal for recently independent countries like India, Kenya and Zimbabwe, with histories of interethnic conflict. I think it is time for us to consider whether it does not have relevance for Britain and British schools too.

Developing a common culture through a common curriculum has long been an aim of liberal and radical educationalists – the 'public educators', Raymond Williams called them, in an analysis now more than 20 years old, but no less pertinent for that. What united them, he suggested, was belief in education as a human right, and among the founding fathers he identified was Matthew Arnold. Arnold's organizing principle for a common curriculum was the 'best that is known and thought in the world', which would certainly yield a multi-ethnic curriculum but seems today too preoccupied with content and the transmission of a body of knowledge. Williams proposed instead 'what a member of an educated and participatory democracy needs' (Williams, 1961 pp.125–154). From this vantage point any changes that might affect the content of culture-bound subjects of the curriculum as a result of multi-ethnic developments are less important than the manner in which children experience them. One of the most striking features of discussions on the multi-ethnic curriculum has been that methods of teaching and learning have been almost entirely ignored. The dominant assumption has been that it is simply a matter of exchanging the 'wrong' for the 'right' content. The outcome too often has been trivial or cosmetic change, replacing Tudors and Stuarts by African empires or Chinese dynasties – what Martin Ballard (1970) called 'juggling with the counters of learning'. In Kenya in the 1960s the literature, history and geography curricula were all Africanized but still taught in the old way – ingestion for regurgitation. More recently, in this country on a visit to a school's exhibition on the multi-ethnic curriculum, I asked a 12-year-old girl who had produced an admirable piece of work on the Indian independence movement what she had made of it all. 'Nothing much,' she replied, 'we only copied it down off the board.' She might just as well have studied the Tudors and Stuarts.

'What a member of an educated and participatory democracy needs' is not so much one content rather than another, but, as Raymond Williams recognized, extensive experience of, and practice in, democratic skills and procedures – in debating and listening to the opinions and experiences of others, and in learning to respect facts and tests for rationality, and to change one's mind in response to these. That is why it is hard to see a place for religion in a common curriculum for a common culture. I do not mean religion as fact, which can be included in history or humanities, but religion as faith and doctrine. The purpose of public education in a democracy is both to teach children to think for themselves and to initiate them into ways of deciding rationally what is true or false, right or wrong, good or bad. The purpose of religious education (for most religious people in Britain anyway) is to persuade children to accept certain propositions about life and morality, by reference not to rational criteria, but to the scheme of a deity or deities as revealed through prophets, sacred texts or earthly representatives.

The incompatibility of democratic and religious education (in this sense) was brought home to me while working on the Open University film referred to earlier, and is vividly illustrated in the film itself. One sequence shows a multi-ethnic primary school class engaged in a comparison of different marriage customs – studying individually, in pairs or in groups; writing, reading, painting, discussing; sitting, standing, moving around, querying a point with the teacher; all the general hubbub of an active British classroom. Another sequence shows some of the Muslim children in that class back at school in the evening for a Quran lesson – ranged in rows round the *imam*, chanting responses in unison, learning by rote. Primary school teachers who object to Muslim children attending Quran classes in the evening do so, in my experience, as much because of the reactionary pedagogy employed there, which they see as undermining what they are trying to achieve during the day, as because of the extra hours of study (often two or three per evening) imposed upon the children.

The Lancaster projects tried to solve this problem by replacing confessionalism (represented in my example by the Quran class) with a combination of teaching for empathetic understanding and subjecting religions to critical evaluation in the classroom. Laudable as this enterprise was, I do not see how it could possibly succeed. Brought up without benefit of religion, I have struggled over the years to familiarize myself with the tenets and rituals of the world's major faiths. Though I can appreciate what motivates or impels the religious spirit – the mystery of existence, the beauty of the world, fear of death – I cannot see an objective reason for subscribing to any of the organized world religions that I am familiar with. The only possible exception might be the Christian Society of Friends, which has at least institutionalized democratic values and procedures. Nor do I see how religious faiths can be fully incorporated into the forum of classroom debate, for they do not acknowledge the publicly accredited criteria for distinguishing truth from falsehood and right from wrong as ultimate arbiters. Moreover, there would be a serious risk of the religious sensibilities of both children and their parents being bruised in the process.

The secularization of the curriculum seems to me to be the only solution. The development of multi-ethnic content for culture-bound subjects could then go forward without impediment to the free play of the critical mind. In addition, this alliance of ethnic diversity and democratic skills could form the basis for a new common culture which could claim cultural neutrality because it had drawn on a variety of traditions yet was in the interests of all. Obviously it would be predominantly British in focus, since that is where we are, but British in the redefined sense (including rather than excluding ethnic minorities) intended by Bhikhu Parekh. This brand of assimilationism is preferable both to the kind that flourished in the 1960s and to the currently popular pluralism.

CHAPTER 7

COMBATING RACISM

> If people would but leave children to themselves; if teachers would cease to bully them; if parents would not insist upon directing their thoughts and dominating their feelings . . . If, I say, parents and masters would leave their children alone a little more, – small harm would accrue . . .
>
> (W.M. Thackeray, 1848, *Vanity Fair*)

> If liberty means anything at all it means the right to tell people what they do not want to hear.
>
> (George Orwell, 1945, Preface to *Animal Farm*)

The idea that schools and local authorities should assemble a systematic response to the phenomenon of racism is a fairly recent one. Of more venerable lineage are narrower educational programmes designed specifically to dispel or reduce racial prejudice. These were developed principally in the United States after the Second World War as adjuncts to psychological investigations of the nature of prejudice directed against Jews and American blacks. Though open to criticism for being short-term and isolated, they were at least evaluated, which is more than can be said for most initiatives in multicultural education. The findings were, on the whole, depressing, with little impact made on deep-seated hostilities and some reports of counter-productive outcomes. However, a measure of success was claimed for strategies that went beyond the instructional or informative to involve members of different groups affectively in simulations and shared tasks (Allport, 1954). There has been one major British contribution to this tradition: the research of Lawrence Stenhouse and his colleagues into the effectiveness of different strategies for teaching race relations to adolescents.

The Stenhouse research

Stenhouse's research originated in the work of the Schools Council's Humanities Curriculum Project (HCP) (1967–1972) of which he was director. The HCP was intended for 14–16-year-olds, with the raising of the school-leaving age in 1972 in view. Its aim was to 'enhance understanding and judgement in those areas of practical living which involve complex considerations of value'. The areas initially identified were war, education, the family, poverty, relations between the sexes, living in cities, law and order, and people and work. A collection of 'value-balanced' printed and visual material attempted to represent the scale and character of the debate on each particular topic. This material was subsequently tested in a wide range of trial schools. The other distinguishing feature of HCP was the pedagogic principle of 'procedural neutrality'. The role of the teachers was to chair discussions on the materials without imposing or even intruding their own opinions. The hope was that the assumption of a non-authoritarian role would render simple-minded conformity and rebellion on the part of pupils equally unlikely, thereby facilitating the search for truth and fostering their own autonomy. This did not mean that the teachers were to abrogate all their normal responsibilities. They were expected to aim for orderly and purposeful discussions, querying and challenging where necessary, restraining the voluble and encouraging the diffident, above all trying to get their pupils to submit to 'the discipline of the evidence'. Their task was summarized as 'the development of open, coherent, and rigorous enquiry'. Clearly being procedurally neutral in chairing discussions of value-balanced materials was not the same as being value-free: 'education is committed to a preference for rationality rather than irrationality, imaginativeness rather than unimaginativeness, sensitivity rather than insensitivity. It must stand for respect for persons and readiness to listen to the views of others' (Stenhouse, 1969; Parkinson and MacDonald, 1972; Ruddock, 1983).

Belatedly the HCP team added the topic of race to the controversial issues already identified. Recognizing that it might prove particularly difficult to handle in the classroom, they proceeded with caution, undertaking a small feasibility study in six schools before deciding to go ahead with production and dissemination. However, in January 1972 the Schools Council's programme committee rejected what came to be known as the 'race pack' (the first time any of its projects' materials had met such a fate). They did this apparently because the teachers unions' representatives on the committee found some of the ingredients extremist and doubted whether the topic of race was really amenable to the HCP approach. Stenhouse and colleagues then refined and expanded their materials in a further project entitled 'The Problems and Effects of Teaching about Race Relations', funded jointly by the Gulbenkian Foundation and the Social Science Research Council between 1972 and 1975. Its aim was to explore the possibilities of three different strategies for teaching about race relations: the HCP strategy of procedural neutrality; the more 'positive' strategy of the 'committed' teacher; and the use of drama.

Like their American antecedents, the two Stenhouse projects stressed the importance of evaluation. The evaluation of the 'race pack' in 1970, and of the three strategies of the later project in 1974, is about all that exists in the way of descriptions and assessments of innovations in multi-ethnic education in Britain. Rather surprisingly both projects persevered with the American practice of administering attitude scales to the students before and after the teaching and comparing the results for experimental and control groups. I say 'surprisingly' because Stenhouse was one of the foremost critics of the behaviourist school of rational curriculum planning, and because controlled experiments and attitude scales did not seem exactly in tune with the open-ended humanism of the HCP philosophy. One of the five major premises of the HCP was that 'the discussion should protect divergence of view among participants'. For what they are worth, the 1970 findings showed 'small but significant shifts in the direction of tolerant attitudes in the post-test situation' for the experimental but not the control groups. The 1974 findings revealed 'a high incidence of negative shifts in the control groups' for both 'committed' and HCP pedagogies, 'compared with a high incidence of positive shifts in the experimental groups'. In other words, if one wishes to make students in the 14–16 age-range less racially prejudiced and more racially tolerant, it is better to teach about race relations than not to, and it does not much matter whether one adopts the strategy of 'neutral' chairman or 'committed' teacher. In the case of drama, the tentative conclusion was that, while attitudes are unlikely to deteriorate as a consequence, it is equally unlikely to be sufficient on its own.

However, the researchers were quick to qualify their general conclusions: 'these broad results mask the tendency of individual schools and individual pupils' ('a fairly substantial minority') 'to change counter to the general tendency'. It would have been surprising, they added, had this not been so, since there is a limit to what schools can realistically purport to accomplish in the fight against racism; there would also have been grounds for disquiet 'on educational grounds if the values, attitudes or outlooks of all our students moved in the direction desired by the teacher'. Nevertheless it was anxiety about counterproductive effects which lay behind some of the reservations expressed by the Schools Council's programme committee in 1972 and explains why so many secondary schools continue to give teaching about race relations a wide berth (Verma and Bagley, 1979; Stenhouse et al., 1982).

Of greater interest and relevance than the experimental data, with their arid calculations of statistical significance, were the case studies of individual classrooms generated by both phases of the research. The concern displayed by Stenhouse and colleagues for the autonomy of pupils was complemented by their concern for the autonomy of teachers. They encouraged the teachers involved in the trials to tape-record their lessons, thereby involving them more actively than normal in the business of classroom research and curriculum evaluation. Self-evaluation was the ideal, and regarded as integral and essential to professional development. One of the published case studies (presented jointly by the teacher and the HCP evaluator) was from the feasibility investigation of the 'race pack' carried out in 1970. The school was a boys' secondary modern in the Midlands. Over 60 percent of its 600 pupils were 'Commonwealth immigrants' according to the official definition of the time, and most of these were South Asians. Both curriculum and discipline were 'traditional' and the 'overwhelming view' among the staff was that 'the best approach to race relations was to play it down'. The discussion group comprised half of the top form in the fourth year and included roughly equal numbers of English and South Asian pupils. The teacher, who had no experience of working within the HCP philosophy, was faced with a number of problems during the six weeks of the course: what to regard as acceptable language; how to draw out reticent pupils and restrain loquacious ones; how to respond to the character assassination of the unrepresented West Indian community indulged in by English and South Asian pupils alike. But the biggest strain on his 'procedural neutrality' was imposed by a debate on a verbatim report of one of Enoch Powell's 1968 speeches on immigration. It was acrimonious, racially polarized and hard to control. Yet the pupils assured both teacher and evaluator afterwards that no harm had been done to inter-racial friendships; all had been given and taken in good part. They also claimed (and were supported by the evidence of the tests administered) that the discussions had made no impact on their attitudes though their understanding had certainly been enhanced (Parkinson and MacDonald, 1972).

The teacher in another case study, taken from the 1974 evaluation of the later Stenhouse research, encountered similar problems over language, responding to prejudiced utterances and the general control of the discussion in a more 'liberal' school with a 'prevailing ethos of reasonableness and rationality'. He differed from the first teacher in being both a 'fervent exponent of', and considerably experienced in, neutral chairmanship; and his group of fourth formers from a Yorkshire mining village were all white. He opted for permissiveness both in regard to his pupils' choice of language, since they applied labels like 'wog' and 'blackie' descriptively not derogatorily, and in regard to the direction of the discussion:

> In a sense it would be true to say that the structure and logical progression of conventional teaching was abandoned as the price to be paid for giving pupils the opportunity to follow their own, particular interests. To suggest to them that there might be a correct order and content could imply that they should also accept a 'correct' set of opinions . . . If pupils are to be given the opportunity to explore their attitudes in any area of controversy, they need to feel free and secure in their ability to express themselves.

'Inelegant' as certain passages of discussion may have been, he felt able to conclude:

> . . . this particular group came to an awareness of the limitations of their own knowledge and understanding . . . and indicated that they were learning to think rationally for themselves rather than to accept passively all that they were told . . . [This] strategy for teaching about race relations . . . cannot claim to be a way of systematically changing opinion. However, it does seem to be consistent with the concept of a society . . . in which the individual has, in the last resort, the freedom to choose.
>
> (Sikes and Sheard, 1978; Stenhouse et al., 1982, pp.234–256)

The Stenhouse research has yet to be accorded due recognition in the field of multicultural education. This is not entirely surprising for on the face of things its contribution to combating racism appears to be slight. Its strengths – the importance attached to developing rationality and autonomy in both teacher and pupil – are of a more general kind. Because they embody some of the virtues of a participatory democracy, 'of a society . . . in which the individual has, in the last resort, the freedom to choose', I shall be using them here as touchstones against which to judge the validity of more recent anti-racist ventures.

The emergence of anti-racism

Anti-racism as a self-conscious educational ideology first emerged in the 1970s. In the early years of the decade an organization called Teachers Against Racism flourished briefly; it was later followed by others such as

Teachers Against the Nazis and All London Teachers Against Racism and Fascism. Anti-racism marked itself off from the liberal tradition of teaching about race relations, exemplified by the Stenhouse research, and from the publicly advocated (but little implemented) integrationist policy of infusing the curriculum with cultural diversity. These were held to be all very well in their own way but inadequate for the pressing task of eradicating racism from the education system and combating negative influences on children in the wider society. In the 1980s anti-racism has made major political advances, recently capturing ILEA, other Labour-controlled local authorities and the influential National Association for Multiracial Education, previously a bastion of multiculturalism.

A number of factors can be detected behind the origin and growth of anti-racism in the 1970s. First, there was the accumulating evidence of underachievement among West Indians. Second, there was David Milner's replication of American research into racial identification and preference on British 5–8-year-olds in the late 1960s. Originally reported in *New Society* in 1971, his findings demonstrated the early onset of racial, and indeed racist, attitudes, with a disquietingly high proportion of West Indian and South Asian children also betraying symptoms of self-rejection (Milner, 1975). Ten years later Alfred Davey and colleagues repeated the experiment, using different tests on a slightly older age-range (7–11-year-olds), and found that although self-rejection had considerably diminished, the level of stereotyping and ethnocentricism displayed by whites, West Indians and South Asians had not (Davey and Norburn, 1980; Davey and Mullin, 1982).

By this time attention had rather shifted from the embryonic racism of infant and junior schoolchildren to the virulent racialism of white, male, working-class adolescents. This provided the third main reason for the growth of the anti-racist ideology in education. White adolescent racialism was popularly associated with the recrudescence of neo-Fascist groups such as the National Front, whose ranks were swelled by dissident Tories after the Conservative government's decision to admit the Ugandan Asians expelled by Idi Amin in 1972. No doubt the far Right, with its overtones of anti-establishment militarism, did make successful appeals to disaffected youth in the recruiting campaigns launched outside football grounds and at rock concerts. But 'Paki bashing' antedated the rise of the National Front and continued after the National Front and the other extremist parties of the far Right had reverted to their customary fissiparous insignificance, following the Conservative electoral victory in 1979 and Mrs Thatcher's promises of even tighter immigration controls. Evidence on the prevalence of these three phenomena – black underachievement, the incipient racism of young children and the full-blown racialism of adolescents (whether associated with the fleeting resurgence of neo-Fascism or not) – has figured prominently in the anti-racist argument that what ILEA has called the 'central and pervasive influence of racism' demands a more forthright, purposeful and unremitting response than has so far been attempted.

The meaning of racism in the context of education

One of the problems anti-racists have in sounding convincing is that racism is used in education, as elsewhere, to cover a multitude of sins. The charge has been levelled at individual teachers and pupils, at schools as institutions and at the entire education system. These different uses need to be identified and distinguished from one another. First of all there is racism in the classical sense of a set of beliefs, largely of nineteenth-century origin, about the categorization, characterization and evaluation of human beings on the basis of their physical appearance ('scientific' racism). Second, there are the unflattering or hostile prejudices and stereotypes an individual may entertain about groups to which he or she does not belong ('popular' racism). Third, there are acts of discrimination, intimidation and violence, which some commentators prefer to describe as racialism rather than racism because they are seen as 'behaviour' rather than 'opinions' or 'attitudes'.

Finally, there is the vexed question of 'institutional' racism. I have already expressed my reservations about this addition to the vocabulary of race relations. Its shortcomings as a tool of analysis in the field of education are only too apparent. Whereas it is relatively clear how 'scientific' and 'popular' racism might manifest themselves in schools – in the attitudes and behaviour of teachers and pupils, in the curriculum and other aspects of school policy – what institutional racism refers to remains as obscure as in other spheres. ILEA's *Policy for Equality* defines it vaguely as a 'web of discriminatory policies, practices and procedures' whose consequence is that 'black people have poorer jobs, health, housing, education and life chances than do the white majority and less influence on the political and economic decisions which affect their lives'. The trouble with this definition is that it is based on a generalized picture of black people's position in society which the evidence cited in Chapters 1 and 3 has shown to be decidedly suspect. Matters have been further obscured in some quarters by the tendency to use 'institutional' racism to refer to patterns of inequality in outcome rather than, or in addition to, the policies, practices and procedures that are alleged to produce them. A good example would be the degree of black underachievement at 16+ revealed by the survey of school leavers in six LEAs undertaken by the DES for the Rampton Committee in 1978–1979 (see Chapter 3). For some this underachievement is per se an indication of institutional racism irrespective of what might have caused it. However, it may (just possibly) be wholly unrelated to 'scientific' and 'popular' racism; or (more probably) racism in these senses may be only one factor in its complex aetiology. Institutional racism has also been applied to curriculum or organizational policy which is inappropriate to a multi-ethnic society. Again, it has to be queried whether this is a useful or valid characterization. Syllabuses in literature, geography and history which limit their choice of content to the British or European are more likely to be reflections of parochialism, teacher ignorance or sheer curriculum inertia, than of anything that could fairly be construed as racism. Similarly, failure to make concessions to ethnic minorities in such areas as school uniform or dress could be motivated as much by a wish not to be seen to favour them, as by antagonism towards them or any belief in the inferiority of their cultures.

Some discussions of institutional racism have compounded the confusion by attaching the phrase to manifestations of racism in the other senses (notably in respect of teachers' attitudes) or by using it to refer to just about anything in the education system the writer or speaker happens to dislike. The book accompanying the recent BBC series on multicultural education has a section on institutional racism which defines it, rather like the ILEA policy document, in terms of 'matters of political power, hierarchy and status. It is the form in which we can be party to racism without being racially prejudiced in our personal relationships.' Thirty-three examples are then listed which emanated from the discussion of a group of Yorkshire teachers during a 'racism awareness' workshop. Most of them are instances of teacher inactivity, insensitivity or ineptitude. Whether they are hypothetical or drawn from actual experience is not made plain. Though almost all are certainly reprehensible, the link with racism (to say nothing of 'political power, hierarchy and status') is in many cases tenuous. I have pencilled 'not necessarily racist' against over half in the margin of my copy of the book. 'Describe an English village' may be an asinine essay title, and confounding 'inadequate English' with 'slow learning' may be a serious pedagogic error (examples 8 and 14 respectively), but to call them 'racist' is to devalue and trivialize the concept itself. Moreover, the second example on the Yorkshire teachers' list – treating all children the same – seems to me to be, if anything, anti-racist. It is their preferred strategy which is racist, in the classical sense: 'for black children, school should support awareness and pride that "Black is beautiful" – or more powerfully, that they are part of the Black Consciousness – as much as it should make white children feel it's good to be white, in some of its own ways, too' (Twitchin and Demuth, 1981, pp. 166–169). School should do no such thing. 'Education', observed Stenhouse and colleagues, 'is committed to a preference for rationality rather than irrationality.' Young people who emerge from school believing it is right and proper to evaluate themselves and others on the basis of skin colour have been grievously miseducated. As to whether black children should regard themselves as 'part of the Black Consciousness' (whatever that may be), that is for them to decide individually.

Anti-racism as obfuscation

Preoccupation with racism to the exclusion of all else, and with outcomes and effects rather than intentions or causation, goes some way to explaining why anti-racists have so frequently misidentified the nature of the problem to be addressed and been found fighting the wrong battle. Take, for example, one frequently cited instance of institutional racism – the congregation of black pupils in bottom streams or sets. Anti-racists are likely to argue not only that this is racist per se, but that it should be replaced by an arrangement which guarantees proportional representation. In fact the over-representation of black pupils in bottom streams or sets is not necessarily a manifestation of racism. No one *knows* why it occurs. The explanation is probably multifactoral and could well include factors falling outside the senses of racism defined earlier. Nor is such over-representation necessarily a manifestation of racial inequality. Working-class pupils have long been shown to 'percolate downwards' through streaming and setting systems. As most black pupils are working class, their position could simply be a more visible representation of this long-standing tendency.

The impression conveyed by the anti-racist argument is that all would be well if black pupils were distributed evenly across forms and sets. Given willingness on the part of the authorities, this outcome could no doubt be readily secured, but only at the expense of undermining the basis of streaming and setting which is supposed to be some kind of objective assessment of ability or aptitude. Moreover it would leave untouched the position of working-class pupils who were not black, and would mean that other children would have to be relegated to make room for the black pupils promoted. In other words the complexion or identity of those suffering the indignity of bottom streams or sets would be changed but the numbers would not. The problem is not that more black children are to be found there than one would expect from their proportion in the overall pupil population, but that any child of whatever colour or ethnic background should be exposed to such public humiliation and to the risk of depressed academic performance that is widely believed to be associated with it.

Similarly, anti-racists have been known to complain that voluntary schools situated in multi-ethnic neighbourhoods too often have fewer pupils from the ethnic minorities than would have been expected had a strict catchment area policy of school allocation been in operation; they have appeared to imply that under-representation is the extent of the problem to be rectified. Sometimes, as I have indicated in Chapter 5, under-representation is certainly at least partly the result of church complicity in the racism of white parents anxious to reduce the incidence of contacts between their children and black people. However, it could also simply be a reflection of admissions policy favouring the faithful. Increasing the proportion of ethnic minority children attending voluntary schools could only come about as a consequence of a reversal of admissions policy (since so many of them are neither Christians nor Jews), which would no doubt somewhat affect the schools' role as institutions to preserve the faith. Yet, even were this to happen, the dual system would remain intact, arbitrarily dividing the nation's young. As in the case of streaming and setting, the problem is not so much the position occupied by pupils from the ethnic minorities, as the invidiousness of the system which their presence has served to highlight.

The superficiality of analysis that can result from a preoccupation with racism is even more evident when we consider those in the field of education who are alleged to be its perpetrators – individual teachers and pupils. In Chapter 3 I commented on the flimsiness of the evidence adduced to substantiate the assertion that the teaching profession is riddled with racism. Most of it is at least 10 years old, anecdotal and dependent on what teachers say in staffrooms or write in response to questionnaires. Very little derives from close observation of teachers in classroom interactions with pupils from the ethnic minorities. One piece of research undertaken in the early 1970s which does fall into this category was Martyn Hammersley's study of a downtown secondary modern school. Hammersley, it will be remembered, queried whether it was right to interpret staffroom outbursts of hostility against West Indians simply at face value. They were, he suggested, partly expressions of resentment at the loss in prestige which these teachers saw as attendant upon the 'changing character of the pupil intake' (Hammersley, 1981).

Paul Willis's (1977) study of a counter-school culture among white working-class boys reached a similar conclusion: 'Many senior staff associate the mass immigration of the 1960s with the break up of the "order and quietness" of the 1950s and of . . . their peaceful, successful schools'. He also noted a curious collusion between the staff and his group of anti-school boys. Despite the teachers' publicly stated opposition to racism, they shared with the 'lads' a sense 'of resentment for the disconcerting intruder'. These studies by Willis and Hammersley are now a decade old. They were undertaken at a time when immigration was a major political issue and Powellism a significant force. Since then both immigration and Powellism have rather receded from the national consciousness. Unfortunately there have been no recent studies to compare with those of Willis and Hammersley and which might enable us to arrive at a more up-to-date assessment of the extent and nature of racism among teachers.

The same is true of racism among pupils where even the impressionistic picture is sketchy. Once again Willis provides some useful insights, at least so far as the racism of white, working-class, male adolescents is concerned. It was one ingredient (albeit not as potent as sexism or the cult of violence) in the 'lads' ' subculture. Willis noted a clear distinction between the racism they directed against West Indians on the one hand, and against South Asians on the other hand. Though West Indians might be resented sexually and dismissed as 'thick', they occupied similar cultural ground and came off a good deal better in the 'lads' ' estimation than the reviled South Asians who were perceived as 'ear 'oles' (i.e. conformist and pro-school), culturally alien and overambitious. As a result it was the South Asians who became 'the target for petty intimidation, small pestering attacks, and the physical and symbolic jabbing at weak or unprotected points in which "the lads" specialise' (Willis, 1977, pp.47–49). I think it would be generally agreed that the problem of racism (or racialism) in school is principally represented by boys like Willis's 'lads' – the disaffected unclubbables, or what the Home Office (1981b) report *Racial Attacks* rather coyly refers to as 'white youths of the skinhead fraternity'.

Yet there has been very little attempt to follow Willis in investigating the significance of such racism. The Home Office report makes the important point that it is in a sense incidental, for even if there were no ethnic minorities in Britain or racialist organizations to latch on to, these boys would still constitute a problem: 'The criminality of youthful hooliganism has worn many different fashions over the past twenty years and combating one particular fashion will not necessarily tackle the violence which uses racialism as the present means through which to express it' (Home Office, 1981b, pp.30–31). 'Paki-bashers' are very unlikely to be just 'Paki-bashers'; their addiction to violence finds its victims throughout the ranks of the weak and unwary. To the extent that they do join racialist organizations (they are notoriously fickle in their loyalties), it is not so much the racist ideology that draws them into the fold as the paraphernalia of membership, the prospect of violence and the general aura of anti-establishment disreputability and defiance. On the other hand there are pupils in school who could be described without exaggeration as budding racist psychopaths. Bob Brett, a teacher in London's East End, has characterized them as follows: 'In every school there are children for whom being racist is central to their sense of their own value. On the whole they are the most pathetic and inadequate kids, those kids that have got so little going for them that they will clutch at anything that will give them a sense of their own worth' (Brett, undated). In other words the racists themselves are as much a social and educational problem as the racialist behaviour they exhibit.

Anti-racism as illiberalism

The main reservations to be expressed about anti-racism concern recent initiatives by a few local authorities and schools which appear to threaten the autonomy of teachers and pupils and to evoke the spectres of indoctrination and totalitarianism. The most blatant example involves the London Borough of Brent. In 1983 its Labour-controlled council announced that, in the event of not enough teachers volunteering for 'racism awareness' courses, it would consider making attendance compulsory. Furthermore, willingness to attend would in future be made a condition of all new appointments to the borough's staff. This stipulation represents a gross infringement of teachers' rights. Traditionally, teachers have attended those in-service courses they thought would benefit their professional development, which is not to say that headteachers or advisers have not drawn their attention to particular courses and encouraged them to attend. But to make a course mandatory, or to make a new appointment conditional on attendance, is quite simply not compatible with education in a democracy – in a society where 'the individual has, in the last resort, the freedom to choose'. Nor for that matter, in this instance, is the course itself. Indeed it is peculiarly apt that courses in 'racism awareness training' should be made obligatory for they do not appear to attach any great importance to individuals thinking for themselves; and it is hard to imagine many self-respecting teachers attending courses bearing such a sinister title of their own accord.

The description of the racism awareness workshop attended by the Yorkshire teachers in the BBC book on multicultural education suggests that the title is by no means misplaced. Conclusions were unmistakably foregone. 'To gain an understanding of the nature and effects of institutional racism' ran the second of three aims. What happened, one wonders, to those (like me) who doubted whether institutional racism was a viable concept and whether the supposed manifestations of it eventually listed were necessarily in many cases even related to racism? The overall impression conveyed is that, notwithstanding the seemingly open-ended exercises in self-exploration, the participants were expected to reach predetermined (and distinctly simple-minded) conclusions: that deep-down they and their schools were racist; that racism is something white people do to black people; that in Britain white people have power while black people do not; that racism and racial inequality are endemic in Britain and inextricably bound in with the histories of slavery and empire; and that institutional racism is more important than other forms. There was no hint of recognition that racism might also be something that West Indians do to South Asians and vice versa, nor that the Irish, Jews and Gypsies might be victims too. The participants appear to have been subjected to a brand of the Marxist version of racism (admittedly somewhat diluted and vulgarized) purveyed through the unlikely methodology of encounter group behaviourism. Those running the course remain elusive. Who were they? Was this another instance (they are plentiful in the anti-racist field) of the self-appointed enlightened few presuming to 'raise the consciousness' of the unenlightened multitude? (Twitchin and Demuth, op. cit., pp.161–173).

Illiberalism is also a feature of several of the recently promulgated anti-racist guidelines and policy documents. But what is more striking is that they should also have found it necessary to state that certain forms of behaviour which have always been regarded as unacceptable and intolerable should be outlawed and punished. I have not worked in a school in which personal abuse, insulting graffiti, bullying and physical assaults were held to be anything other than serious disciplinary offences. Yet the NUT, ILEA and a number of schools have all been moved to state publicly that racialist behaviour of these kinds should be proscribed and the perpetrators chastised. I am puzzled by their motivation, for such an unwarranted intervention could well be taken to imply that racialist bullying is more reprehensible than bullying which is not racialist – surely an untenable position.

The absurdity of this position can be readily illustrated from the chapter in the BBC's book describing a school policy on racism. A London teacher, Shaun Doherty, emphasizing the necessity systematically to confront racist remarks, quotes the following example from his own experience:

> 'You fucking paki curry eater, I'll kill you.' When I heard this remark in a second year class I was doubly disturbed because it combined racist abuse . . . with an apparent threat of physical violence. I stopped the lesson and called the speaker out to the front, making my own sense of outrage clear to the rest of the class. This was necessary to reassure the pupil at the receiving end of such language that teachers are not neutral to it, and are ready to protect any pupil from apparent physical threats. I then publicly explained why his remarks were offensive to me; fortunately he was receptive to argument and in fact was ready subsequently to apologise.
>
> (Twitchin and Demuth, op.cit., pp.111–112)

The teacher appears to believe that other members of the profession (including me, to judge by a reference to my book *Positive Image*) would find the abuse quoted acceptable classroom behaviour. If so, I have yet to meet such teachers. More to the point is whether his own behaviour would have been different had the abuse not been racist. Let us suppose that the pupil had shouted instead 'You fucking fat bastard' or 'You fucking four-eyed git'. Would he have reacted any differently? If so, how would he have justified this to children, with their keenly developed sense of fair play? If not, why has he made such an issue out of behaviour which all teachers would find intolerable and would seek to control?

Later in the chapter the same teacher gives what he calls 'a less obvious, and more typical, example' of racism about which teacher opinion would be far from unanimous. A fourth-year boy is quoted as saying: 'Sir, I think black people should be sent back home because this country is overcrowded'. Doherty is less explicit about exactly how he responded than in the first example, but his comment conveys some impression of what ensued:

> If I had failed to respond to such a view with the facts to indicate the ignorance, as well as insensitivity, it is based on, I would be guilty of fostering racist attitudes through omission. Silence may not imply agreement, but it does imply no serious disagreement, and so serves to create an atmosphere in which racist attitudes are apparently an acceptable part of classroom discourse. The intervention need not be heavy and should seek to win over the

offender, but it is so important that the teacher makes his or her attitudes clear.

(Twitchin and Demuth, op.cit., p.112)

Doherty fails to make the crucial point that the offending remark here belongs to a quite different category to the one in the first example. It is not racialist abuse but an expression of political opinion. As such it should certainly be expected to submit to the 'discipline of the evidence', though what the relevant facts are we are not told. I can imagine inviting the author of the remark to reconsider his opinion in the light of information about Britain's black population and the likely problems and effects of implementing his proposal. Conceivably, he might modify it as a result to the kind of voluntary repatriationism favoured by some members of the Conservative Party. But I cannot imagine impressing upon him that his view ('racist attitude' seems a bit of an overstatement) was an unacceptable part of 'classroom discourse'. As the Stenhouse research implicitly recognized, the classroom is precisely the place where adolescents should be encouraged to express and explore opinions on controversial issues such as race and immigration, for it is there that democratic procedures are most likely to be respected and tests of rationality most rigorously applied.

For some reason anti-racists appear to lose faith in normal democratic practice when it comes to engaging with racist opinions and beliefs. For example, several local authority and school anti-racist policies state that racist literature should be confiscated. One quotes the following extracts from a National Front leaflet found in school:

> 'Unfortunately, East End discos are very much multi-racial. White youths entering a discotheque in the East End might be approached by a gang of blacks who ask for some money, if the white refuses he would very probably be "done over". . . . We in the Young National Front think it's time that discos in East London and the whole of Great Britain were designed for us. They should not be designed especially for black invaders. . . . The YNF will welcome all young patriots to one of our "ALL WHITE" discos.'
>
> 'The National Front wants Britain to remain a white country and for this reason it opposes all coloured immigration to Britain. Furthermore, the National Front wants to send all coloured people back home, to their own countries, by the most humane means possible.'
>
> (Quoted in NUT, 1983, p.17)

The justification given for confiscation in this instance is that such literature is like pornography – 'directly offensive and degrading to many of our pupils'. In fact the extracts quoted are decidedly *un*like pornography. The closest approximation to racialist abuse is the phrase 'black invaders'. Essentially they amount, like the fourth-year boy's remark quoted earlier, to an expression of opinion, here on the desirability of all-white youth clubs and an all-white Britain. In other words, they are an example of the type of 'racialist propaganda' that successive governments have consistently refused to include under the offence of incitement to racial hatred. 'False and evil publications of this kind,' argued the 1975 Home Office White Paper *Racial Discrimination*, 'may well be more effectively defeated by public education and debate . . . Due regard must also . . . be paid to allowing the free expression of opinion.'

Five years later a Green Paper amplified on the threat to democracy posed by proscription:

> It would make no allowance for genuine discussion and debate or for academic consideration of such proposals. To single out political proposals for proscription by law regardless of how they are expressed, and in what circumstances, and of the possible consequences would be a new departure. In the Government's view such a departure would be totally inconsistent with a democratic society in which – provided the manner of expression, and the circumstances, do not provoke unacceptable consequences – political proposals, however odious and undesirable, can be freely advocated.
>
> (Home Office, 1980, para.112)

The critical point is that pupils should feel free to express their opinions in the classroom, no matter what their political or ideological content may be, learning at the same time (one hopes) to test them out against publicly accredited criteria of truth and rationality and to observe the rules of democratic procedure. It would, of course, be naive not to recognize that, where the content is racist, particularly fraught classroom moments may arise. Stenhouse and colleagues acknowledged that there was likely to be something especially sensitive about race as a controversial issue; and their classroom research shows their apprehension to have been well founded. But this is an argument not for proscription or evasion but for developing the skill and confidence to cope.

Another London teacher, Martin Francis (1981), has provided a good example of what can be achieved within the best traditions of child-centred primary school practice. One day a 10-year-old child walked into his class sporting a swastika armband:

> I did not spot it at first. Some of his friends (who are white) came to me and complained. Because we have talked about racism before, because they have heard from black children about harassment and because we have read *The*

> *Diary of Ann Frank*, they knew what the swastika meant and felt it should not be allowed in school.
>
> Because discussion is an accepted part of the school today, they asked for a discussion about it and we stopped the work we were doing to get round in a circle to talk. This is something that we had done before when an important issue had come up in the classroom. What followed was not a moralistic lecture from me the teacher, but the children themselves saying what they felt. White children argued that it was insulting to wear the armband and recalled some of what they had heard about the Second World War, Asian children who were friends with the boy said that people in the NF had threatened them or their families and challenged him to say whose side he was really on. He listened but did not reply and we went back to other work. The children continued to work with him but occasionally brought up the subject again.
>
> At the end of the day he told me that I could keep the armband and I was quite warm towards him. He did not recant that day – it was a gradual process. Now, six months later, he has abandoned the group of old children who were in the National Front, despite them threatening to beat him up if he left. Other children in the class admire him for having left and his status has been enhanced.
>
> (Francis, 1981)

Francis concedes that such stories do not always have happy endings. I can readily understand how considerations of public order impel schools and local authorities to ban the insignia of racialist organizations, the Home Secretary or a Chief Constable to ban their marches. The need to avert threats to life and limb must obviously take precedence. But it is important to be clear that the ground for proscription in such cases is concern for public order and not the dangerous argument (often heard in anti-racist circles in the late 1970s) that racists, because they are racists, have forfeited their democratic rights. Ultimately one would hope that we might have something on the statute book resembling the First Amendment to the United States Constitution, which guarantees the right to freedom of speech and assembly of all citizens including racists. In 1977 the American Civil Liberties Union (with its many Jewish sponsors, members and officials) successfully pleaded the First Amendment, despite strong opposition, in defending the right of the American Nazi Party to hold a march through the Chicago suburb of Skokie which had the largest number of Holocaust survivors outside New York. In October 1983 the *Spectator's* correspondent in Washington described with astonishment how he had seen a 'puny' Ku Klux Klan march protected from a 'substantial crowd of counter-demonstrators' by lines of black police officers under the orders of a black police chief who also pleaded the First Amendment.

Another area of anti-racist activity where illiberalism has been prominent in recent years is the evaluation of school textbooks and children's literature. Several organizations have published criteria or guidelines for eradicating biased material and choosing new books which are not wholly consistent with cardinal educational values. Much admired in certain quarters are the guidelines for the production of anit-racist and non-racist books published by the World Council of Churches (WCC) in 1980. A 'good book' is defined as one that satisfies the following 16 conditions:

1. Strong role models with whom third world children can identify positively are presented.
2. Third world people are shown as being able to make decisions concerning the important issues that affect their lives.
3. The customs, life-styles, and traditions of third world people are presented in a manner which explains the value, meaning, and role of these customs in the life of the people.
4. Those people considered heroes by the people of the third world are presented as such and the way they influence the lives of the people are clearly defined.
5. Family relationships are portrayed in a warm supportive manner.
6. Efforts of third world people to secure their own liberation are acknowledged as valid rather than described as illegal activities which should be suppressed.
7. The material is presented in such a manner as to enhance the self-image of the third world child.
8. The material is presented in such a manner as to eliminate damaging feelings of superiority – based on race – in the European child.
9. The illustrations provided are non-stereotypes and portray third world people in active and dominant roles.
10. The illustrations reflect the distinctive features of third world groups rather than presenting them as 'coloured Caucasians'.
11. The role of women in the development of third world societies and their impact on history is adequately presented.
12. The history of third world people and their role in developing their own society and institutions are accurately presented from their own perspectives.
13. The role of third world people in shaping historical events in their own country and in the world is accurately portrayed.
14. The content is free of terms deemed insulting and degrading by third world people.
15. The language of the people is treated with respect and presented in the proper rhythm and cadence.
16. The material has been developed by an author of recognized scholarship, valid experience, skill and sensitivity.

(Preiswerk, 1980, pp.144–145)

I would have thought that the only conditions to be borne in mind when choosing (say) a new history, geography or social studies textbook for use in secondary school would be that it should be accurate and truthful, admit to the impossibility of telling the 'whole' truth, distinguish clearly between facts and its author's opinions, indicate the empirical basis for any judgements made and conclusions reached and, above all, encourage and assist pupils to think for themselves. A few of the conditions in the WCC list show some regard for accurate and truthful presentation of people and events, but most seem to be preoccupied with compensating for the stereotypical and ethnocentric portraits of an earlier generation of textbooks or with the likely effects of verbal and visual content on children's attitudes. There is also a distinct strain of 'strong' relativism and 'full-blooded' pluralism running throughout, while any concern for critical enquiry or independent thought is conspicuously absent. Altogether I can well envisage the implementation of such criteria leading to the production and adoption of narrowly conformist curriculum material. Consider, for instance, the first part of condition 4 – 'Those people considered heroes by the people of the third world are presented as such'. This condition seems to make no allowance for divergence of opinion among 'people of the third world' nor for the possibility that they might be as mistaken as anyone else in the assessment of their heroes.

At a recent conference on multicultural education I came across a booklet called *They Fought for Freedom* on the bookstall of the Children's Book Trust of New Delhi. The booklet was intended, I would guess, for the middle-school age-range and consisted of brief biographies of the main leaders of India's independence movement. It appeared to me to be not so much history as hagiography. Included in the pantheon was one very controversial character indeed – Subhas Chandra Bose, a radical Bengali politician who fell out with Gandhi and Nehru in the 1930s and left India in 1942 to throw in his lot with first the Germans and then the Japanese. Bose formed and eventually became supreme commander of the Indian National Army (INA) whose troops were drawn from the ranks of Indian prisoners in Japanese hands and fought alongside their captors in the invasion of India in 1944. His ambition was to be installed as dictator of his liberated homeland. The Children's Book Trust booklet made no mention of this ambition and played down Bose's conflict with Gandhi and Nehru. No indication was given of the nature of the regimes he forged alliances with, nor was the young reader invited to consider the morality of his actions or the soundness of his judgement. He and his INA were, quite simply, 'heroic'. Such uncritical adulation is unlikely to get very far in the average British classroom. There one would hope that pupils found it possible to assess Bose's case – whether he was a hero or not – objectively, treating his posthumous deification and the contemporary British view that he was a traitor with equal scepticism.

Anti-racism and the curriculum

So far as curriculum development is concerned, there are very few examples of anti-racist teaching available that might enable one to evaluate its worth. The existing examples appear to combine multicultural content with the second of the three Stenhouse strategies for teaching about race relations – that of the committed teacher. Where the commitment is of an overtly socialist kind, the result seems to be indoctrination. This is not the place to embark on a philosophical disquisition about the necessary and sufficient conditions of indoctrination. I think I.A. Snook (1972) captured its essence when he wrote that it 'suggests that someone is taking advantage of a privileged role to influence those under his charge in a manner which is likely to distort their ability to assess the evidence on its own merits'. Stenhouse and colleagues also identified it in terms of attempts to 'evade', 'disarm' or 'subvert' the judgement of pupils.

Using Snook's definition as a yardstick one very clear case of indoctrination is the anti-racist material published in 1982 by the Institute of Race Relations (IRR). This consists of two booklets for use in secondary school – *Roots of Racism* and *Patterns of Racism* – which purport to foster children's 'critical judgement' by radically re-examining 'white society and history in the light of the black experience'. What they actually do is survey 'white society and history' from a Marxist viewpoint sometimes labelled 'black vanguardism' (Insititue of Race Relations, 1982). This might please the compilers of the WCC checklist but is hardly compatible with recent trends in history teaching which stress the importance of nurturing children's capacities for independent historical enquiry. Another case of socialist indoctrination is the anti-racist humanities course developed by Chris Searle and colleagues in an East End secondary school whose outcome was the compilation of children's writing *The World in a Classroom* (Searle, 1977). In Searle's own version of the programme the socialist purposes are undisguised and from a rival Marxist stable to that of the Institute of Race Relations – one that aims to subordinate race consciousness to class consciousness. I have criticized Searle's intentions and the IRR's materials elsewhere (Jeffcoate, 1979, 1984). I do not propose to do so again, but to look instead at another version of the Searle course provided by one of his colleagues, Bob Brett.

Somewhat oddly Brett (undated) states no socialist objectives and carries little of the Marxist flavour of Searle's prose. Indeed in some ways his version is decidedly liberal-minded – as, paradoxically, is Searle's – combining child-centredness with integrationism ('A harmonious multi-racial classroom is a living denial of racism'). But one is left at the end with a sense of unease. Brett makes much of the need to establish 'a reasonably relaxed and non-authoritarian relationship with the kids' in order to get them to 'open up' on race and racism, not however (or so it seems) because they should feel free to speak their minds in the classroom but for strategic reasons. He recognizes that there is only a slight chance of moving the minority of die-hards (those 'for whom being racist is central to their sense of their own value', referred to earlier in this chapter), and that working-class children alienated from school values can all too easily see anti-racism as just another set of institutional rules. Brett argues for the importance of building up 'a relationship of trust' so that the teacher can strengthen 'the anti-racism of those kids who are already anti-racist' and operate in the space provided by the 'many children' who 'have contradictory attitudes to race'. His targets are the racism of white children and 'the lies, distortions and half truths of the NF and the electioneering of right wing politicians and media' which are at least partially responsible. His strategy is to combat the first by exposing the latter through a process of 'persuasion'.

One cannot escape the impression that non-authoritarian classroom relationships and child-centred classroom techniques are advocated not so much because they are good in themselves as because they are likely to facilitate this process. In other words their value is perceived to be instrumental rather than intrinsic. One pauses too over whether persuasion, even if confined to rational argument and the exposure of lies and myths, is compatible with child-centredness and non-authoritarian classroom relationships. Children are, of course, entitled to expect to acquire knowledge at school, and to find irrationality and untruth challenged in the classroom, but there is more to the National Front, right-wing politicians and the media than misinformation and faulty logic. What of their opinions and attitudes? If Brett was, as he seems to have been, attempting to change opinions on political issues such as immigration control and race relations policy or alter attitudes towards ethnic minorities and their cultures, then he was 'taking advantage of a privileged role' to infringe his pupils' autonomy. Unfortunately it is hard to form firm conclusions about the classroom activities of either Brett or Searle. Although they are both reasonably explicit on the content of their course (the experience of the pupils and their families, East End history, slavery, migrant workers in Europe, oppression and resistance in the Third World) and although *The World in a Classroom* incorporates a generous selection of children's written work, neither of them conveys a clear or detailed picture of the *enactment* of the course. I think it can be generally said that anti-racist teaching has yet to furnish a corpus of descriptions and evaluations of curriculum in action to set beside those furnished by Stenhouse and colleagues between 1970 and 1975 and (more modestly) by myself and colleagues on the Schools Council multiracial education project between 1973 and 1976.

The targets of anti-racism

A major problem confronting anti-racists is the absence of consensus on precisely what should be fought. About controlling and disciplining racialist behaviour there has never been any disagreement; and I have already expressed my bewilderment as to why some local authorities and schools should have thought it necessary to make such an issue of proscribing actions (personal abuse, bullying, physical assault) which, in my experience, have always been disciplinary offences. The same applies to the behaviour of teachers. I am equally puzzled why the NUT should have recently added to its codes of professional ethics and conduct a clause which states: 'A teacher should not behave in a racially discriminatory manner or make racist remarks directed towards or about ethnic minority groups or members thereof'. Does this mean that there has been a time when discriminatory behaviour and insulting remarks, at whomsoever directed, have not been contrary to these codes or that they are held to be reprehensible and punishable only when the content is racist? I would be interested in hearing the NUT's justification for either position.

I would also be interested in hearing ILEA's justification for its recent decree that staff who engage in racist activities will face disciplinary action. If this simply refers to racialist conduct at school, then I can only again wonder why such a decree should have been thought necessary. If, however, it refers, as I rather suspect it does, to members of staff joining racialist organizations and participating in their legal activities – attending meetings, distributing leaflets, going on demonstrations – then it is a breach of democratic rights and an early step on a totalitarian road. It will not be

ILEA's only one, for it has also decreed that 'all pupils should be learning to identify, resist and remove racism'. This decree is, of course, guilty of the 'essentialist' fallacy I commented on in the opening chapter – the misapprehension that there is something out there called racism waiting to be identified by those with sufficient knowledge and perspicacity. More to the point is the extraordinary presumption that an LEA is entitled to prescribe what pupils should seek to 'resist and remove'.

Political action, which is what it amounts to, is pupils' own prerogative. It is for them to decide how to respond to racism, depending on which sense of the word is intended. Herein lies the nub of the matter. Everyone might agree on the need to combat racism in the sense of racialist behaviour, and on the need to expose the irrationality of racial prejudice and stereotyping (differing only over choice of strategy). However, that still leaves a vast area of opinion and belief, represented by the ideology of racism in the original sense and the politics of immigration control and race relations, where, as often as not, it is not just a question of separating truth from falsehood, myth from reality, rationality from irrationality. If, during the course of the debate, and in possession of the relevant facts, some children argue that white people are as a group intellectually superior to black people, or come out in favour of repatriation and oppose racially mixed youth clubs or whatever, we have to accept that as their privilege. As concerned adults we may abhor these opinions. But, as teachers, our job is not to combat opinions we do not like but to uphold democratic principles and procedures.

Anti-racism and democracy

Unfortunately, as Brett (op.cit.) noted, although individual teachers may succeed in developing their classrooms into democratic workplaces, schools tend to be rather undemocratic institutions. The poet W.H. Auden once observed that the best reason he had for opposing Fascism was that at school he lived in a Fascist state. The same point has been made less flamboyantly by Raymond Williams:

> It is clear, on balance, that we do not get enough practice in the working of democracy, even where its forms exist. Most of us are not expected to be leaders, and are principally instructed, at school and elsewhere, in the values of discipline and loyalty, which are real values only if we share in the decisions to which they refer.
>
> (Williams, 1961, p.309)

Auden made his remark almost 50 years ago and Williams's analysis is now over 20 years old. Since then much has undoubtedly changed. Schools today are, in general, less authoritarian and more open, relaxed and informal. Both teachers and parents are represented on governing bodies, and many schools have parent–teacher associations, staff committees and pupil councils. There has also been an increase in consultation, and a proliferation of academic hierarchies, management structures and working parties generating piles of paper (reports, proposals, minutes, prospectuses) where previously there was none. However, it is a moot point whether these developments have been accompanied by any genuine increase in democratic participation. After a brief flirtation the teachers' unions ran away from the idea of teacher participation 10 years ago; the much heralded 'partnership' between schools and parents has yet to emerge from the realms of rhetoric; and pupils are still effectively excluded from any say in the direction of institutions ostensibly established for their benefit.

To the best of my knowledge no state school has made a serious attempt to emulate the models of pupil democracy laid down by pioneers in the independent sector like Homer Lane and A.S. Neill in the period after the First World War. Democratic participation – what Raymond Williams called 'extensive practice in democratic procedures' – is, of course, a good thing in itself, quite apart from providing the ideal training for adulthood in a democratic society. But it has a particular significance for combating racism too, as Bob Brett appeared to acknowledge. Organized racism is historically associated with totalitarianism and individual racism with the authoritarian personality. Moreover the few ethnographic studies so far undertaken rather suggest that both teacher and pupil racism may be at least to some extent expressions of powerlessness and disaffection from institutions in which their status and valuation are low. Thirty years ago the American psychologist Gordon Allport, in his classic study *The Nature of Prejudice*, was one of the first to recognize that the school's hidden curriculum might actually be more important than the formal curriculum of syllabuses and lessons:

> . . . the atmosphere that surrounds the child at school is exceedingly important. If segregation of the sexes or races prevails, if authoritarianism and hierarchy dominate the system, the child cannot help but learn that power and status are the dominant factors in human relationships. If, on the other hand, the school system is democratic, if the teacher and child are each respected units, the lesson of respect for the person will easily register. As in society at

> large the *structure* of the pedagogical system will blanket, and may negate, the specific intercultural lessons taught.
>
> (Allport, 1954, p.511)

More recently a British psychologist, Alfred Davey, argued along very similar lines:

> Purging the textbooks of black stereotypes, boosting the black child in our teaching materials and telling improving stories about children of other lands will not have the slightest effect on how children treat each other – if teachers make rules without explanation, if they command needlessly and assume their authority is established by convention. We learn to respect each other's individuality not by hearing about tolerance, or reading about tolerance or even discussing tolerance but by being tolerated by others and being tolerant in return.
>
> (Davey, 1977, p.261)

I do not know why anti-racists are so distrustful of democracy. It could be the strongest weapon in our armoury.

CHAPTER 8

CONCLUSION: LIBERTY, EQUALITY, FRATERNITY

> At this point in our history we must enter once again into the debate that preceded mass schooling over a century ago, namely: what kind of society do we want to create and how can the education system help us to realize such a society?
>
> (David Hargreaves, 1982)

In his 1977 Reith Lectures A.H. Halsey suggested that we could do worse than examine questions of social policy in the light of the ancient principles of liberty, equality and fraternity. This in a way is what I have tried to do in this book – substituting, however, the more mundane aim of social integration for the now quaintly archaic concept of fraternity. Liberty, equality and fraternity (or integration) sound an admirable triad of principles, and the phrase trips off the tongue, or pen, harmoniously enough. But in practice the alliance has proved both fragile and fraught. Tension between equality and liberty has been particularly acute. Socialist egalitarians have ridden rough-shod over individual liberties, while right-wing libertarians have defended the existence of social inequalities as the price to be paid for freedom. There is also some tension between integration and liberty, as will have been apparent from Chapter 5, where I argued that a degree of parental freedom might have to be sacrificed to the greater good of a more integrated (and more equal) society.

Integration and equality seem a better match; the integrationist philosophy has often appealed to egalitarian considerations. Twenty years ago in the United States the desegregationist campaign was premised on the assumption that segregated schools necessarily denied black students equality of opportunity. On the other hand there are those who would claim to be egalitarian separatists – some feminists, for example, and some black radicals, and Marxists generally still wedded to class conflict and the development of a distinctive working-class consciousness. They, no doubt, would dismiss my substitution of integration for fraternity, preferring the original in the case of male chauvinist trades unionists or sisterhood in the case of feminists or solidarity in the case of socialists seeking a more all-embracing shibboleth. I favour integration essentially because it is what Halsey calls a 'universal' rather than an 'exclusive' principle for social cohesion. Whatever the formulation, there is no escaping the fact that in specific situations we may have to rank the three principles in order of priority, choosing one at the expense of one or both of the others. In Halsey's words, 'it is a matter of finding the best balance between the revolutionary triad' (Halsey, 1978, p.160).

At the beginning of Chapter 3 I suggested that the most important issue in the field of ethnic minorities and education was that of equality. This view would, I think, be widely shared among parents, teachers, activists of one kind or another, and the pupils themselves. However, the evidence, such as it is, summarized in that chapter, leads one to conclude that the educational inequalities between children from the ethnic minorities and those from the ethnic majority are comparatively insignificant when set against those associated with region, social class and (to a lesser extent) gender. Indeed the former are, in large measure, a reflection of the latter (gender excepted), in so far as underachievement among pupils from recently settled ethnic minorities is a product of their concentration in underachieving schools in local authorities scoring highly on indices of deprivation. This concentration is, in many instances, a consequence of the fact that their parents or grandparents were recruited to perform poorly paid jobs in the manufacturing and service sectors and obliged by the location of their employment, and its low level of remuneration (among other factors), to take up residence in some of the most deprived parts of our towns and cities. The evidence also makes plain that there is more to the ethnic minority experience of education than underachievement. Both Jews and South Asians have been conspicuously successful, overcoming a range of disadvantages, though in the case of the Jews the evidence relates to economic and social, not educational, success (there being no data on how Jewish children fare at school), while the general success of South Asians may mask underachievement among particular communities like the Bangladeshis in London's East End. With respect to gender, both South Asian and West Indian girls appear to be less vulnerable in certain respects to the stereotypes of what is appropriate, educationally and occupationally, for females than their counterparts from the ethnic majority.

The inference for social policy that I have drawn from the evidence is that positive discrimination in favour of ethnic minorities as such, in the form of directing extra money, staff and resources in their direction, is totally unwarranted. However, this is not to say that short-term interventions to support newly arrived and especially underprivileged groups, such as the Bangladeshis or the Vietnamese, might not be justified, nor that the Gypsies might not, by virtue of their nomadic way of life, constitute a special case. But, on the whole, what is required is a reinvigorated assault on those well-entrenched inequalities of region and social class. In other words, a fresh commitment is needed to the simple egalitarianism of the 1940s – 'equal shares for all', 'an equal chance to take one's chance' – and to the philosophy of the Plowden Report of 1967. The Plowden Committee envisaged that positive discrimination might make 'schools in the deprived areas as good as the best in the country', thereby narrowing 'the gap between the educational opportunities of the most fortunate and least fortunate' children. Such a major task has yet seriously to be attempted. Whether its implementation would make a visible dent in working-class underachievement, or go any way towards reducing the substantial differences in educational outcomes between north and south or inner city and suburbia, we really have no means of knowing. Desirable as this result undoubtedly would be, it is not essentially the purpose of the exercise, which is to try and ensure, so far as possible, that one school is as well staffed, resourced and administered as another and hence that one child's experience of statutory education is as rewarding, enriching and enjoyable as that of the next. David Hargreaves (1982) has made the point well, from a slightly different perspective: 'Education has little to contribute directly to a more just distribution of wealth . . . But (it) can and should have a central role to play in the redistribution of dignity' (p.184).

A positive experience of school needs to be seen as a good thing in itself, rather than as only instrumentally valuable to the extent that it conduces to success in 16+ and 18+ examinations and entry into higher education and socially prestigious employment. It might be objected that an initiative of the kind I have proposed is bound to appear somewhat chimerical under a Conservative government happily presiding over the pauperization of public education, while further subsidizing, through the assisted places scheme, the already privileged independent sector. However, there can be no harm, and some benefit, in setting out a programme for future reform, and a Conservative government might at least be persuaded of the wrong-headedness of positive discrimination in favour of ethnic minorities, to which it at present seems as dedicated, though possibly for different reasons, as its political opponents.

The point about ethnic minorities and positive discrimination can be illustrated from my native city, and the city in which I have written this book – Liverpool. As race relations workers never tire of reminding us, Liverpool's prosperity in the eighteenth and nineteenth centuries was founded in its participation in the transatlantic slave trade and the importation of colonial products – sugar, tea, tobacco and cotton. Historically, Merseyside's economy has been based on ships, the port and related activities. Since the ending of the slave trade that economy has been in decline and has now virtually collapsed. Miles and miles of dockland stand derelict. Manufacturing industry has fared no better. Always small and vulnerable, due to the preponderance of a handful of national and international firms, its base has been much eroded in recent years by a series of closures. Since 1976 over 100,000 jobs have been lost in manufacturing industry on Merseyside. The consequence has been a calamitous increase in unemployment in an area long notorious for limited job opportunities. The overall unemployment rate is currently estimated at 20 percent, but in the inner city and on some council estates it is at least twice as high. In 1981 F.F. Ridley, Professor of Political Theory and Institutions at Liverpool University, wrote that 'There are areas of Merseyside where . . . unemployment has become as normal as work'. He calculated that on one estate, not far from where I live, almost half the adult population was dependent on the state for an income. As elsewhere, the young have suffered disproportionately from the deepening of the recession. Of the 8000 young in Liverpool who reached school-leaving age in the summer of 1982, one-third remained in full-time education and another third joined the Youth Opportunities Programme, the forerunner of the Youth Training Scheme. Only 6.5 percent were in paid employment six months after leaving. 'The only booming industry in Merseyside', observed Professor Ridley, 'is crime.' The most visible sign of economic collapse is the disappearance of the city's 'rush hour'.

The economic decline has been mirrored in a physical decline. Between the mid-1960s and the mid-1970s the heart was ripped out of the centre of Liverpool under the guise of slum clearance. Cynics commented that the city planners had wreaked more havoc than Hitler's bombers during the blitz. The inner-city population was halved, and it was a moot point whose plight was worse, that of those left behind in an environment of squalid dilapidation or that of those moved to outer-city estates on which, in the words of Professor Ridley (1981), 'the visiting Southerner might think he was in parts of New York rather than Britain'. Not surprisingly educational standards in many parts of the city are abysmal. Professor Ridley suggests that the gap in attainment between Liverpool and the national average 'is almost as wide as between Britain and some Third World States'. Under-achievement has been accompanied by high levels of truancy, vandalism and indiscipline. Matters have been very much exacerbated by falling rolls and 10 years of political stalemate on a 'hung' local council, which has meant that the city has kept open seven or eight more secondary schools than are required by the numbers of children in the age-group. Liverpool's best known multi-ethnic comprehensive school, Paddington, built for 1700, had 320 pupils on roll in 1983. Following several sharply critical HMI reports on the state of education in the city, government ministers summoned local council leaders in the same year to voice their concern. Everything considered – economic collapse, environmental blight, educational under-achievement – there seem good grounds for regarding Merseyside as the United Kingdom's most deprived region after Northern Ireland.

The composition of Liverpool's ethnic minority population is quite different from that of most other multi-ethnic towns and cities. Because of the state of the local economy, it attracted very little of the mass immigration of the 1950s and 1960s, and those who did come were mainly professionals. There are, therefore, very few West Indians or South Asians in the city. Nor are there many Italians or Cypriots or Europeans generally. The communities that exist are of nineteenth- or early twentieth-century origin and, with the exception of the Jews, solidly working class. The largest single group is of Irish Catholic ancestry and represents somewhere between one-third and one-half of the city's total population. Besides them, and the Jews, there are a number of relatively small but long-established 'coloured' communities – Chinese, Africans and Arabs – which owe their beginnings to the settlement of foreign seamen almost 100 years ago. The most prominent of these is Liverpool's black community, descendants of marriages and relationships between African sailors and local working-class women. The size of Liverpool's 'coloured' population is unknown. DES statistics place the proportion of non-white and non-UK born 0–17-year-olds at 3.48 percent, but the local community relations council estimates the size of the ethnic minority population, excluding the Irish and the Jews, as twice that figure.

One thing is clear. Liverpool Irish, Liverpool Jews, Liverpool blacks and Liverpool Chinese are as much Liverpudlians as myself or anyone else. This is not to say the story of their presence is one of interethnic harmony. Far from it. There is a long history of sectarian animosity and violence between Catholics and Protestants, though much abated in recent years, while Liverpool's blacks have consistently faced discrimination in employment and elsewhere, to say nothing of the major assaults launched against them in the race riots of 1919 and 1948. But there is a common sense of shared identity, of being Liverpudlians, yet to be achieved in towns and cities with shorter histories of a multi-ethnic presence. Also, there is now a common sense of shared deprivation against a backcloth of conspicuous national prosperity. In the summer of 1981 Liverpool experienced some of the worst of the country's inner-city riots. Though concentrated in Toxteth, a glaringly impoverished multi-ethnic area popularly associated with crime and prostitution, and though taking the visible form of violent confrontation with the police, these were essentially neither anti-police nor black riots (most of those charged with offences were white not black). Essentially they represented precisely the kind of eruption predicted by Professor Ridley six months before – 'not revolution, but simple undirected violence and pointless destruction' – a spontaneous expression of bitterness and disaffection on the part of the city's undereducated and unemployed working-class youth (Ridley, 1981).

For these reasons, whilst I would be more than sympathetic to any systematic campaign to eradicate discrimination (whether racial, religious or whatever) from the shrinking labour market and other aspects of city life, I would find it a very peculiar initiative indeed which proposed positive action in support of Catholics, blacks or ethnic minorities as a whole, in isolation from a general regenerative programme to alleviate Liverpool's severe economic, environmental and educational difficulties. Indeed, I would regard such an initiative as an unhelpful diversion from more pressing concerns.

Liverpool can also be used to illustrate the issues surrounding the principle of integration. I commented in an earlier chapter on religious apartheid in the city's educational provision. It is vividly symbolized at two places within a mile of one another on the ring road. Two pairs of comprehensive schools stand shoulder to shoulder. In each case one is a non-denominational county school, the other a voluntary-aided Roman Catholic school. When I drive past, I cannot help wondering if the pupils, parents and teachers ever pause to reflect on the desirability of a school system which has divided them on such an arbitrary basis. There is very little, of course, that a local authority can do about religious segregation in education. It requires a bold move by central government, which is unlikely to be forthcoming so long as the established religious minorities (Anglicans, Catholics and Jews) continue to wield disproportionate power and influence. However, there is a good deal that a local authority can do to secure other kinds of integration within the county sector. In the summer of 1983 the deadlock on Liverpool's council was broken when the local elections brought a Labour Party dominated by the Militant Tendency to power. One of their immediate tasks was to introduce a semblance of rationality into the city's provision of secondary education. The scheme eventually submitted for the approval of the Secretary of State (at the time of writing he had still to deliver judgement) proposed the closure of all the existing secondary schools in the county sector, including the 11 single-sex schools and the two surviving grammar schools. Seventeen of the 25 schools would then be reopened the following academic year as coeducational 11–18 neighbourhood comprehensives.

After 10 years of indecision and *laissez-faire*, during which parental choice had become the predominant factor in determining secondary school allocation, any attempt at rationalization was bound to have excited parental protest. But the city council appeared more than slightly taken aback by the volume and vociferousness of the objections they received. Whether these were directed principally at the closure of the selective schools, the single-sex schools or particular local schools, was hard to say. The council was right, in my view, to propose a wholly coeducational and comprehensive system, such as has existed in a number of other authorities for many years, but misguided in its preference for the neighbourhood school principle. This preference reflected the influence of the council's left-wing ideology. Commitment to 'community' schools, in the interests of fostering shared identity and local solidarity, has long been a feature of that specific brand of socialist thinking about education. I expressed my reservations about its parochialism in Chapter 5, as well as my own commitment, on a mixture of integrationist and egalitarian grounds, to a system of allocation by catchment area which tried, so far as possible, to achieve socially, academically and ethnically balanced intakes in all schools. In Liverpool, with falling rolls and broad catchment areas, this should not prove too difficult to accomplish. Equalizing opportunity in this sense seems to me the perfect complement to equalizing opportunity in the other sense, mentioned above, of trying to ensure that one school is, so far as possible, as good as another, in terms of staff quality, facilities and resources. Both ideals are products of the 1960s. For some reason I have never quite managed to fathom, the race relations industry, whilst remaining generally enthusiastic about equalization of opportunity, has lost faith in integrationism, notwithstanding its egalitarian credentials. It is as well to remember that the integrationist dream is precisely the one evoked so memorably by Martin Luther King more than 20 years ago. Where I am entirely in agreement with Liverpool City Council is in the relatively low priority attached to meeting the wishes of individual parents. Egalitarian and integrationist considerations are both more important. Were the wishes those of the group directly affected – the pupils – I would think rather differently.

Liberty has figured centrally in my argument twice: first, in my support for pupils' right to cultural and ideological self-determination and, second, in my support for teachers' right to control the curriculum in their classrooms. My concern to defend the former is inspired not so much by fear that maintainers of culture and anti-racists (the enemies of an open society identified in Chapters 6 and 7 respectively) might actually succeed in indoctrinating the nation's young (the chances of that are mercifully pretty slim), as by anxiety lest the academic pursuit of truth and rationality be impeded and children's capacity to participate in it be diminished. The threat to teachers' autonomy is represented by recent moves by central government to increase its influence over the public examination system, and over the curriculum. In addition, there are encroachments by local authorities (to some extent undertaken as a result of central government's prompting) in the shape of policy statments and recommendations. Local authorities are perfectly entitled to remind their schools of the state of the law, under the various Education Acts or the 1976 Race Relations Act for example, as indeed they are to remind parents of legal rights. However, provided the law is being observed, I can see no good reason for their recent incursions into the curriculum and other areas of school policy making. Fortunately their chances of success in seeking to augment their power in this way are about the same as those of anti-racist teachers seeking to indoctrinate the nation's young. Local authority policy statements on anti-racist and multicultural education seem destined to finish up in wastepaper baskets or gathering dust in cupboards, and rightly so. Strengthening teachers' control over the curriculum does not mean they should be inattentive to the suggestions of others, nor does it imply that they should teach in a didactic or authoritarian way or that pupils should be discouraged from taking control over their own learning. It simply means that the final decision on what is taught and how rests properly with them. Teacher and pupil autonomy are the two key, and complementary, pillars of a democratic education system. At present both are seriously frustrated by virtue of the fact that schools remain hierarchical and undemocratic institutions.

The principles of liberty, equality and fraternity (or integration) are particularly germane to David Hargreaves's question, quoted at the beginning of this chapter: 'What kind of society do we want to create and how can the education system help us to realize such a society?' The immediate reason for entering 'once again into the debate that preceded mass schooling over a century ago' is that the original justification for mass schooling – the need to produce an adequately trained industrial workforce – has evaporated. The bottom has dropped out of the youth labour market in a post-industrial society, and the link between school and paid employment has been severed. Early returns in the autumn of 1983 suggested that less than 10 percent of the 846,000 who reached school-leaving age by the summer had moved directly into jobs. Moreover, it seems highly probable that the present generation of young people will spend much less of their adult lives working for money than did either their parents or grandparents. By some weird logic of its own, central government's response has been to pretend that the opposite was the case. How else is one to interpret the burgeoning of job training schemes, the Technical and Vocational Education Initiative or the stress laid upon improving relationships between school and industry?

An alternative, and more realistic, response would be to welcome the decline in the significance of paid employment as a form of liberation. 'It is the purpose of education', wrote George Sampson over 60 years ago, 'not to prepare children *for* their occupations, but to prepare children *against* their occupations' (Sampson, 1921, p.11). He came from a long tradition of anti-industrialist thought in education, and had in mind precisely the sort of tedious occupations, on production lines and in offices, now threatened, or eliminated, by the recession and the new technology. The liberation of the school system from the role of job preparation means that central government will have to forego much of its cherished rhetoric about education as a form of economic investment, and parents and pupils will have to renounce much of what faith they have in school as a means to secure upward social mobility.

Unlearning the work ethic, and the work ethic's view of public education, may prove especially difficult for the newly established ethnic minorities. Most of the immigrants of the 1950s and 1960s came for economic reasons, and many of them settled for menial jobs in the hope that their children and grandchildren would achieve occupational and social advancement as a consequence of scholastic success. That kind of success was only ever guaranteed to a minority; it now seems likely to be even further restricted. Liberation for the schools themselves should mean that they can now concentrate on the individual and social aims of education frequently stated, but little implemented, in the past, and on the concept of 'being educated' as an intrinsically worthwhile goal. Being educated in the latter part of the twentieth century should include the development of all 'talents and abilities to the full', and of skills in rational discourse and democratic procedure, mentioned in earlier chapters. It should also obviously include familiarity with, and adeptness in, the new technology.

However, perhaps the most important function of school will remain, as it always has been, social. It introduces us to a far wider range of individuals and activities than we would otherwise encounter. Most of us can probably recall very little of lessons at school. Yet we can often recall in graphic detail our friendships and 'extracurricular' life generally. This is one reason why I have attached such significance to the unfashionable aim of integration; it broadens rather than narrows the scope of social experience at school. This, in turn, explains why those unfortunate enough to be educated in the independent and selective sectors can genuinely be described as socially and culturally deprived. My answer to David Hargreaves' question is that I should like to see a more egalitarian, more integrated and more democratic society than the one we now have. I believe that the education system could do more than is commonly supposed to help realize such a society if it was more elalitarian, more integrated and more democratic than at present. Ethnic minorites would derive far greater benefit from a programme of reform with these objects in view than from positive discrimination programmes designed to ameliorate their position alone.

BIBLIOGRAPHY

Allport, G.W. (1954) *The Nature of Prejudice*. Reading, Mass.: Addison-Wesley.

Avon NUT (1980) *After the Fire: a Report on Education in St Paul's, Bristol, and Multi-ethnic Education in Avon*. Bristol: Avon NUT.

Ballard, M. (1970) *New Movements in the Study and Teaching of History*. London: Temple Smith.

Banton, M. (1970) The Concept of Racism. In: Zubaida, S. (ed.) *Race and Racialism*. London: Tavistock.

Berkshire Advisory Committee for Multicultural Education (1982) *Education for Equality*. Berkshire Education Authority.

Brett, R. (undated) Charcoal and Chalk. *Teaching London Kids* **11**.

Brittan, E.M. (1976) Multiracial Education 2 – Teacher Opinion on Aspects of School Life: Pupils and Teachers. *Educational Research* **18**(3).

Cashmore, E. (1982) Black Youth, Sport and Education. *New Community* **10**(2).

Castles, S. and Kosack, G. (1973) *Immigrant Workers and the Class Structure in Europe*. London: Oxford University Press.

Central Advisory Council for Education (CACE) (1967) *Children and Their Primary Schools*. London: HMSO.

Centre for Contemporary Cultural Studies (1981) *Unpopular Education: Schooling and Social Democracy in England since 1944*. London: Heinemann.

City of Bradford Metropolitan Council (1982) *Education for a Multi-Cultural Society: Provision for Pupils of Ethnic Minority Communities*.

Commission for Racial Equality (1981) *Local Authorities and the Educational Implications of Section 71 of the Race Relations Act 1976*. London: CRE.

Commission for Racial Equality (1983) *Secondary School Allocation in Reading: Report of a Formal Investigation*. London: CRE.

Committee of Inquiry into the Education of Children from Ethnic Minority Groups (1981) *West Indian Children in our Schools*. London: HMSO.

Craft, M. and Craft, A. (1983) The Participation of Ethnic Minority Pupils in Further and Higher Education. *Education Research* **25**(1).

Davey, A. (1973) Teachers, Race and Intelligence. *Race* **XV**(2).

Davey, A.G. (1977) Racial Awareness and Social Identity in Young Children. *Mental Health and Society* **4**.

Davey, A.G. and Norburn, M.V. (1980) Ethnic Awareness and Ethnic Differentiation amongst Primary School Children. *New Community* **VIII**(1/2).

Davey, A.G. and Mullin, P.N. (1982) Inter-ethnic Friendship in British Primary Schools. *Educational Research* **24**(2).

DES (1965a) *The Education of Immigrants*. Circular 7/65. London: HMSO.

DES (1965b) *The Organization of Secondary Education*. Circular 10/65. London: HMSO.

DES (1971) *The Education of Immigrants*. Survey 13. London: HMSO.

DES (1974) *Educational Disadvantage and the Educational Needs of Immigrants*. London: HMSO.

Dhondy, F. (1974) The Black Explosion in Schools. *Race Today* February.

Douglas, J.W.B. (1967) *The Home and the School*. London: Panther Books.

Driver, G. (1979) Classroom Stress and School Achievement. In: Khan, V.S. (ed.) *Minority Families in Britain*. London: Macmillan.

Driver, G. (1980) *Beyond Underachievement*. London: Commission for Racial Equality.

Dummett, A. and McNeal, J. (1981) *Race and Church Schools*. London: Runnymede Trust.

Floud, J.E. et al. (1957) *Social Class and Educational Opportunity*. London: Heinemann.

Foot, P. (1965) *Immigration and Race in British Politics*. Harmondsworth: Penguin Books.

Francis, M. (1981) Talking about Racism. *Times Educational Supplement* October 30th.

Fuller, M. (1980) Black Girls in a London Comprehensive. In: Deem, R. (ed.) *Schooling for Women's Work*. London: Routledge & Kegan Paul.

Gartner, L.P. (1960) *The Jewish Immigrant in England 1870–1914*. London: George Allen & Unwin.

Glazer, N. (1975) From Equal Opportunity to Statistical Parity. Reprinted in Braham, P., Rhodes, E. and Pearn, M. (eds) (1981) *Discrimination and Disadvantage in Employment*. London: Harper & Row.

Halsey, A.H. (1978) *Change in British Society*. Oxford: Oxford University Press.

Hammersley, M. (1981) *Staffroom Racism*. Unpublished manuscript.

Hannon, V. (1979) Education for Sex Equality: What's the Problem? In: Rubinstein, D. (ed.) *Education and Equality*. Harmondsworth: Penguin Books.

Hargreaves, D.H. (1967) *Social Relations in a Secondary School*. London: Routledge & Kegan Paul.

Hargreaves, D.H. (1982) *The Challenge for the Comprehensive School: Culture, Curriculum and Community*. London: Routledge & Kegan Paul.

Hiro, D. (1973) *Black British White British*. Harmondsworth: Penguin Books.

Hobsbawm, E.J. (1969) *Industry and Empire*. Harmondsworth: Penguin Books.

Hobsbawm, E.J. (1977) *The Age of Capital 1848–1875*. London: Abacus.

Home Office (1964) *Second Report of Commonwealth Immigrants Advisory Council*. London: HMSO.

Home Office (1975) *Racial Discrimination*. Cmnd 6234. London: HMSO.
Home Office (1978a) *The West Indian Community*. London: HMSO.
Home Office (1978b) *Proposals for Replacing Section 11 of the Local Government Act 1966*. London: HMSO.
Home Office (1980) *Review of the Public Order Act 1936 and Related Legislation*. Cmnd 7891. London: HMSO.
Home Office (1981a) *The Brixton Disorders 10–12 April 1981: The Scarman Report*. London: HMSO.
Home Office (1981b) *Racial Attacks*. London: HMSO.
House of Commons Home Affairs Committee (1981) *Racial Disadvantage*. London: HMSO.
Huxley, E. (1964) The Silent Italian. *Punch* **CCXLVII** (6482).
Inner London Education Authority (1977) *Multi-Ethnic Education*. London: ILEA.
Inner London Education Authority (1979) *Multi-Ethnic Education: Progress Report*. London: ILEA.
Inner London Education Authority (1983) *Policy for Equality: Race*. London: ILEA.
Institute of Race Relations (1982) *Roots of Racism*; *Patterns of Racism*. London: Institute of Race Relations.
Jackson, B. and Marsden, D. (1962) *Education and the Working Class*. London: Routledge & Kegan Paul.
Jeffcoate, R. (1979) *Positive Image: Towards a Multiracial Curriculum*. London: Writers and Readers.
Jeffcoate, R. (1984) Ideologies and Multicultural Education. In: Craft, M. (ed.) *Education and Cultural Pluralism*. Brighton: Falmer Press.
Jewish Educational Development Trust (1981) *Jewish Education 1981/82*.
Jones, C. (1977) *Immigration and Social Policy in Britain*. London: Tavistock.
Jones, D.K. (1977) *The Making of the Education System 1851–1881*. London: Routledge & Kegan Paul.
Kettle, M. and Hodges, L. (1982) *Uprising: the Police, the People and the Riots in Britain's Cities*. London: Pan Books.
King, R. (1979) Italians in Britain: an Idiosyncratic Immigration. *Association of Teachers of Italian Journal* **29** (Autumn).
Kirp, D.L. (1979) *Doing Good By Doing Little*. Berkeley, Calif.: University of California Press.
Krausz, E. (1964) *Leeds Jewry: its History and Social Structure*. Cambridge: Heffer.
Lacey, C. (1970) *Hightown Grammar*. Manchester: Manchester University Press.
Mabey, C. (1981) Black British Literacy: a Study of Reading Attainment of London Black Children from 8 to 15 years. *Educational Research* **23**(2).
Milner, D. (1975) *Children and Race*. Harmondsworth: Penguin Books.
Ministry of Education (1963) *English for Immigrants*. London: HMSO.
National Union of Teachers (1983) *Combating Racism in Schools*. London: NUT.
Okley, J. (1983) *The Traveller–Gypsies*. Cambridge: Cambridge University Press.
Parekh, B. (ed.) (1974) *Colour, Culture and Consciousness*. London: George Allen and Unwin.
Parkinson, J.P. and MacDonald, B. (1972) Teaching Race Neutrally. *Race* **XIII**(3).
Preiswerk, R. (ed.) (1980) *The Slant of the Pen: Racism in Children's Books*. Geneva:

World Council of Churches.

Ratcliffe, P. (1981) *Racism and Reaction: a Profile of Handsworth*. London: Routledge & Kegan Paul.

Reiss, C. (1975) *Education of Travelling Children*. London: Macmillan.

Rex, J. and Tomlinson, S. (1979) *Colonial Immigrants in a British City*. London: Routledge & Kegan Paul.

Ridley, F.F. (1981) View from a Disaster Area: Unemployed Youth in Merseyside. *The Political Quarterly* **52**(1).

Rose, E.J.B. et al. (1969) *Colour and Citizenship*. London: Institute of Race Relations/ Oxford University Press.

Rutter, M. et al. (1979) *Fifteen Thousand Hours: Secondary Schools and their Effects on Children*. London: Open Books.

Sampson, G. (1921) *English for the English*. Cambridge: Cambridge University Press.

Searle, C. (1977) *The World in a Classroom*. London: Writers and Readers.

Ruddock, J. (1983, revised edition) *The Humanities Curriculum Project: an Introduction*. Norwich: School of Education, University of East Anglia.

Shipman, M. and Raynor, J. (1972) *The Curriculum the Teacher and the Child*. Unit 5 of Course E283 *Perspectives on the Curriculum*. Milton Keynes: Open University Press.

Sikes, P.J. and Sheard, D.J.S. (1978) Teaching for Better Race Relations? *Cambridge Journal of Education* **8**(2/3).

Smith, D.J. (1976) *The Facts of Racial Disadvantage*. London: PEP.

Smith, D.J. (1977–8) The Housing of Racial Minorities: its Unusual Nature. *New Community* **6**(1–2).

Snook, I.A. (1972) *Indoctrination and Education*. London: Routledge & Kegan Paul.

Stenhouse, L. (1969) The Humanities Curriculum Project. *Journal of Curriculum Studies* **1**(1).

Stenhouse, L., Verma, G.K., Wild, R.D. and Nixon, J. (1982) *Teaching About Race Relations: Problems and Effects*. London: Routledge & Kegan Paul.

Stone, M. (1981) *The Education of the Black Child in Britain: The Myth of Multiracial Education*. London: Fontana.

Tawney, R.H. (1964, first published 1931) *Equality*. London: George Allen & Unwin.

Taylor, M. (1981) *Caught Between: a Review of Research into the Education of Pupils of West Indian Origin*. Slough: NFER.

Thompson, E.P. (1968) *The Making of the English Working Class*. Harmondsworth: Penguin Books.

Tomlinson, S. (1980) The Educational Performance of Ethnic Minority Children. *New Community* **8**(3).

Townsend, H.E.R. and Brittan, E.M. (1973) *Multiracial Education: Need and Innovation*. London: Evans/Methuen.

Troyna, B. (1978) Race and Streaming. *Educational Review* **30**(1).

Twitchin, J. and Demuth, C. (1981) *Multi-cultural Education: Views from the Classroom*. London: BBC Publications.

Vellins, S. (1982) South Asian Students in British Universities: a Statistical Note. *New Community* **10**(2).

Verma, G.K. and Bagley, C. (1979) Measured Changes in Racial Attitudes Following the Use of Three Different Teaching Methods. In: *Race, Education and Identity*. London: Macmillan.

Walker, E.C. (1966/7) The Education of Immigrant Children in Bedford *Bedfordshire Magazine*. **10**(79–80).

Ward, R.H. (1978) Race Relations in Britain. *British Journal of Sociology* **29**(5).

Westergaard, J. and Resler, H. (1975) *Class in a Capitalist Society*. Harmondsworth: Penguin Books.

Williams, J. (1967) The Younger Generation. In: Rex, J. and Moore, R. *Race, Community and Conflict*. London: Institute of Race Relations/Oxford University Press.

Williams, R. (1961) *The Long Revolution*. London: Chatto and Windus.

Willis, P. (1977) *Learning to Labour: How Working Class Kids Get Working Class Jobs*. Farnborough: Saxon House.

Young, K. and Connelly, N. (1981) *Policy and Practice in the Multiracial City*. London: Policy Studies Institute.

Zec, P. (1980) Multicultural Education: What Kind of Relativism is Possible? *Journal of Philosophy of Education* **14**(1).

INDEX

ability, segregation by, 36, 38–40, 109–10
achievement, *see* educational performance
Africans, 14, 119, 168
  see also Uganda
aided schools, *see* dual system
Aliens Act (1905), 7, 29
Allport, G., 139, 162–3
Amin, Idi, 9, 144
Anglicans, 135–6,
  see also Protestants
  anti-racism, *see* racism, combating
    anti-school culture, 69–72, 149
  anti-semitism, 6–7, 26, 34
  see also Jews
Arabs, 168
Arnold, M., 128, 136
artistic achievement, 73–4
Asians, *see* South Asians; Uganda
assimilation, 122–7
attainment, *see* educational performance
Auden, W.H., 161–2
autonomy of teachers, 48–50
  of teachers and pupils, 172–173

Bagley, C., 142
Ballard, M., 137
Bangladeshis, 81, 85, 166
  assimilation, 165
  educational performance, 56, 72
  employment, 17Î8, 20
  numbers of 14
  see also South Asians
Banton, M., 22, 26, 174
Bedford
  integration in, 123–4
  Italians in, 5–6, 27–8, 105
  religious segregation in, 105
  school allocation in, 101
Belfast, 107, 115
Bentinck, Lord W., 119–20
Berkshire, 102–4, 114
Bernstein, B., 95
Birmingham, 32, 64, 123
black, culture, 69, 147
  educational performance 147–8 *see also* 'coloured'; South Asians; West Indians
Boyle, Sir E., 52–3, 97–8
boys, West Indian, 60–1, 66, 70
Bradford, 101, 106–7, 125–7, 131
Brett, R., 150, 159–61
Bristol, 14, 41, 102, 114
British Deaf Association, 110
British Nationality Act (1981), 10, 25
British Union of Fascists, 7
Brittan, E., 65, 67–8, 124
Buckinghamshire, 42
Bullock Report (1975), 93
Burnham Committee, 77
Burt, C., 38
'bussing', 101, 105

Callaghan, J., 48
Cardiff, 14
Caribbean, *see* West Indians
Cashmore, E., 73–4, 174
Castles, S., 3
Catholics, 3–4, 36, 105, 107–9, 111, 115; *see also* religion
CED, *see* Centre for Information, etc

Centre for Information and Advice on Educational Disadvantage, 79
Chileans, 10
Chinese, 1, 9, 12–14, 55, 83, 91, 105, 168
Christians, *see* Catholics; Protestants; religion
CIAC, *see* Commonwealth Immigrants Advisory Council
Circular 7/65 on education of immigrants, 98–100, 114
Circular 10/65 on comprehensive education, 99
circumcision and infibulation, 119
class: educational performance and, 57, 66, 69, 72, 147
  examination results, 42–7
  Labour Party and, 17
  maintenance of, 30–1, 35, 39–42
  middle, 4, 6, 17, 19
  nationality and, 2–4, 6, 17–20
  segregation and, 40–2, 97, 113
  West Indians, and 61, 66, 69, 72
  working, 2–3, 6, 17–20, 45–6
colonialism, 119
'coloured' minorities, 13–20
  economic context, 15–17
  as 'underclass' 17–20
  see also black; South Asians; Œest Indians
Commission for Racial Equality, 19, 48;
  and positive discrimination, 88, 90–1
  and secondary school allocation, 102–4
Commonwealth Immigration Act (1962), 25
Commonwealth Immigrants Act (1968), 25, 78
Commonwealth Immigrants Advisory Council, 96, 99, 116, 122–3
comprehensivization, 37, 39–41, 101, 110, 113
Connelly, N., 49, 81, 92
Conservative Party:
  and comprehensives, 39
  and curriculum 48
  and integration, 97
  and positive discrimination, 76–9, 81–2
  and repatriation, 153
  and state education, 31
Corby, 16
counter-school culture, 69–72, 149
Cowper-Temple clause in 1870 Education Act, 32, 35
Craft, M. and A., 57–8
CRE *see* Commission for Racial Equality
Cromwell, O., 6
Crosland, A., 39
cultural:
  adaptation, 10
  drift, 9–10
  maintenance, 8–9, 12, 88, 130, 134
  needs, 87–8
  pluralism, 94, 128–37
  practices and colonialism, 119
  relativism, 121
  strength, 66–7
  transformation, 129
culture: black, 69, 147
  non-literate, 8
  religion and, 133–8
  of resistance, 69–72, 148
  working class, 17, 45–6
curriculum: anti-racist, 140–2, 158–60
  Conservatives and, 48
  ethnocentric, 63–4
  'Great Debate', 48–9
  hidden, 47
  multi-ethnic, 94
  and pluralism, 128–38
Cypriots, 1, 12, 55, 59, 72, 83

Davey, Alfred, 29, 144, 163
decentralization, 47–50
Defoe, D., 1
democracy: and anti-racism, 161–3
  model of, 116–17
  values, 116–20
Demuth, C., 147, 151–3
Department of Education and Science: on educational performance, 56–9
  on integration, 98–101
  on positive discrimination, 77, 79–80, 82, 88, 92
Department of Employment, 19
deprivation *see* disadvantage
Dhondy, F., 69–71
disadvantage, 42–3, 82–4
discrimination *see* racism
dispersal, 97–101, 105
Doherty, S., 152–3
Douglas, J.W.B., 44–5, 59
Driver, G., 59–60, 65–70, 133
dual system of education, County and voluntary schools, 30–1, 35–41, 105–9, 112; *see also* segregation
Dudley, 43
Dummett, A., 77, 109

Eccles, D., 49
economic context of 'coloured' minorities, 15–17
Education Acts: (1870), 30–2, 34–5, 122
(1944), 35–6, 48, 75, 111, 127, 129, 134
(1980), 48, 111, 113
(1981), 37, 48
Scotland (1918), 108
Educational Disadvantage Unit, 79
educational performance, 46–7, 55–9, 66, 69, 72, 147–8
Educational Priority Areas, 76, 78, 85–6
educational context, 29–51
decentralization, 47–50
inequality, 42–7
Jewish children in London Borad Schools, 31–5
segregation, 35–41
state education, origins of 30–1
unemployment, youth 50–1
educational subnormality, 37, 41, 68
egalitarianism, *see* equality
equality, liberty and fraternity, 164–73
equality of opportunity, 48, 52–76
culture of resistance, 69–72
educational performance, 55–9
limitations to philosophy 52–4
reconsidered, 72–4
underachievement concept of, 59–69
women, 89
ESN *see* educational subnormality
essentialism, 23
ethnic minorities in Britain, 1–28
'coloured', 13–20
Gypsies, 7–8
Irish, 2–4
Italians, 5–6
Jews, 6–7
meaning of, 8–11
ethnic segregation, 97
ethnocentrism, 23, 63–4
European Economic Community, 87–8, 92, 124
evaluation of books and materials (in anti-racism), 141
examinations, 11, 38
class and, 42–7
geographical differences in results, 42–3
obsession with, 73
expenditure on education, 36, 85
Eyesenck, H., 62
Fair Employment (Northern Ireland) Act (1976), 89
fascism, 7; *see also* neo–fascism
Floud, J., 69
folk racism, 23–4; *see also* popular racism
Foot, P., 7
Forster, W.E., 31
France, 9
Francis, M., 154–5
fraternity, liberty and equality, 164–73
Friends, Christian Society of, 138; *see also* religion
Fuller, M., 70, 133
further education, 58–9, 68

Gaitskell, H., 25
Gandhi, 157
Gartner, L.P., 33–4
Garvey, M., 133
gender, *see* women and girls
geographical inequality, 42–3
Germany, 7
'ghettoization', 101
girls *see* women and girls
Glasgow, 36, 105, 107, 115; *see also* Scotland
Glazer, N., 26
Gordon, Major W.E., 6–7
government and education, 30–1, 47–50
assimilation or pluralism, 122–7
and positive discrimination, 79–82
see also dual system legislation
Greek: Cypriots, 10, 55, 72
language, 129
Griffiths, P., 26
Gypsies, 7–10, 13, 166
educational performance, 55, 72, 86
numbers, 8
positive discrimination and, 90
segregation of, 115
stereotypes of, 24

Hadow Report (1931), 38
halal meat, 125
Halsey, A.H., 44, 164–5
Hammersley, M., 66, 148–9
handicapped people, 85
segregation of, 36–7, 40–8, 109–10
Hannon, W., 47
Hargreaves, D.H., 69, 73, 114, 164, 166, 172–3
Hattersley, R., 77–8, 83
HCP *see* Schools Council Humanities etc

Hertfordshire, 42
hidden curriculum, 47
Hinduism, 23, 36, 105–7, 112, 119, 131; *see also* India; religion
Hiro, D., 100
Hobsbawm, E.J., 2–4, 15, 22–3, 30–1
Hodges, L., 71
Holland, 6
home-ownership, 6, 18
Hong Kong Chinese, 1, 12, 14, 83, 91
House of Commons Affairs Committee on Racial Disadvantage, 84
housing, 18
Hungary, 9
Huzley, E., 123
Huxley, T.H., 52–3, 58

ILEA *see* literacy study; London
illiberalism, 150–8
immigrants, 24–6, 76–8, 98–9
  advisory council for, 96, 99, 116, 122–3
  legislation, 7, 9, 25, 29, 78, 85
India, ix–x, 119, 131–3, 136, 157
Indians, 1
  educational performance, 55
  employment, 17–18
  numbers, 14
  Sikhs, 131–2, 134
  see also Hinduism
  South Asians
industrialization and state education, 30
inequality, 36–47
inflation, 15
inner city decline, 17
  riots, 169
Inspectorate, HM, 55, 168
Institute of Race Relations, 158
institutional racism, 26, 63–4, 88, 145–7
integration or segregation, 37, 39, 96–115
  case for integration, 109–15
  dispersal in 1960s 97–101
  religious segregation, 105–9
  secondary school allocation, 101–4, 113–14
intelligence tests, 12, 62
International Convention on Elimination of All Forms of Racial Discrimination, 117
Irish, 2–4, 9–10, 12–13
  Catholics, 3–4
  excluded from positive discrimination, 80, 91
  numbers, 2, 4, 9
  stereotypes, 24
  see also Northern Ireland
IRR *see* Institute of Race Relations
Italians, 5–6, 9–10, 13, 80, 129

Jackson, B., 69
Jamaica, 61, 70; *see also* West Indians
Jeffcoate, R., 159
Jensen, A., 62
Jews, 6–7, 9–11, 13
  integration, 10–11, 130, 165
  London Board Schools and, 29, 31–5
  numbers, 6–7
  positive discrimination, 86, 90
  religious segregation, 106–8, 112
  schools for, 32–3, 36
  stereotypes, 24
  violence against, 6–7, 26
John Paul, Pope, 108
Johnson, L.B., 76
Jones, C., 30, 33–5, 75–6
Jones, D.K., 30–1
Joseph, Sir K., 48–9

Kenya, 136
Kettle, M., 71
King, M.L., 171
King, R., 6
Kirklees, 42–3
Kirp, D.L., 20
Kosack, G., 3
Krausz, E., 34

Labour Party: and class, 17
  and comprehensives, 39, 170
  integration and 98–100
  positive discrimination and, 76–8, 80–1, 83, 89
Lacey, C., 69
Lancashire, 19, 32, 42, 97; *see also* Liverpool
Lane, H., 162
languages, 123, 128–31
  teaching, 92–4, 96
Leeds, 42
legislation, 3, 30
  aliens, 7, 29
  anti-discrimination, 117
  education, 30–2, 34–7, 48, 75, 111, 113, 122, 127, 129, 134, 171
  employment, 89
  immigration, 7, 9, 25, 29, 78, 85
  local government, 77–8, 80, 89, 92

nationality, 10, 23
race relations, 8, 24, 27, 48, 78, 87–9, 91–3, 102–3, 115, 124, 171
resettlement, Polish, 9, 85
sex discrimination, 88
Leicester, 72
liberals and state education, 30–1
libertarianism and proscriptiveness, tension between 117–18
liberty, equality and fraternity, 164–73
Literacy Survey, ILEA (1968–75), 55, 57, 59, 61–2
Liverpool: blacks in, 14, 168–8
Catholics in, 4, 36, 168–70
Chinese in, 14, 168
Irish in, 2, 4, 168
Jews in, 32, 106, 109, 168, 170
Protestants in, 169–70
religious segregation in, 106–7
school allocation in, 102, 115, 170–1
unemployment in, 167–8
local authorities, 47–8, 91–5
Local Government Act (1966), 77–8, 80, 89, 92
London and south–east: anti-racism, 144–6, 151–2, 160–1
blacks in, 14–15, 19–20, 25, 27, 57–60, 68, 72, 165
'bussing', 101
Chinese in, 14
curriculum in, 133
dispersal, 100
educational performance in, 57–8, 60
examination results, 42–3
Jews in, 29, 31–5, 96
literacy survey, 55, 57, 59, 61–2
positive discrimination in, 91–4
racism in, 150–1
religious segregation in, 106
riots in, 25, 27, 77
South Asians in, 19–20, 72, 165
West Indians in, 57–8, 60, 68

Mabey, C., 57, 62
MacDonald, B., 140, 142
McNeal, J., 109
Macmillan, H., 15
maladjusted, segregation of, 37
Maltese, 1, 83
Manchester, 32, 42
Manpower Services Commission, 49–50
Marsden, D., 69
marriage, beliefs about, 119–20, 131–2
Marx, K. and Marxism, 3
on class, 44, 46–7
on culture of resistance, 69–70
feminist, 47
and post-industrialism, 51
and racism, 22–3, 158–9
and state education, 35
Mazzini, G., 5
middle class, 4, 6, 17, 19; *see also* class
Midlands: anti-racism in, 142
blacks in, 14, 72, 142
counter-school culture, 69–70
educational performance, 65
examination results, 42–3
Jews in, 32
schools, 123
teachers in, 64
unemployment in, 16
Mill, J.S., 31, 112, 117–18
Milner, D., 63, 144
Ministry of Education on English for Immigrants, 123, 128
mixed-ability teaching, 40, 110
MPA *see* Muslim Parents Association
Mullin, P.N., 144
multi-ethnic curriculum, 94
music, 10, 73–4
Muslims, 36, 105–7, 111–12, 124–7, 133, 135, 138
Parents Association, 106–7 *see also* Pakistanis; religion

National Association for Multiracial Education, 144
National Child Development Study, 19, 44, 57, 59, 61–2, 110–11
National Dwelling and Household Survey, 17
National Foundation for Educational Research, 56–7, 60, 103–4
National Front *see* neo-fascism
National Union of Teachers, 151, 160
NCDS *see* National Child Development Study
Nehru, 157
neo-fascism, 26, 144–5, 153, 159, 161
Newsom Report (1963), 52
NFER *see* National Foundation, etc
Norburn, M.V., 144
north-east, 16

Northern Ireland, 16, 42, 107, 111, 115; *see also* Irish
Norwood Report (1943), 38
Nottingham, 25, 77

obfuscation, anti-racism as, 147–50
Office of Population Census and Surveys, 14
oil crisis, 15
Okely, J., 8
Open University, 134, 137
Opinion Research Centre, 19
opportunity *see* equality of opportunity
organizations against racism, 143–4
Orwell, G., 139
overachievement, 61, 64

Pakistanis, 9, 82
  'bussing', 105
  and Local Government Act (1966) (and excluded from positive discrimination), 81, 85
  educational performance, 55–6
  employment, 17–18
  numbers 14–15
  see also Muslims; South Asians
Parekh, B., 118, 120, 138
parents, 48, 111–14; West Indian 67–9
Parkinson, J.P., 140, 142
phenomenological approach, 134
Plato, 112
Plowden Report (1967), 55, 76, 80, 87, 166
pluralism, limits to, 116–38
  and assimilation, 122–7
  and curriculum, 128–38
  'full-blooded' or 'modified', 118–22
Poland, 9, 91
policy *see* government
Polish Resettlement Act (1947), 9, 85
Political and Economic Planning, 21, 88
politics, 3–4, 7, 50
popular racism, 23–4
Portuguese, 55, 91
positive discrimination, 75–95
  case for, 84–7
  cultural needs, special, 87–8
  government policy in 1970s, 79–82
  in 1960s, 76–8
  local authority policies, 91–5
  racial disadvantage concept, 83–4
  racial discrimination, combatting, 88–9
  statistics collection, 77, 82–3
Powell, E. and Powellism, 78, 142, 149
Preiswerk, R., 156
proscriptiveness and libertarianism, tension between, 117–18
Protestants, 36, 105, 107–9, 115, 135; *see also* religion
pupils: racism of, 149–55
  West Indian views, 67–9

Race Relations Acts: (1965), 87, 88
  (1968), 78, 88, 100
  (1976), 8, 24, 27, 48, 87–9, 91–3, 102–3, 115, 124, 171
Race Relations Board, 101
race: meaning of, 145–7
  question of, 11–13
racial disadvantage, 82–4; racial discrimination, *see* discrimination
racism and racialism, 20–8, 48, 63–6, 74, 154
racism, combating, 139–63
  curriculum and, 140–2, 158–60
  democracy and, 161–3
  emergence of anti-racism, 143–5
  illiberalism, anti-racism as, 150–8
  meaning of race and, 145–7
  obfuscation, anti-racism as 147–50
  Stenhouse research, 140–3
  targets of anti-racism, 160–1
radicals and state education, 31–3, 36
Rampton (later Swann) Committee of Enquiry, 56, 59–61, 68, 80, 146
Rastafarianism, 132–3
Ratcliffe, P., 68
Raynor, J., 40
Reading, 102–4, 114
recession, 15–17
Reform Act (1867), 30
refugees, 9–10
Reiss, C., 8
relativism, 121–2, 134
religion and education: and culture, 133–8
  and dispersal, 105
  segregation, 31–6, 40, 48, 105–9, 148
  see also Catholics; Hinduism; Muslims; Protestants; Sikhs
repatriation, 153
resistance, culture of, 69–72, 149
Resler, H., 19–20
results *see* educational performance
Rex, J., 64–5, 67–8
Ridley, F.F., 167–9
riots, race, 77
Rose, E.J.B., 67, 98

Royal Commission on Alien Immigration (1930), 29, 33
Ruddock, J., 140
Russia, 6
Rutter, M., 60–1

Salford, 42
Sampson, G., 172
Sandwell, 42
Scarman, Lord, and Report, (1981), 27, 75, 94–5
Schools Council, 135
Humanities Curriculum Project, 140–2, 160
'scientific racism', 23–4
Scotland, 36, 105, 107–8, 111, 115
Searle, C., 159–60
secondary school allocation, 101–4, 113–14
secularism, 108, 112
segregation, 36–42
  by ability, 36, 38–40, 109–10
  by class, 40–2, 97, 113
  ethnic, 97
  by gender, 36–8, 40
  of handicapped, 36–7, 40–8, 109–10
  of maladjusted, 37
  religious, 31–6, 40, 48, 105–9, 148
Select Committee on Immigration and Race Relations (1971), 27, 79–80
self–concept and self-esteem, 63–4
sex *see* gender
Sex Discrimination Act (1975), 88
Sheard, D.J.S., 143
Shipman, M., 40
Short, E., 100
Sikes, P.J., 143
Sikhs, 10, 36, 89, 105–7, 112, 131–4; *see also* India; religion
single sex schools, 38
slave trade, 23
Smart, N., 134
Smith, D.J., 18, 21
social class *see* class
Social Darwinism, 22
Socialist Sunday School Movement, 68
South Asians, 9, 11–13, 81–2, 86
  integration, 165
  'bussing', 105
  educational performance, 55–9, 61–4, 67–8, 72, 81, 85, 144
  employment, 17–18, 20
  further education, 58
  home ownership, 18
  numbers, 14–15
  positive discrimination, 81, 90
  school allocation, 103, 114
  single-sex schools, 38
  women and girls, 38, 58, 119–20, 126–7, 131–2
Southall, 97, 99, 122
Southampton, 5
Spanish, 55, 91
special:disruptive units, 37
  educational needs, 86–8
Spens Report (1938), 38
sport, 73–4
state education, 30–1; *see also* government
statistics, collection of, 77, 82–3
Stenhouse, L., 139–43, 147, 158, 160
stereotyping, 65–6, 68, 74
Stone, M., 63–4, 67–8, 70–1
streaming, 40
Surrey, 42
Sussex, 42
suttee, suppressed, 119
Swann Committee *see* Rampton
Swift, J., 112

Taunton Commission (1867), 39
Tawney, R.H., 29, 53
Taylor, M., 56, 60
teachers: assimilation, opinions on, 123–4
  autonomy, 48–50
  politics, 50
  racism and, 148–9, 152
  stereotyping of and by, 65–6, 68, 74
Technical and Vocational Education Initiative, 50, 172
tests; intelligence, 12, 62
  NFER, 103–4
  USA, 63
textbooks, evaluation of, 156–7
Thackeray, W.M., 139
Thatcher, M., 131, 144
Thompson, E.P., 3
Tomlinson, S., 56, 64–5, 67–8
Townsend, H.E.R., 65, 124
tripartite system, 38–40
Troyna, B., 69, 71
Turkish Cypriots, 55, 59, 72
TVEI *see* Technical and Vocational, etc
Twitchin, J., 147, 151–3

Uganda and East Africa, Asians from, 9, 14, 17, 56, 72, 144

underachievement, 42–6, 55–69
'underclass' concept of, 17–20
unemployment, 15–20, 50–1
United States, 1
  'bussing', 101
  combating prejudice in, 139, 141, 155, 164
  constitution, 117, 155
  economy, 30
  positive discrimination, 86
  racialism, 26
  religious education, 107
  teachers, 64
  tests, educational, 63
  war on poverty, 76
Universal Declaration of Human Rights, 108, 112
Urban Aid Programme, 77

Vellins, S., 58
Verma, G.K., 142
Vietnamese, 10–13, 86, 166
  excluded from positive discrimination, 81, 85, 91
  unemployment, 20
voluntary schools *see* dual system

Wales, 14, 16, 42, 130
Walker, E.C., 124
Walker, P.G., 77
Ward, R.H., 19
WCC *see* World Council of Churches
West Indians, 11–13
  anti-racism and, 142
  boys, 60–1, 66, 70
  'bussing', 105
  class and, 61, 66, 69, 72
  counter-school culture, 69–71
  dispersal of, 100
  educational performance, 55–73, 144
  employment of, 17–18
  further education of, 59, 68
  girls, 59–60, 64, 70, 132–3, 165
  government policy, 80
  hostility to, 148–9
  numbers, 14–15
  positive discrimination, 90
  Rastafarianism, 132–3
  school allocation and, 103
  ESN schools, 37, 68, 71
  stereotypes, 73–4
  under-achievement, 62–9
  unemployment, 19
Westergaard, J., 19–20
White Papers: educational disadvantage, 82
  equality for women, 89
  immigration from Commonwealth, 77–8, 98–9
  racial discrimination, 154
Williams, J., 123–4
Williams, R., 136, 161–2
Willis, P., 69, 71, 149
Wilson, H., 78
Wolverhampton, 42
women and girls: achievement, 46–7
  circumcision, 119
  further education of, 58
  role beliefs, 119–20, 131–2
  separate education, 37–8
  Sikh, 131–2
  South Asian, 38, 58, 119–20, 126–7, 131–2
  West Indian, 59–60, 64, 70, 132–3
  working, 16, 18
working class: blacks, 17–20
  culture, 17, 45–6
  Irish, 2–3
  Italians, 6
World Council of Churches, 156–8

Yorkshire: anti-racism, 143, 146, 151
  blacks in, 14
  'bussing', 101
  examination results, 42
  integration, 125–6, 131
  Muslims in, 106–7, 126–7, 131
Young, K., 49, 81, 92
Youth Opportunities Programmee, 50, 167
Youth Training Scheme, 50, 167

Zec, P., 121, 134
Zimbabwe, 136